THE ALEXY-POSCHER DEBATE ON LEGAL PRINCIPLES

This collective work provides a chronological and up-to-date reconstruction of the three-round debate between Robert Alexy and Ralf Poscher.

The debate represents the German development of an enduring jurisprudential controversy over the concept and adjudicatory role of legal principles, classically addressed by HLA Hart and Ronald Dworkin. Alexy's principles theory, which has initially defined 'legal principles' as optimisation requirements, currently argues that they express an 'ideal ought'. Poscher's critique challenges the soundness of Alexy's principles theory by questioning its ontological and epistemological commitments.

As legal principles are directly related to constitutional rights, the Alexy-Poscher debate has significant implications for constitutional adjudication. For instance, proportionality analysis – which incorporates a highly controversial balancing test – and the legitimate boundaries of judicial power, hinge on the debate's two opposing views. Yet despite the centrality and pervasiveness of this topic, German contributions to the theoretical and practical impact of legal principles remain generally overlooked by English-speaking scholars.

Concluding with David Duarte's critical and meticulous assessment of the debate, this collection bridges that important scholarly gap. Whether or not conversant in the debate on legal principles, legal researchers and advanced law students with interdisciplinary interests in jurisprudence and constitutional law will find in this book a timely and distinctive introduction to leading developments in German legal thinking.

The Alexy–Poscher Debate on Legal Principles

Robert Alexy and Ralf Poscher

Edited by
Rafael Giorgio Dalla-Barba

Conclusion by
David Duarte

•HART•

OXFORD • LONDON • NEW YORK • NEW DELHI • SYDNEY

HART PUBLISHING

Bloomsbury Publishing Plc

Kemp House, Chawley Park, Cumnor Hill, Oxford, OX2 9PH, UK

1385 Broadway, New York, NY 10018, USA

Bloomsbury Publishing Ireland Limited, 29 Earlsfort Terrace, Dublin 2, D02 AY28, Ireland

First published in Great Britain 2025

First published in hardback, 2025

Paperback edition, 2026

A catalogue record for this book is available from the British Library.

A catalogue record for this book is available from the Library of Congress.

Library of Congress Control Number: 2025933510

ISBN: PB: 978-1-50998-057-4
ePDF: 978-1-50998-059-8
ePub: 978-1-50998-060-4

Typeset by Compuscript Ltd, Shannon

Perhaps no study equals debate in the acquirement of the power of logical thinking combined with clear expression.

Edwin Shurter

ACKNOWLEDGEMENTS

This collective work would not have been feasible without the support of a select group of people. Their efforts must be acknowledged. First and foremost, I am deeply grateful to Professor Ralf Poscher not only for his unwavering encouragement throughout the editing process, but also for providing the creative spark to compile the scholarly articles that form the Alexy–Poscher debate into a single volume. My heartfelt thanks also go to Professor Robert Alexy, whose endorsement and great enthusiasm for the book proposal from the very beginning exemplify the true spirit of scientific collaboration. This work would not have been possible without their unrestricted and indispensable support.

I extend my thanks and sincere appreciation to Professor David Duarte, whose scholarly contribution to the project presents invaluable criticisms of both protagonists' views of the debate whilst proposing an alternative approach for distinguishing rules and principles. David's input is noteworthy not only for its substantive engagement with the Alexy–Poscher debate, but mainly for having trusted in the consistency and the positive impact of the book even before its approval for publication. I firmly expect that this fruitful teamwork with the Lisbon Legal Theory Research Group is just the first of many to come.

I also want to express my gratitude to those who helped me navigate the obstacles along the way, especially some of my academic colleagues and closest friends: Artur Fernando Wagner Junior, Artur Ferrari de Almeida, Dr Matheus Pellegrino da Silva, Dr Randall Lee Stephenson, Dr Rodrigo Garcia Cadore, Dr William Galle Dietrich, Eduardo Kronbauer, Guilherme Henrique Mariani de Souza, Heydegger Francisco, and Samuel Matthias Hartwig. If the famous German philosopher Friedrich Nietzsche once said that 'without music, life would be a mistake', I would just like to add to his line that 'without friendship as well'.

In addition, my thanks go to the institutions that were (directly or indirectly) involved in this project. Firstly, I am especially grateful to the Foundation of German Business (Stiftung der Deutschen Wirtschaft), which not only granted me a generous scholarship for my doctoral thesis at the University of Freiburg, but was also understanding about the development of this parallel work. Not least, I would like to sincerely thank the Department of Public Law at the Max Planck Institute for the Study of Crime, Security and Law (MPI-CSL), which has provided all resources and research support to turn the project into reality. Here I would like to mention the assistance of Caroline Hillemanns, Inga Chrétien, and Tanja Tippach with the administrative issues during the course of the editing process and the expertise of Sarah Norman in translating into English one of the articles that had not yet been translated. Andrea Neisius and Pastor Georg Alexy were also very supportive by facilitating the communication between Freiburg and Kiel in the ending phase of the process.

Genuine thanks also go to Hart Publishing for their remarkable support and dedication throughout the journey of bringing this project to fruition. The insightful remarks from the peer reviewers were invaluable, providing critical feedbacks that greatly enriched the final product. The editorial team's commitment has been particularly involved in refining the manuscript and ensuring that every detail is meticulously addressed. A special acknowledgment is owed to Kate Whetter, Sarah Skinner, Verity Stuart, Joanne Choulerton, and Linda Goss, whose thoughtful inputs and suggestions have made a significant impact on the work in terms of editorial quality. It has been an honour to work with such a talented and dedicated group of professionals.

Grateful acknowledgment is also due to Franz Steiner Verlag and Nomos Verlag for their understanding and flexibility in authorising the republication of key texts for the Alexy–Poscher debate. Their willingness to collaborate and accommodate this project has been instrumental in ensuring that these important scientific contributions could be reused, enriching the discussion and broadening its audience. I am also appreciative of the collaboration from Oxford University Press and Wiley, who have kindly granted permission to reuse additional texts. The cooperation and professionalism of these esteemed publishers have been vital to the success and continuation of this thought-provoking legal debate.

With love and thanks to my parents, Italo and Vilma, for their enduring patience and for letting me find my own way.

Rafael Giorgio Dalla-Barba

CONTENTS

EDITOR'S NOTE

This collective work compiles chronologically the six principal scholarly articles that constitute the legal debate between Robert Alexy and Ralf Poscher on the concept of 'legal principles'. They are reorganised here in three separate rounds of academic discussion over the last two decades.

These articles have been originally published in leading international journals specialising in Jurisprudence and Constitutional Law. Both their full original references and the publishers who have graciously authorised their republication are indicated on the respective front pages.

The terminological choices made by all contributors have been faithfully preserved. Given that certain German terms may be translated differently into English, readers are encouraged to consult the 'Table of Translations' for clarification, ensuring precise understanding throughout.

TABLE OF TRANSLATIONS

English	German
Balancing	Abwägung
Balancing law Law of balancing	Abwägungsgesetz
Basic Law	Grundgesetz
Collision law Law of competing principles	Kollisionsgesetz
Constitutional rights Fundamental rights	Grundrechte
Constitutional rights doctrine Fundamental rights doctrine	Grundrechtsdogmatik
Commands to be optimised Requirements to be optimised	Zu optimierende Gebote
Commands to optimise Requirements to optimise	Gebote zu optimieren
Decisions of the Federal Constitutional Court (BVerfGE)	Entscheidungen des Bundesverfassungsgerichts (BVerfGE)
Definitive commands Definitive requirements	Definitive Gebote
Exception clause	Ausnahmetatbestand
Existence objection	Existenzeinwand
Fulfilment requirement	Erfüllungsgebot
'Ideal ought'	Ideales Sollen
Interference	Beeinträchtigung Eingriff
Legal doctrine	Rechtsdogmatik
Necessity thesis	Notwendigkeitsthese

(continued)

(Continued)

English	**German**
Non-fulfilment Non-satisfaction	Nichterfüllung
Non-necessity objection Superfluity objection	Überflüssigkeitseinwand
Ontological objection	Ontologischer Einwand
Optimisation commands Optimisation requirements	Optimierungsgebote
'Ought'	Sollen
Possibility thesis	Möglichkeitsthese
Principle of necessity	Grundsatz der Erforderlichkeit
Principle of proportionality	Verhältnismäßigkeitsgrundsatz
Principle of proportionality in a broad sense	Verhältnismäßigkeitsgrundsatz im weiteren Sinne
Principle of proportionality in a narrow sense	Verhältnismäßigkeitsgrundsatz im engeren Sinne
Principle of appropriateness Principle of suitability	Grundsatz der Geeignetheit
Principles theory Theory of principles	Prinzipientheorie
Prohibition of gross disproportionality	Verbot grober Disproportionalität
Protected area	Schutzbereich
'Real ought'	Reales Sollen
Rule of law principle	Rechtsstaatsprinzip
Scope of rights	Tatbestand
Weight formula	Gewichtsformel

Introduction

A Brief Overview of the Alexy–Poscher Debate

RAFAEL GIORGIO DALLA-BARBA*

The jurisprudential debate between Robert Alexy and Ralf Poscher focuses on *legal principles*; more precisely, what their ontological status is, to what extent they are epistemically relevant, and – no less decisive – how exactly they differ from legal rules. The so-called 'principles theory' developed by Alexy is based on a *categorical* (or, in Alexy's terminology, *qualitative*) *distinction* between rules and principles. In his book *A Theory of Constitutional Rights*,[1] originally published in 1986, Alexy proposed the thesis according to which legal rules and principles are structurally different: while rules are applicable in an 'all-or-nothing fashion', principles require something to be realised to the greatest extent possible given the legal and factual possibilities. Since then, the principles theory has undergone a number of conceptual adjustments in response to different sorts of criticism. One of the harshest critics (if not *the* harshest) has been Poscher, who defends the traditional and opposite thesis of a merely *gradual distinction* between rules and principles. In his *habilitation* thesis *Constitutional Rights as Defensive Rights*,[2] published in 2003, Poscher questioned both theoretical and doctrinal foundations of the principles theory and, by extension, its soundness as a theory of constitutional rights. This was the starting point of an intense and long-standing debate across six scholarly publications, which are chronologically organised in this collective work in three successive rounds. They form what can be called the 'Alexy–Poscher debate on legal principles'.[3]

* I should like to thank Sarah Norman again for her careful revision and writing suggestions.

[1] See R Alexy, *A Theory of Constitutional Rights* (J Rivers trans, Oxford, Oxford University Press, 2002) 47–61. For the original version, see R Alexy, *Theorie der Grundrechte* (Frankfurt, Suhrkamp, 1986) 75–93.

[2] See R Poscher, *Grundrechte als Abwehrrechte. Reflexive Regelung rechtlich geordneter Freiheit* (Tübingen, Mohr Siebeck, 2003) 73–84.

[3] For the Portuguese and Spanish translations, see RG Dalla-Barba (ed), *Princípios Jurídicos: O Debate Metodológico entre Robert Alexy e Ralf Poscher* (Belo Horizonte, Casa do Direito, 2022); RG Dalla-Barba and JA García Amado (eds), *Principios Juridicos: El Debate Metodológico entre Robert Alexy y Ralf Poscher* (Lima, Palestra, 2022). See also M Hong, *Abwägungsfeste Rechte. Von Alexys Prinzipien zum Modell der Grundsatznormen* (Tübingen, Mohr Siebeck, 2019) 81–103, who coined the label 'Alexy–Poscher debate'.

I. First Round

Alexy's *On the Structure of Legal Principles*[4] opened what was to become the first round of the debate with Poscher by reaffirming the cornerstone of the principles theory: every legal norm is either a rule or a principle. According to Alexy, this distinction is not gradual, but qualitative. While rules are *definitive requirements* – norms applicable in a way that they are either fulfilled or not – principles are *optimisation requirements*. They require that something be realised to the greatest extent possible given the legal and factual possibilities. Thus, this concept of 'legal principles' would capture the nature of constitutional rights and establish that a balancing test (developed within the 'proportionality analysis') should be used by courts to resolve cases where such rights collide. Alexy then responded to two initial objections to his principles theory. Firstly, he reacted to Klaus Günther's critique that rules differ from principles because they have a 'different kind of use'. Secondly, he replied to the objection raised by both Aulis Aarnio and Jan Sieckmann that optimisation requirements are actually rules and therefore cannot be defined as principles. Alexy maintained that his concept of 'legal principles' can still be upheld if it is understood as 'requirements to be optimised'. Legal principles become the object of optimisation requirements that implies an 'ideal ought'. Different from the 'real ought' that characterises legal rules, the 'ideal ought' is an 'ought' that lacks reference to the limited possibilities of the empirical and normative worlds.

Poscher was not convinced by Alexy's attempt to hold onto his modified concept of 'legal principles'. By taking the objection previously raised by Aarnio and Sieckmann to its ultimate logical conclusion, Poscher argued that the principles theory lacks an object. In *Insights, Errors, and Self-Misconceptions of the Theory of Principles*,[5] he firstly questioned the thesis that legal principles are norms to be optimised by other norms; that is to say, that they would be requirements to be optimised by optimisation requirements. While Poscher did not deny that optimisation requirements may address both facts and other norms, he pointed out that constitutional rights, at least in Germany, address solely facts. For instance, Article 2 (2) of the Basic Law,[6] which guarantees the right to life and physical integrity, does not aim to optimise the norm itself that establishes these values, but rather the *factual means* by which life and physical integrity of individuals and groups can be protected. Therefore, if legal principles were the normative object of optimisation requirements (which supposedly imply an 'ideal ought'), then they would fail to characterise exactly what they were designed for: constitutional rights. Secondly, Poscher contended that, by determining conflicts involving constitutional rights to be resolved by an optimisation-based balancing test, the Alexyan definition of 'legal principle' ends up suppressing all other argumentative tools available to

[4] See below Chapter 1 pp 17–27.

[5] See below Chapter 2 pp 29–55.

[6] 'Every person shall have the right to life and physical integrity. Freedom of the person shall be inviolable. These rights may be interfered with only pursuant to a law'.

resolve such disputes. Constitutional adjudication, he concluded, is rather a matter of legal hermeneutics than of ontology of norms.

II. Second Round

In *Ideal Ought*,[7] Alexy replied to Poscher's critique by reframing it into two main objections. The *ontological objection* questions the existence of an ideal dimension of law that characterises legal principles. It questions whether there is an 'ideal ought' beyond the 'real ought' that addresses facts (and, in theory, even other norms). Countering this objection, Alexy argued that the 'ideal ought' is no mysterious entity, but rather an abstract 'ought' that can be morally justified. In turn, the *non-necessity objection* affirms that, even if such an 'ideal ought' were to exist, it would be unnecessary to explain the factual object of legal norms, such as constitutional rights. Alexy responded that the existence of an 'ideal ought' is necessary since one can only optimise an object – both facts and norms (eg 'it is obligatory to help those in need') – if one has an abstract idea of what has to be optimised (eg 'helpfulness'). It is necessary, he argued, to initially assume an ideal dimension of law where conflicts of certain legal norms (more precisely, legal principles as requirements to be optimised) occur in a completely abstract manner. The optimum outcome of the balancing test used to resolve such conflicts provides a rule to be applied in individual cases. Thus, Alexy concluded that there must be a reciprocal implication between legal principles characterised as requirements to be optimised and an 'ideal ought'. They are the object of the principles theory.

In *Theory of a Phantom*,[8] Poscher reacted to Alexy's second attempt to defend his concept of 'legal principles' by reformulating it as two main theses. The *possibility thesis* claims that legal principles are actually the normative object of optimisation requirements, ie requirements to be optimised that imply an 'ideal ought'. He questioned that claim, firstly, because optimising a legal norm (eg 'helping people in need') is different from optimising the ideal representation of that norm (eg 'helpfulness as such'); and, secondly, because while the optimisation of a norm is contingent upon factual and legal possibilities, the optimisation of an 'ideal ought' – given its own purely abstract character – is not. Poscher also restated that a normative object of optimisation requirements is just a superfluous notion for constitutional rights, which are ultimately aimed at optimising facts (not norms): if 'helping people in need' is an optimisation requirement, it demands that the factual means to help people in this situation be optimised (eg by distributing tents and food supplies); if it were a requirement to be optimised, it would demand instead that penalties for failure to comply with it be increased. Against the *necessity thesis*, Poscher maintained that neither the normative status of optimisation requirements nor the 'collision rules' to resolve disputes where legal norms conflict

[7] See below Chapter 3 pp 59–77.
[8] See below Chapter 4 pp 79–100.

need a normative object, let alone the assumption of an 'ideal ought'. If this is the case, then the principles theory indeed has no object.

III. Third Round

Alexy presented his subsequent reply to Poscher's objections in *Ideal 'Ought' and Optimisation*.[9] Surprisingly (or not), Alexy conceded that Poscher had been partially correct in the previous rounds, but insisted on a qualitative distinction between rules and principles. Alexy now defends what he calls the 'index model', a notion according to which legal rules – including optimisation requirements – express a 'real ought'. They are applied in an all-or-nothing fashion. By contrast, legal principles express an 'ideal ought', ie a purely 'prima facie' or '*pro tanto* ought'. The main difference is that legal principles are no longer defined as the normative object of optimisation requirements. This new explanation is justified by 'two basic axioms of the principles theory'. The *first axiom* affirms that normative conflicts in the ideal dimension – abstracted from both factual and normative possibilities – are possible because the legal norms involved in the conflict preserve their validity. Thus, when legal principles collide, the defeated one remains valid. The *second axiom* states that normative conflicts in the real dimension are impossible because both conflicting rules cannot be valid at the same time. When they clash, it is factually necessary to either create an exception or invalidate one of them. As normative conflicts in which both norms involved preserve their validity *do* occur, one can infer not only the existence, but also the necessity of an 'ideal ought' and the consequent soundness of the first axiom.

It was Poscher's turn to respond to Alexy's latest reaction, and he did so with a provoking title: *Resuscitation of a Phantom?*[10] Following conceptual clarifications and a brief reconstruction of the debate to date, he presented two arguments against Alexy's 'index model'. The *formal argument* questions the relevance of and ultimately the need for an 'ideal ought' to explain optimisation requirements, which – in Alexy's new terminology – constitute rules (and therefore express a 'real ought'). Poscher contended that, properly understood, conflicts of optimisation requirements do not result in logical contradictions. He uses the example of an obligation to optimise darkness and lightness when painting a room, which can be satisfied by choosing a lighter or darker shade of grey. That is, apparently contradictory optimisation requirements are realised in the real world precisely in the way Alexy described the 'ideal ought'. The *substantive argument* speculates that the insistence on an 'ideal ought' can be justified by the need to have a direction for the optimisation. Poscher contested this possible claim by pointing to – morally questionable – norms requiring something to be optimised in

[9] See below Chapter 5 pp 103–116.
[10] See below Chapter 6 pp 117–133.

the opposite direction to its ideal counterpart. For instance, instead of demanding the realisation of actions that maximise the ideals of 'efficiency' and 'life', the optimisation of certain legal norms requires the use of war weapons to minimise both financial costs and human lives. Ultimately, Poscher reiterates his previous conclusion that the principles theory remains a theory with no object.

IV. Implications for Legal Scholarship

There are at least two fields of legal research directly impacted by the Alexy–Poscher debate. The first is *jurisprudence*, where this intellectual exchange can be charitably interpreted as a German development of the famous debate between HLA Hart and Ronald Dworkin.[11] As late as at the end of the 1970s,[12] Alexy had drawn on the distinction between rules and principles previously sketched by Dworkin in his 'general attack' on legal positivism.[13] Although Alexy's definition of 'legal rules' is virtually identical, his concept of 'legal principles' represents a significant change (and, for adherents to the principles theory, also an improvement[14]) in relation to Dworkin's. Its initial redefinition as optimisation requirements and its reference to an 'ideal ought' prompted the above-described three-round controversy that enhances considerably the study of legal norms – particularly the distinction between rules and principles – in terms of analytical clarity and scientific rigour.

[11] See SJ Shapiro, 'The Hart–Dworkin Debate: A Short Guide for the Perplexed' in A Ripstein (ed), *Ronald Dworkin* (Cambridge, Cambridge University Press, 2007) 22–55; N Stavropoulos, 'The Debate That Never Was' (2017) 130 *Harvard Law Review* 2082, 2082–95. For a more critical assessment, see B Leiter, 'Beyond the Hart/Dworkin Debate: The Methodology Problem in Jurisprudence' in B Leiter (ed), *Naturalizing Jurisprudence: Essays on American Legal Realism and Naturalism in Legal Philosophy* (Oxford, Oxford University Press, 2007) 153–82.

[12] For the original version, see R Alexy, 'Zum Begriff des Rechtsprinzips' in W Krawietz et al (eds), *Rechtstheorie, Argumentation und Hermeneutik in der Jurisprudenz* (Berlin, Duncker & Humblot, 1979) 79–82.

[13] See RM Dworkin, 'The Model of Rules' (1967) 35 *The University of Chicago Law Review* 14. Later republished as 'The Model of Rules I' in RM Dworkin (ed), *Taking Rights Seriously* (Cambridge MA, Harvard University Press, 1977).

[14] See eg M Borowski, 'Reconstruction of Formal Principles' in JA de Oliveira et al (eds), *Alexy's Theory of Law* (Stuttgart, Franz Steiner, 2015) 97. See also M Klatt, 'Taking Rights Less Seriously: A Structural Analysis of Judicial Discretion' (2007) 20 *Ratio Juris* 517, who stresses Alexy's improvements regarding the notion of discretion; VA da Silva, 'Comparing the Incommensurable: Constitutional Principles, Balancing and Rational Decision' (2011) 31 *Oxford Journal of Legal Studies* 277, relying on Alexy's distinction for analysing value incommensurability. For more critical assessments of Alexy's distinction and its implications for legal reasoning, see JR Sieckmann, 'Is Balancing a Method of Rational Justification *sui generis*? On the Structure of Justification by Balancing' in C Dahlman and E Feteris (eds), *Legal Argumentation Theory: Cross-Disciplinary Perspectives* (Dordrecht, Springer, 2013) 190ff; and F Leal, '"Less is More": Against Argumentative Saturation in Legal Decision-Making' in Miguel N de Brito et al (eds), *The Role of Legal Argumentation and Human Dignity in Constitutional Courts* (Stuttgart, Franz Steiner, 2019) 52, who raises concerns about excessive justificatory requirements in Alexy's theory of argumentation. A more comprehensive critique is elaborated in F Leal, 'Irracional ou Hiper-Racional? A Ponderação de Princípios Entre o Ceticismo e o Otimismo Ingênuo' (2014) 14(58) *Revista de Direito Administrativo & Constitucional* 177, 186ff.

The second field of legal scholarship affected by the Alexy–Poscher debate is *constitutional law*. Although in part highly theoretical, this debate has particularly relevant implications for constitutional rights and their adjudication process. Proportionality analysis, for instance, depends on a theory that explains the nature of constitutional rights and explains how to resolve disputes in which they conflict. As the principles theory aims to provide such a theory, embracing or rejecting it also translates to adhering to or rejecting mechanisms for interpreting, construing, and applying constitutional rights in individual cases. The implications of the debate for these two fields of study will be analysed in more detail below.

A. Implications for Jurisprudence

At least three main themes of jurisprudence – across the Anglosphere and Continental Europe – are under consideration in the Alexy–Poscher debate. One of them is indirectly related to more abstract questions, such as the concept (and the 'nature', as some might prefer) of law and its relationship to morality. The other ones, at a lower level of abstraction, touch directly upon the general theory of legal norms. Although the leading legal scholars involved in the debate have by no means exhausted all possible approaches to these themes, their differing views have become established in the contemporary jurisprudential landscape.

The first question raised by this controversy is whether the law *does* indeed encompass an 'ideal ought'. Alexy's position implies that an account of legal principles as well as the very concept of law claim and necessarily require the existence of an ideal dimension. This is directly at odds with positivistic theories of law, which are mainly characterised by the rejection of a necessary connection between law and morality. Thus, Alexy's defence of an ideal dimension of law is not exclusively a response to Poscher's critique, but also represents a fundamentally non-positivistic theory of law.[15] Poscher's position seems to be epistemically more modest. He does not explicitly deny the existence of an ideal dimension of law, but questions the need for it to explain legal principles and, consequently, the concept of law itself. This line of reasoning does not automatically side with legal positivism (whether

[15] See eg R Alexy, *The Argument from Injustice: A Reply to Legal Positivism* (SL Paulson and BL Paulson trans, Oxford, Oxford University Press, 2002) 20ff. For more recent criticisms, see J Raz, 'The Argument from Justice, or How Not to Reply to Legal Positivism' in G Pavlakos (ed), *Law, Rights and Discourse: The Legal Philosophy of Robert Alexy* (Oxford, Hart Publishing, 2007) 17–35; BH Bix, 'A Critique of Alexy's Claim to Correctness' (2020) 33 *Ratio Juris* 124, 125–30. Alexy's non-positivistic theory was drawn up in R Alexy, *Law's Ideal Dimension* (Oxford, Oxford University Press, 2021). For Alexy's legal debate with Eugenio Bulygin on the critique of legal positivism, see E Bulygin, 'Alexy Between Positivism and Non-Positivism' (2011) 2011 *Law of Ukraine: Legal Journal* 51, 51–59; R Alexy, 'Between Positivism and Non-Positivism? A Third Reply to Eugenio Bulygin' in J Ferrer Beltrán et al (eds), *Neutrality and Theory of Law* (Dordrecht, Springer, 2012) 225–38; P Gaido (ed), *La Pretensión de Corrección del Derecho: La Polémica Completa entre Alexy y Bulygin sobre la Relación entre Derecho y Moral*, 2nd edn (Bogotá, Universidad del Externado, 2022).

in its 'exclusive' or 'inclusive' version[16]), but can be interpreted as reinforcing the so-called 'separation thesis' in the overall discussion.[17] In a nutshell, Poscher's arguments seem to suggest that, if there is a necessary connection between law and morality, it can hardly be justified by resorting to Alexy's 'ideal ought'.

Secondly, the debate highlights the question of according to which criterion legal norms can be distinguished; more precisely, by which specific criterion rules and principles – as different types of legal norms – differ from each other. As explored in more detail by Duarte,[18] there seem to be various criteria, both qualitative and gradual, by which legal norms can be distinguished. The question then becomes: which one provides the best explanation for distinguishing rules from principles? Is this achieved by Alexy's principles theory, by another qualitative criterion (eg indeterminacy in the variable 'action'[19]), or, as Poscher proposes, by a distinction in gradual degrees of generality and importance? This question could be considered obsolete if it had no doctrinal or practical impact. Yet qualifying a legal norm as a 'rule' or a 'principle' may entail different justificatory requirements that have to be met when it comes to legal adjudication.[20] What specific requirements are effectively necessary, in which context they apply, and who is – directly and indirectly – bound by them are questions that explain why the distinction became so contested in legal scholarship. Despite its theoretical character, the 'rule-or-principle' distinction has an undeniable substantive impact.

Thirdly, the debate has been paving the way for further developments in connection with optimisation requirements. Importantly, neither Alexy nor Poscher deny the existence and the possibility of legal norms whose content requires a certain object (regardless of whether this be facts or other norms) to be

[16] For further reading on exclusive legal positivism, see A Marmor, 'Exclusive Legal Positivism' in JL Coleman (ed), *The Oxford Handbook of Jurisprudence and Philosophy of Law* (Oxford, Oxford University Press, 2004) 104–24. For inclusive legal positivism, see WJ Waluchow, 'The Origins of Inclusive Legal Positivism' in T Spaak and P Mindus (eds), *The Cambridge Companion of Legal Positivism* (Cambridge, Cambridge University Press, 2021) 487–511. For a critique of the divide, see eg D Priel, 'Farewell to the Exclusive-Inclusive Debate' (2005) 25 *Oxford Journal of Legal Studies* 675, 677–96.

[17] For more details, see R Poscher, 'The Principles Theory: How Many Theories and What is Their Merit?' in M Klatt (ed), *Institutionalized Reason: The Jurisprudence of Robert Alexy* (Oxford, Oxford University Press, 2012) 224.

[18] See below, Conclusion pp 137–160.

[19] ibid 152ff. Similarly, adopting a 'genericity criterion', PM Lopes, 'The Syntax of Principles: Genericity as a Logical Distinction Between Rules and Principles' (2017) 30 *Ratio Juris* 471, 472–83. For a qualitative distinction based on defeasibility, although maintaining an optimisation-based status of legal principles, see C Bäcker, 'Rules, Principles, and Defeasibility' in M Borowski (ed), *On the Nature of Legal Principles* (Stuttgart/Baden-Baden, Franz Steiner/Nomos, 2010) 81ff.

[20] For further reading on 'rules' and 'principles', see F Schauer, *Playing by the Rules: A Philosophical Examination of Rule-Based Decision-Making in Law and in Life* (Oxford, Oxford University Press, 1993) 167–206, who pays particular attention to the former concept; HB Ávila, *Theory of Legal Principles* (Dordrecht, Springer, 2007) 83ff, who develops the distinction further by adding a third category: 'normative postulates'; M Neves, *Constitutionalism and the Paradox of Principles and Rules* (Oxford, Oxford University Press, 2021) 72ff, who sees principles as reflexive mechanisms in a circular relationship with rules against the background of 'transconstitutionalism'.

optimised. Rather, their disagreement centres on whether or not this phenomenon requires the assumption of an ideal dimension in order to be properly understood. Even if the answer is 'no', optimisation requirements can still find their place in legal systems if they can be underpinned by other legal arguments (doctrinal, historical, systematic, etc); that is, if a given legal system allows for an interpretation or construction that justifies this outcome. There are no a priori reasons that prohibit the adoption of optimisation-based content in, for instance, a statutory or even a constitutional norm.

B. Implications for Constitutional Law

Another field of study directly impacted by the Alexy–Poscher debate is constitutional law. Both the status of constitutional rights and the argumentative tools for resolving judicial disputes in which these rights collide are intimately related to the jurisprudential controversy over legal principles. The 'idealised' dimension underlying Alexy's optimisation-based approach to constitutional rights – and its implications for proportionality analysis (thus including the balancing test) – is persistently challenged by Poscher, who maintains a traditional, 'defensive' understanding of these concepts and mechanisms. These diverging views are briefly explained below.

Despite the successive conceptual adaptations of the principles theory over the last two decades, one of its cornerstones has remained untouched: the 'double aspect of constitutional rights'.[21] According to Alexy, legal norms such as constitutional rights are both rules – currently including optimisation requirements – and principles, characterised by expressing an 'ideal ought'. Thus, constitutional rights not only have an optimisation-based content due to their 'rule aspect', but necessarily imply an ideal dimension by virtue of their 'principle aspect'. This line of reasoning can be justified insofar as the answers to conflicts of constitutional rights require both a quest for an optimum outcome and the preservation of the outweighed right's validity in individual cases. To resolve conflicts of constitutional rights on these grounds, Alexy has developed three central concepts; more precisely, two laws and one formula.

In line with a notion of normative conflict in which no principle takes absolute precedence over another, Alexy's 'law of competing principles' reads as follows:

> If principle $P1$ takes precedence over principle $P2$ in circumstances C: $(P1\ \mathbf{P}\ P2)\ C$, and if $P1$ gives rise to legal consequences Q in circumstances C, then a valid rule applies, which has C as its protasis and Q as its apodosis: $C \rightarrow Q$.[22]

This law's main purpose is to clarify how colliding legal principles are converted from the ideal dimension – in which their respective weights (not their validity)

[21] Alexy (n 1) 84.
[22] ibid 54.

are assessed – to the real dimension of actual individual cases, where only one of them can be ultimately applied. Bearing in mind that such an assessment has to consider the degrees of both epistemic certainty and normative satisfaction of formal and substantive principles,[23] Alexy proposed a 'law of balancing' that, in his view, amounts to the doctrinal figure known as 'proportionality in a narrow sense' (also called the 'balancing test'). It has the following wording:

> The greater the degree of non-satisfaction of, or detriment to, one principle, the greater must be the importance of satisfying the other.[24]

Alexy's balancing proposal is further developed through a fine-grained triadic scale of intensities ('light', 'moderate', and 'serious') that aims to determine the 'concrete weight of the principle P_i relative to the colliding principle P_j' ($W_{i,j}$) by measuring their respective interference (I), abstract weight (W), and the reliability of the empirical and normative assumptions at play (R). It is called the 'weight formula':[25]

$$W_{i,j} = \frac{I_i \cdot W_i \cdot R_i}{I_j \cdot W_j \cdot R_j}$$

Poscher's understanding of constitutional rights and adjudication is significantly different. His position is that the constitutional rights enshrined in the Basic Law are not optimisation requirements, nor do they require the assumption of an 'ideal ought' in order to be properly interpreted. Rather, they are individual and group protections – translatable as 'defensive claims'[26] – against state powers. In addition to other doctrinal disagreements (eg multipolar legal relationships and the link between constitutional law and other areas of law), Poscher's position also entails an alternative approach for interpreting constitutional disputes.[27] According to him, instead of being almost invariably confined to a balancing test, conflicts of constitutional rights can be resolved by means of a much wider range of argumentative tools. They may demand, for instance, a case-by-case analysis, an appeal to classical interpretive canons, an appeal to a doctrinal system, or even an adjustment to a more comprehensive theory of political morality. In the end, their application is contingent upon one's understanding of what is substantially at stake in each individual case rather than a 'rule-or-principle categorisation'.

Moreover, divorcing the nature of constitutional rights from the assumption of an 'ideal ought' might open up other approaches to proportionality analysis

[23] ibid 82.
[24] ibid 102.
[25] See R Alexy, 'On Balancing and Subsumption: A Structural Comparison' (2003) 16 *Ratio Juris* 433, 446.
[26] Poscher (n 2) 1ff.
[27] ibid 198–202.

(both in Germany[28] and in other jurisdictions[29]). Throughout the debate, Poscher has pointed to a doctrinal construction of the proportionality in a narrow sense according to which the balancing test is understood as a 'prohibition of gross disproportionality'.[30] Rather than being orientated towards the optimum outcome when balancing both abstract and concrete weights of conflicting constitutional norms, Poscher's alternative demands that courts merely assess whether state measures that interfere with these rights are not grossly disproportionate to the aims pursued by the legislator. It manifests the notion that the responsiveness of proportionality testing terminates at the moment when these discrepancies can no longer be measured in intersubjective grounds. Hence, its 'prudential spirit' limits judges' decision-making powers when balancing constitutional rights and state interests, while leaving greater scope for political decisions made by – democratically elected – legislative bodies. In short, the divorce of legal principles from an ideal dimension ultimately facilitates the development of doctrinal constructions that, by recognising unavoidable incommensurabilities in constitutional adjudication, urge a more 'self-restrained attitude' from the judicial branch.

V. Closing Remarks

The German legal debate between Robert Alexy and Ralf Poscher presents different and substantial challenges for future legal research. On the one hand, Alexy and his followers owe a response to Poscher's main objections. They have to

[28] Listing a number of theoretical and doctrinal problems with the principles theory, M Jestaedt, 'The Doctrine of Balancing: Its Strengths and Weaknesses' in M Klatt (ed), *Institutionalized Reason: The Jurisprudence of Robert Alexy* (Oxford, Oxford University Press, 2012) 159–72; pointing to a tendency to undermine the distinction between state and society, KH Ladeur, 'A Critique of Balancing and the Principle of Proportionality in Constitutional Law – A Case for "Impersonal Rights"?' (2016) 7 *Transnational Legal Theory* 228, 247–51. For more recent views, see N Petersen, *Proportionality and the Review of Legislative Rationality: Fundamental Rights Adjudication in Canada, Germany and South Africa* (Cambridge, Cambridge University Press, 2017) 158–82; M Kumm, 'Global Constitutionalism, Human Rights and Proportionality: Institutionalizing Socratic Contestation' (2022) 9 *Journal of Constitutional Justice* 193, 198ff.

[29] See eg DM Beatty, *The Ultimate Rule of Law* (Oxford, Oxford University Press, 2004) 169ff; K Möller, *The Global Model of Constitutional Rights* (Oxford, Oxford University Press, 2012) 99–133; A Barak, *Proportionality: Constitutional Rights and their Limitations* (Cambridge, Cambridge University Press, 2012) 243ff. For a general overview, see JS Sampaio, 'Proportionality: Measuring Impacts on Fundamental Rights' in M Sellers and S Kirste (eds), *Encyclopedia of the Philosophy of Law and Social Philosophy* (Dordrecht, Springer, 2023) 2863–69.

[30] See R Poscher, 'What Would It Take? The Potential and Limits of Proportionality in Law' (2025) *Jurisprudence* 1, 1–34. See also R Poscher, 'Proportionality and the Bindingness of Fundamental Rights' in E Billis et al (eds), *Proportionality in Crime Control and Criminal Justice* (Oxford, Hart Publishing, 2021) 60–64; T Kingreen and R Poscher, *Grundrechte. Staatsrecht II*, 38th edn (München, CF Müller, 2022) 106–7 [Rn 431]. Similarly, see B Schlink, *Abwägung im Verfassungsrecht* (Berlin, Duncker & Humblot, 1976) 76–78, 192ff, who argued against the balancing test within the proportionality analysis. In a more recent contribution, Schlink upheld that 'the process of balancing remains methodologically obscure'. See B Schlink, 'Proportionality (1)' in M Rosenfeld and A Sajó (eds), *The Oxford Handbook of Comparative Constitutional Law* (Oxford, Oxford University Press, 2012) 725.

answer why the concept of 'legal principle' necessarily requires the assumption of an ideal dimension of law; more precisely, to clarify what properties the 'ideal ought' has that cannot be explained by the 'real ought' that characterises optimisation requirements (which, according to Alexy himself, have become rules). On the other hand, those who are not convinced by the principles theory can follow at least two paths that are not mutually exclusive: in jurisprudence, they can either embrace a different qualitative criterion for distinguishing rules from principles or maintain a gradualist view (as supported by Poscher). In constitutional law, they have the option of highlighting the various argumentative tools beyond optimisation-based approaches and developing a normative alternative to the balancing test that responds to contemporary – both theoretical and doctrinal – challenges. Either way, those hesitant about the principles theory also have to clarify what legal principles are, how they differ from rules, and what impact they have on constitutional adjudication.

First Round

1

On the Structure of Legal Principles*

ROBERT ALEXY**

The distinction between rules and principles had already been thoroughly considered in Germany by Josef Esser during the 1950s, albeit with a slightly different terminology.[1] In Austria, Walter Wilburg in the 1940s had anticipated major developments in his theory of flexible systems.[2] Still, it was Ronald Dworkin's major challenge to HLA Hart's version of legal positivism, initially in 'The Model of Rules', that marked the beginnings of a broad discussion.[3] During the past three decades the distinction between rules and principles – including its implications for legal methodology, the concept of the legal system, the relation between law and morality, and legal dogmatics, especially that of basic rights – has been subject to a great number of in part very detailed studies. Two main positions have emerged. One is that principles express the idea of optimisation. This can be expressed in the short formula that principles are optimisation commands, and it is this feature that represents the main distinction between principles and rules. This understanding may be termed 'principles theory'. The other position is less uniform. But there is a consensus of opinion to the effect that either the optimisation thesis is wrong, or at any rate its explanatory power is greatly exaggerated.

The number and variety of contrary positions is such that I cannot discuss all of them. Instead, I will consider just a few objections concerning the structure

* Formerly published as R Alexy, 'On the structure of legal principles' (2000) 13 *Ratio Juris* 294. Copyrights granted by John Wiley & Sons and Copyright Clearance Center.

** I should like to thank Bonnie Litschewski Paulson and Stanley L Paulson for help and advice on matters of English style.

[1] J Esser, *Grundsatz und Norm in der richterlichen Fortbildung des Privatrechts*, 3rd edn (Tübingen, Mohr Siebeck, 1974).

[2] W Wilburg, *Die Elemente des Schadenrechts* (Marburg, Elwert, 1941). See also W Wilburg, *Entwicklung eines beweglichen Systems im bürgerlichen Recht* (Graz, Kienreich, 1950); W Wilburg, 'Zusammenspiel der Kräfte im Aufbau des Schuldrechts' (1964) 163 *Archiv für civilistische Praxis* 346, 346ff. For a comparison of the theory of principles with Wilburg's doctrine of elements, see L Michael, *Der allgemeine Gleichheitssatz als Methodennorm komparativer Systeme. Methodenrechtliche Analyse und Fortentwicklung der Theorie der „beweglichen Systeme"* (Berlin, Duncker & Humblot, 1997) 105ff.

[3] RM Dworkin, 'The Model of Rules' (1967) 35 *University of Chicago Law Review* 14, 14ff. Reprinted as RM Dworkin, 'The Model of Rules I' in RM Dworkin (ed), *Taking Rights Seriously* (London, Duckworth, 1978) 14ff.

of principles as norms. First, however, I shall provide a sketch of the three main theses of principles theory; they delineate the core of the controversy.

I. Three Theses

A. The Optimisation Thesis

According to the standard definition of principles theory,[4] principles are norms commanding that something be realised to the highest degree that is actually and legally possible. Principles are therefore *optimisation commands*. They can be fulfilled to different degrees. The mandatory degree of fulfilment depends not only on actual facts but also on legal possibilities. The field of legal possibilities is determined by countervailing principles and rules. Contrariwise, rules are norms that can only be either complied with or not. If a rule is valid, it requires that one do exactly what it demands, nothing more and nothing less. Rules therefore comprise a decision in the fields of actual and legal possibilities. They are *definitive commands*. This means that the difference between rules and principles is a difference in quality and not only one of degree. Every norm is either a rule or a principle.[5]

B. The Collision Law

The difference between rules and principles emerges most clearly when one turns to collisions of principles and conflicts of rules. Collisions of principles and conflicts of rules share the feature that two norms, when applied separately, lead to incompatible results, namely to two contradictory specific or concrete legal 'ought'-judgements. But they differ most fundamentally in their respective solutions to the conflict.

(i) Conflicts of Rules

A conflict between two rules can only be solved by either introducing an exception clause into one of the two rules or declaring at least one of them invalid. An example of the first is a school regulation that prohibits one's leaving the classroom before the signal but requires that one do just that in the event of a fire alarm. This conflict is easily solved, namely by introducing, for the case of the fire alarm, an exception into the prohibition from leaving the classroom before the signal. If such

[4] R Alexy, *Theorie der Grundrechte*, 3rd edn (Frankfurt, Suhrkamp, 1996) 75ff.

[5] ibid 77. See also R Alexy, 'Zum Begriff des Rechtsprinzips' in R Alexy (ed), *Recht, Vernunft, Diskurs* (Frankfurt, Suhrkamp, 1995) 177, 203.

a solution is out of reach, the only remaining possibility is to declare at least one of the rules invalid. This is the main purview of collision rules such as '*lex posterior derogat legi priori*', '*lex superior derogat legi inferiori*', and 'Federal law shall override Land law' (Article 31 of the Basic Law).

(ii) Collisions of Principles

A collision of principles is solved in an altogether different way. An example is a decision of the German Federal Constitutional Court concerning the inability to attend sessions of a court proceeding.[6] This decision takes up the question whether a trial may be held in the case of an accused who would be in danger of suffering from a stroke or heart attack owing to the stress of the trial. The colliding norms are, on the one hand, Article 2 (2) first sentence of the Basic Law, guaranteeing to everyone the right to life and the inviolability of one's body, and on the other, the rule-of-law principle (*Rechtsstaatsprinzip*) in so far as it obligates the state to provide for a functioning system of criminal justice. If only the basic right existed, the conduct of the trial could easily be qualified as prohibited owing to the danger posed to the life and health of the accused that is connected therewith. If, vice-versa, the only obligation that existed were that of the state to provide for a functioning system of criminal justice, the performance of the trial would be classified without difficulty either as obligatory or at least as permitted. Now, the court could have solved the case by either declaring the basic right or the rule-of-law principle, in so far as it comprises the obligation to provide for a functioning system of criminal justice, as invalid. In this case the court would have treated the collision as a conflict of rules and solved it in terms of validity. It is obvious, however, that neither the invalidation of the basic right to life and inviolability of the body nor of the principle of a functioning criminal justice system as a sub-principle of the rule-of-law principle is a live option here. The second possibility for solving a conflict of rules, namely introducing an exception, also fails to comprehend what is to be done in this case. The basic right to life and inviolability of the body does not count as an exception to the principle of a functioning system of criminal justice, nor does this principle count as an exception to the right to life and inviolability of the body. Rather, the court solves the problem by determining a conditional priority of one of the colliding principles over the other with respect to the circumstances of the case. The basic right to life and to the inviolability of the body shall have priority over the principle of a functioning system of criminal justice as a sub-principle of the rule-of-law principle where 'there is a clear and specific danger that the accused will forfeit his life or suffer serious bodily harm if the trial is held'.[7] Under these conditions the basic right has greater weight and

[6] BVerfGE 51, 324 – Verhandlungsfähigkeit des Angeklagten.
[7] ibid 324 (346).

therefore takes priority; under different conditions precisely the opposite may well be the case.

The priority of the basic right implies that its legal effects are mandatory. The fulfilment of the conditions of priority brings about the legal effects of the preceding principle. This can be formulated as a general *collision law*. It runs:

> The conditions under which one principle takes priority over another constitute the operative facts of a rule giving legal effect to the principle deemed prior.[8]

A more technical version is:

> If principle P_1 takes priority over principle P_2 under conditions C: $(P_1 \mathbf{P} P_2)$ C, and if P_1 under conditions C implies legal effect R, then a rule is valid that comprises C as the operative facts and R as legal effect: $C \rightarrow R$.[9]

The collision law expresses the fact that the priority relations between the principles of a system are not absolute but only conditional or relative. The task of optimising is to determine correct conditional priority relations. The fact that a determination of a conditional priority relation in accordance with the collision law is always the determination of a rule formed on the occasion of the case demonstrates that the respective levels of principles and rules are by no means unconnected. To solve a case by weighing is to decide by means of a rule that is substantiated by giving priority to the preceding principle. In this respect, principles are necessarily reasons for rules.

C. The Balancing Law

The practical significance of principles theory in the form of the optimisation thesis is found above all in its equivalence to the principle of proportionality (*Verhältnismäßigkeitsgrundsatz*). Principles theory implies the principle of proportionality, and the principle of proportionality implies principles theory.[10] The fact that principles theory implies the principle of proportionality means that the three sub-principles it contains – the principle of appropriateness, of necessity, and of proportionality in a narrow sense – follow logically from it; hence, they are deducible from it in a strict sense. The same is true if we proceed from the other side of the equivalence relation, namely, that the principle of proportionality implies principles theory. Thus, one who rejects principles theory must reject the principle of proportionality, too. The dispute over principles theory can therefore be seen as a reflection of the dispute over the proportionality principle.

[8] This phrasing of the law of competing principles relates to the case in which the legal effect of the preceding principle comes fully into force. If it does not come fully into force, modifications are necessary. See Alexy (n 4) 83 (fn 42).

[9] ibid 83.

[10] ibid 100ff.

The implications of the proportionality principle turn on the definition of the concept of principle. Principles *qua* optimisation commands demand realisation as far as is possible relative to the actual and legal possibilities. A relativisation in the direction of the actual possibilities leads to the principles of appropriateness and necessity. Let us assume a measure M that encroaches on the freedom of trade, occupation, or profession (P_1) in order to promote consumer protection (P_2), but which is not appropriate to promoting P_2 in any way whatever. It is possible to abandon M at no cost to P_2, consumer protection. The optimisation of P_1 and P_2 demands, then, that M not be used. This is exactly the content of the principle of appropriateness. The principle of necessity says that a measure M_1 is prohibited in respect of P_1 and P_2 if there is an alternative measure M_2 that promotes P_2 approximately as well as M_1 but encroaches less intensively on P_1. Let us assume that P_2 stands, again, for consumer protection; in particular, for the consumers' protection against buying products that they do not in fact want. Let us also assume that M_1 is an absolute prohibition of goods that look like chocolate but are not chocolate. M_2 stands in this case for the obligation clearly to designate the nature of the goods. This obligation, namely (M_2), obviously encroaches less intensively on the freedom of trade, occupation, or profession (P_1) than would an absolute prohibition (M_1), and it serves consumer protection more or less equally well; therefore, the absolute prohibition (M_1) is prohibited in relation to P_1 and P_2 as an unnecessary means.[11]

The principles of appropriateness and necessity stem from the obligation of a realisation as great as possible relative to the actual possibilities. They express the idea of Pareto-optimality. The principle of proportionality in a narrow sense stems from the obligation of a realisation as far as possible relative to the legal possibilities; that is, relative most of all to the countervailing principles. Here we are concerned with balancing or weighing in a narrow and true sense. This is necessary whenever the fulfilment of one principle leads to the non-fulfilment of another; hence, whenever one principle is only realisable at the cost of another. For this kind of case the following *balancing law* can be formulated: 'The more intensive the interference in one principle, the more important the realisation of the other principle'.[12] The problems connected with this formula are the main topics of the discussion concerning the question whether balancing is a rational procedure.

II. Two Objections

Balancing and collision law are attempts to describe the core idea of principles theory – namely the optimisation thesis – more precisely. This thesis claims that principles are norms that, owing to their structure, are fundamentally distinct

[11] BVerfGE 53, 135 (145ff) – Schokoladenosterhase.
[12] Alexy (n 4) 146.

from rules. Numerous arguments have been adduced against this position. Two are discussed here.

A. Principle Structure and Norm Application

A radical 'norm theoretic' criticism would have us believe that principles do not exist at all; rather, only norms exist, albeit norms that are used in different ways. Klaus Günther thus asserts that the difference between rules and principles is not a difference in structure but merely a 'different kind of use'. Whether 'we treat a norm as a rule by using it without regard to the unequal characteristics of the situation or whether we treat a norm as a principle by considering all (actual and legal) facts',[13] is a question of the 'conditions of action'[14] or of the 'conditions of conversation'.[15] In legal systems, the conditions of conversation and of action are institutional in nature. The separation of powers and the rule-of-law require that the decisions of the legislator be treated as rules and that exceptions be admitted only in special cases.

The heart of Günther's criticism is the thesis that, independently of the institutional frame, one can 'direct the claim that a norm be used relative to the actual and normative (legal) possibilities present in a situation, … to any norm whatever'.[16] This is true, but it fails to address the decisive point. By a 'use relative to the actual and normative (legal) possibilities present in a situation', Günther understands the 'consideration of all circumstances'.[17] To consider something, however, is different from optimising. This is demonstrated by the fact that the consideration of all circumstances is also possible using norms that can either be fulfilled or not, whereas optimisation requires that one be able to adhere to a norm to a greater or lesser extent. While optimisation implies the consideration of all circumstances, the consideration of all circumstances does not imply optimisation. It is this point that makes clear why Günther's criticism fails to meet what is essential – optimisation itself.

Gradual fulfilment is not the only reason for constructing principles in terms of the structure of norms. Only principles theory can explain why a norm, set aside in a balancing decision, is neither violated nor partially or totally rendered invalid.[18]

[13] K Günther, *Der Sinn für Angemessenheit: Anwendungsdiskurse in Moral und Recht* (Frankfurt, Suhrkamp, 1988) 270.

[14] ibid 273.

[15] ibid 270. Stelzer argues along the same lines, contending 'that "rule" and "principle" characterise, ultimately, the argumentative use of norms'. M Stelzer, *Das Wesensgehaltsargument und der Grundsatz der Verhältnismäßigkeit* (Vienna, Österreich Verlag, 1991) 215.

[16] Günther (n 13) 272.

[17] ibid 272.

[18] Habermas has raised against the optimisation thesis the objection that it cannot take account of the case in which 'one right can "yield" to another right, without loss of validity, when the two happen to conflict'. Precisely the opposite is the case. See J Habermas, 'Reply to Symposium Participants, Benjamin N. Cardozo School of Law' in M Rosenfeld and A Arato (eds), *Habermas on Law and Democracy* (Berkeley CA, University of California Press, 1998) 429.

The idea of optimisation is necessary if we are to comprehend the dimension of weight in the case of a norm, in contrast to its validity. This has a great many consequences in legal dogmatics. An adequate theory of the limits of a right, for example, is not possible without principles theory.[19]

One can grant that Günther is right when he says that there are cases in which is not easy to decide whether a norm should be treated as a rule or as a principle.[20] This is a question of interpretation, and, as is usual with interpretation, there are no criteria providing for simple and clear answers in all cases. But this is not an objection to the point that 'principle' captures a characteristic of norm structure. The very question whether a norm is a rule or a principle presupposes that norms *qua* principles be possible entities.

B. Optimisation Commands

(i) Commands to Optimise and Commands to be Optimised

The discussion of Günther's 'norm theoretic' objection has shown that the distinction of rules and principles generally is dependent on the character of principles as commands to optimise. Aulis Aarnio and Jan-Reinard Sieckmann have raised the objection that the concept of a command to optimise is ill-suited for distinguishing between rules and principles. According to the standard definition presented above, principles are optimisation commands – that is, commands to optimise – because they impose the obligation that something be realised to the highest degree that is actually and legally possible. This obligation has, indeed, a definitive character. It can only either be fulfilled or not fulfilled, and its complete fulfilment is always obligatory.[21] Aarnio puts this point as follows: 'Either one does or one does not optimise. For example, in the case of conflict between two value principles, the principles must be brought together in the optimum manner, and only in the optimum manner'.[22] Optimisation commands therefore have the structure of rules.

This in no way says that principles theory in the guise of the optimisation thesis collapses; it simply gives it a sharper focus. A distinction is to be made between *commands to be optimised* and *commands to optimise*. Commands to be optimised are the objects of balancing or weighing. They can be termed 'the ideal "ought"' or 'ideals'.[23] An ideal 'ought' is something that is to be optimised and thereby transformed into a real 'ought'.[24] As the object of optimisation, it is placed on the

[19] Alexy (n 4) 249ff.
[20] Günther (n 13) 272.
[21] JR Sieckmann, *Regelmodelle und Prinzipienmodelle des Rechtssystems* (Baden-Baden, Nomos, 1990) 65.
[22] A Aarnio, 'Taking Rules Seriously' (1990) 42 *Archiv für Rechts- und Sozialphilosophie – Beihefte* 180, 187.
[23] Alexy (n 5) 203ff.
[24] Alexy (n 5) 204.

object level. Contrariwise, the commands to optimise, that is, the optimisation commands, are placed on a meta-level. On this level they prescribe what is to be done with that which is found on the object level. They impose the obligation that their subject-matter, the commands to be optimised, be realised to the greatest extent possible. As optimisation commands, they are not to be optimised but to be fulfilled by optimisation.

Principles, therefore, as the subject-matter of balancing are not optimisation commands but rather commands to be optimised. As such they comprehend an ideal 'ought' that is not yet relativised to the actual and legal possibilities. In spite of this, it is useful to talk about principles as optimisation commands or obligations. It expresses in an altogether straightforward way the nature of principles. In saying what is to be *done* with principles, one says all that matters from the point of view of legal practice. This practical aspect is lent support by a theoretical consideration. There is a necessary connection between the ideal 'ought' – that is, the principle as such – and the optimisation command as a rule. The ideal 'ought' implies the optimisation command and vice versa. These are two sides of the same coin. The question 'whether the command to weigh, necessarily accompanying a principle, is "inside" or "outside" of the meaning of this principle', thus formulated by Peczenik,[25] can be answered by pointing out that the optimisation command is comprised in the concept of principle. To abolish it would mean that the principle had lost its character as a principle. Peczenik adds that the question of whether or not principles should be called 'optimisation commands' has no substantial consequences for moral or legal philosophy.[26] All this seems to show that it is advisable, for reasons of simplicity, to designate principles as 'optimisation commands' and to employ more precise distinctions only where necessary.

(ii) Reiterated Validity Obligations

One might well think that none of this leads to clarity where the structure of principles is concerned. Certainly, one knows that they are to be optimised and, therefore, that they are commands or obligations to be optimised, but one knows nothing about the nature of whatever is to be optimised. Sieckmann tries to answer this question with his theory of reiterated validity obligations. His starting point is a distinction among three kinds of sentences: (1) norm formulations, (2) validity sentences, and (3) validity obligations.[27] Norm formulations or norm sentences[28] express norms semantically – that is, norms as simple meaning-contents – without saying anything about their validity. Here the basic form can be represented with the help of the obligation operator '*O*' (It is obligatory …) and the letter '*p*'

[25] A Peczenik, *On Law and Reason* (Dordrecht, Springer, 1989) 78.

[26] ibid.

[27] JR Sieckmann, 'Zur Analyse von Normkonflikten und Normabwägungen' in G Meggle (ed), *Analyomen 2: Perspektiven der Analytischen Philosophie* (Berlin, Walter de Gruyter, 1997) 352.

[28] Alexy (n 4) 42.

standing for what is obligatory. For example, '*Op*' can express: 'It is obligatory to return the thing'. Instead of '*Op*' one can insert a simple '*n*' for norm formulations or norm sentences. Validity sentences or norm-validity sentences[29] have a more far-reaching content than norm formulations. They not only represent norms semantically but also express that these norms are valid. Using the validity predicate '*V*', they can be represented as '*VOp*' or, more simply, as '*Vn*'.[30] Finally, validity obligations are obligations expressing that a specific norm (*n*) ought (*O*) to be valid (*V*), which can be captured by '*OVn*'. Once these distinctions have been made, the question arises: How, employing this machinery, are principles best represented? It is easy to see that the first alternative has to be eliminated. A principle is more than simply a norm in the semantic sense – that is, a mere norm content (*n*) – if its role as a reason in balancing or weighing is to be captured. For this, it must, in one way or another, have validity.[31] Now, one might assume that this could be accomplished by attaching to the norm sentence '*n*' the validity predicate '*V*', which would imply the classification of the principles as '*Vn*', the second of the alternatives stated above. According to Sieckmann, however, precisely this is not permissible. Validity sentences, that is, sentences of the form '*Vn*', express what Sieckmann calls 'normative statements'. One who utters such a sentence gives expression to an assumption about the definitive validity of a norm.[32] If principles had definitive validity, they would not lend themselves to, and would not be in need of, balancing, and they would therefore not be principles at all.

Now, one might ask whether it really is cogent to reserve validity predicates like '*V*' solely for definitive validity. There is the possibility of introducing different validity predicates, for example, one for definitive and one for prima facie validity. Nothing in our normative language precludes such a possibility; the language is sufficiently flexible to give expression to the differing strengths of different kinds of validity. The point of Sieckmann's effort, however, is to obstruct this very path. If one chose it, the problem concerning the argumentative power of principles would be concealed without being analysed in a specific validity predicate. Seen from an analytical point of view, the interpretation of principles as reiterated validity obligations is said to be superior to this.

If the validity predicate '*V*' is understood solely in the sense of definitive validity, a dilemma arises between the first and second alternatives representing the point of departure of the thesis of reiterated validity obligations. Simple norm sentences of the sort '*n*' or '*Op*' are not sufficient to represent the argumentative power of principles. They merely express norms as the content of thought *sans* validity. Anyone could come up with a norm, thus understood. This alternative is, therefore, too weak. On the other hand, validity sentences of the sort '*Vn*' or

[29] ibid 51.
[30] In the following the simpler form is used. For '*n*' one can always substitute '*Op*'.
[31] JR Sieckmann, 'Zur Abwägungsfähigkeit von Prinzipien' in HJ Koch and U Neumann (eds), *Praktische Vernunft und Rechtsanwendung. ARSP-Beiheft 53* (Stuttgart, Franz Steiner, 1994) 209.
[32] Sieckmann (n 27) 351.

'*VOp*' are too strong. This is indeed the case where the validity predicate '*V*', as Sieckmann stipulates, is to be reserved solely for definitive validity. Principles, after all, are the opposite of definitive obligations.

According to Sieckmann, the solution to the dilemma lies in the third alternative, that is, in the interpretation of principles as validity obligations. Problems, however, arise at once. According to Sieckmann, validity obligations have the form of '*OVn*'. That which begins with '*O*', not '*V*', is nothing other than a norm in the semantic sense, thus, a mere content of thought without validity, and this will be true even if the thought refers to validity. It is of no help, here, to insert another '*V*' before the '*O*', for this would lend to the thought, initially too weak, the strength of definitive validity. Sieckmann, therefore, has to find a path between the too weak '*O*' and the too powerful '*V*' – he does, at any rate, if he wants to stay within the co-ordinates of his elements '*n*', '*V*', and '*O*'. It is said that this middle course can be found in the connection of '*O*' and '*V*', namely, in an infinitely reiterating connection. The true logical form of the principle is therefore said to be '... *OVOVn*'.[33]

Now it may be asked: Is this an answer to the question of what principles come to that goes beyond what we already know? To be sure, it is clearly said what principles are not. They cannot be either definitely valid or non-obligatory norms. But this is nothing new. Only a positive answer would have real interest. The thesis of reiterated validity obligations offers us a positive answer, however, in only a very limited way. Reiteration illustrates the problem in an interesting manner but does not solve it. It is interesting, for the two things that principles cannot be are connected by infinite reiteration in such a way that a continuous oscillation takes place between them. '*Vn*' says that '*n*', for example, a norm sentence of the form '*Op*', is definitely valid. This is too much. '*OVn*' weakens this radically. It is only a norm without validity that turns up in the world as a mere thought of a norm. This is too little. '*VOVn*' overcomes this insufficiency, but goes beyond the target, for definitive validity – and this according to Sieckmann is what '*V*' stands for – exceeds that which can be claimed of a principle. Thus, '*O*' must immediately be poured like water on the fire once again, and the game continues endlessly, for the quenched fire is to be rekindled straightaway, ad infinitum. It seems as though the reiteration thesis describes in a relatively complicated way the notion that principles stand somewhere between definitive validity and non-obligation.

A different position would be close at hand if it were possible to explain, by appeal to reiteration, distinctive features of principles that could not be explained without it. This is, however, not the case. Sieckmann regards principles as validity obligations, that is, as obligations expressing that specific norms ought to be valid, a state of affairs that can be captured by '*OVn*'. In so doing, he gives the infinite reiteration of the form '... *OVOVn*' a certain priority over the form '... *VOVOVn*'. This, however, is not at all evident and does not follow from the assumption of infinity, since the assumption speaks on behalf of a balance between validity (*V*)

[33] ibid 352.

and 'ought' (*O*). How can an obligation operator (*O*) that stands ahead of the validity predicate (*V*), and thus does not include validity, substantiate validity? Sieckmann's answer is plain. Thanks to infinite reiteration, there is no obligation operator (*O*) standing alone ahead of a validity predicate (*V*), for ahead of every obligation operator there is always a validity predicate that also does not stand alone – and this for the reason that it is immediately connected to an obligation operator. Perhaps one has to imagine that all this takes place at one time. None of this, however, serves as an explanation of the character of the principle. That question is, indeed, encapsulated neither by a validity predicate nor by some deontic operator, but is left undecided between '*V*' and '*O*'. In the end, nothing is claimed other than that the argumentative power of principles is to be found somewhere between definitive validity and non-obligation.

Still, Sieckmann's attempt to capture the character of principles with the help of the reiteration thesis is not without value. It deserves attention as a painstaking effort to understand the nature of principles by means of classical deontic logic and a binary validity predicate. However, nothing said in this connection alters the fact that there is, presently, no explanation of what principles come to that is more promising than a construction of them as obligations to be optimised, where this corresponds to obligations to optimise. This construction seems to be the best expression of the idea of an ideal 'ought' and of ideal validity.

2

Insights, Errors, and Self-Misconceptions of the Theory of Principles*

RALF POSCHER

The topic of principles first attracted attention in the context of German legal theory with Josef Esser's work *Principle and Norm* from 1956,[1] in which Esser attacked the positivist concept of adjudication by redirecting attention to the role played in private law by fundamental legal principles that were neither written norms nor formally enacted by any legislator. About 20 years later – certainly without reference to and probably without knowledge of Esser's work – Ronald Dworkin used the argument of principles in his attack on HLA Hart.[2] He used the argument of principles to show that the positivist conception of pedigree was unable to explain the role of principles in adjudication. This was one of his major arguments against positivism in general. As one of his examples of a principle in law, Dworkin referred to the freedom of speech.[3] Again, about eight years later, Robert Alexy took up Dworkin's remarks on the character of some fundamental rights as principles to develop a theory of fundamental rights. According to this theory, fundamental rights in general should be understood as principles, from which it follows that they must be understood as optimisation requirements.[4] In his later work and in that of his students, the theory of principles has not only

* Formerly published as R Poscher, 'Insights, Errors, and Self-Misconceptions of the Theory of Principles' (2009) 22 *Ratio Juris* 425. Copyrights granted by John Wiley & Sons and Copyright Clearance Center.

[1] A predecessor could be seen in W Wilburg, *Entwicklung eines beweglichen Systems im bürgerlichen Recht* (Graz, Kienreich, 1951); for an early critique, see J Esser, 'Review: W Wilburg, *Entwicklung eines beweglichen Systems im bürgerlichen Recht*' (1950–51) 151 *Archiv für die civilistische Praxis* 555; J Esser, 'Review: W Wilburg, *Entwicklung eines beweglichen Systems im bürgerlichen Recht*' (1953) 18 *Rabels Zeitschrift für ausländisches und internationales Privatrecht* 165.

[2] RM Dworkin, 'The Model of Rules I' in RM Dworkin (ed), *Taking Rights Seriously* (Cambridge MA, Harvard University Press, 1977) 22.

[3] ibid 90.

[4] R Alexy, *Theorie der Grundrechte* (Frankfurt, Suhrkamp, 1986) 47–49.

been applied to constitutional law in general[5] and other areas of law such as Administrative Law,[6] Private Law[7] and the Law of the European Union,[8] but also as a general theory of law which claims to reveal the fundamental structures of law and legal practice.[9]

In a nutshell, the claim of the theory of principles as developed by Alexy is that in law there are two types of norms: rules and principles. Whereas rules do not pose any specific problems, since they can be applied by mere subsumption, principles are more interesting. Rules are easy; principles do all the work. Principles must be applied by balancing them against other principles and rules.[10] Principles are balanced by optimisation in those individual cases where they collide.[11] Principles were thus characterised by Alexy as optimisation requirements.[12] Alexy initially developed his theory of principles as a doctrinal theory of the fundamental rights of the Basic Law. Due to the open nature of the constitutional text, fundamental rights serve as the paradigm case of principles, from which it follows that they must be applied by optimisation in a process of balancing. In German constitutional law, the theory of principles competes with a whole range of doctrinal approaches to fundamental rights, which are resistant to or at least sceptical about the theory of principles' tendency to transform all constitutional issues into a matter of optimisation by balancing.[13] One major concern is the tendency of

[5] R Alexy, 'Rechtsregeln und Rechtsprinzipien' (1985) 25 *Archiv für Rechts- und Sozialphilosophie* 13; JR Sieckmann, 'Zur Abwägungsfähigkeit von Prinzipien' (1994) 53 *Archiv für Rechts- und Sozialphilosophie* 227; M Borowski, *Grundrechte als Prinzipien. Die Unterscheidung von Prima-facie Position und definitiver Position als fundamentaler Konstruktionsgrundsatz der Grundrechte* (Baden-Baden, Nomos, 1998); M Borowski, 'Prinzipien als Grundrechtsnormen' (1998) 53 *Zeitschrift für öffentliches Recht* 307; R Alexy, 'Zur Struktur der Rechtsprinzipien' in B Schilcher et al (eds), *Regeln, Prinzipien und Elemente im System des Rechts* (Vienna, Verlag Österreich, 2000) [ed note: see Chapter 1 for the translated version].

[6] JH Park, *Rechtsfindung im Verwaltungsrecht: Grundlegung einer Prinzipientheorie des Verwaltungsrechts als Methode der Verwaltungsrechtsdogmatik* (Berlin, Duncker & Humblot, 1999); M Ryter-Sauvant, *Allgemeine Rechtsgrundsätze – Analogien zum Privatrecht. Ein Beitrag zur richterlichen Rechtsfortbildung im Verwaltungsrecht* (Bern, Stämpfli, 2005) 136–42.

[7] An argument for fundamental norms of justice as principles is given by N Jansen, *Die Struktur der Gerechtigkeit* (Baden-Baden, Nomos, 1998) 140–62; N Jansen, *Die Struktur des Haftungsrechts* (Tübingen, Mohr Siebeck, 2003) 598–606; N Jansen, 'Theoriebildung in der europäischen Privatrechtsdogmatik' in R Alexy (ed), *Juristische Grundlagenforschung* (Stuttgart, Franz Steiner, 2005) 35; N Jansen, 'Dogmatik, Erkenntnis und Theorie im europäischen Privatrecht' (2005) 13 *Zeitschrift für Europäisches Privatrecht* 750; N Jansen, 'Zum Gedanken einer juristischen Strukturtheorie' (2006) 91 *Archiv für Rechts- und Sozialphilosophie* 277; N Jansen, 'Die normativen Grundlagen rationalen Abwägens' in JR Sieckmann (ed), *Die Prinzipientheorie der Grundrechte. Studien zur Grundrechtstheorie Robert Alexys* (Baden-Baden, Nomos, 2007) 39–57.

[8] J Pietsch, *Das Schrankenregime der EU-Grundrechtecharta. Dogmatik und Bewertung auf der Grundlage einer Prinzipientheorie der Rechte* (Baden-Baden, Nomos, 2006).

[9] JR Sieckmann, *Regelmodelle und Prinzipienmodelle des Rechtssystems* (Baden-Baden, Nomos, 1990) 18ff.

[10] R Alexy, *A Theory of Constitutional Rights* (J Rivers trans, Oxford, Oxford University Press, 2002) 50–56.

[11] ibid 47ff.

[12] ibid 47.

[13] EW Böckenförde, 'Grundrechte als Grundsatznormen: Zur gegenwärtigen Lage der Grundrechtsdogmatik' (1990) 29 *Der Staat* 1, 13, 20ff; B Schlink, 'Grundrechte als Prinzipien?' (1992) 39 *Osaka University Law Review* 41, 41–45. Fundamentally critical of balancing doctrines in

balancing to dissolve more concrete doctrinal structures and open them up to opportunistic decisions in individual cases. Opponents of the theory contest, for example, the idea that the guarantee of human dignity or the provision for content neutrality of state regulation concerning the freedom of speech in the Basic Law should be subject to balancing, and not absolute, for theoretical reasons. Another major reservation stems from concerns about the division of power[14] and democratic theory. The idea of a constitutional requirement to optimise fundamental rights leaves little room for legislative decision-making. If an optimum is required in each conflict, the legal solution seems to be predetermined with no room for political manoeuvring. Parliaments could simply apply the constitution with at best a special margin of error, which would be the only safeguard against comprehensive political rule by the constitutional courts.

Despite the doctrinal critique, Alexy's theory of principles became influential not only in Germany but also in South America and Asia via translations of his book *A Theory of Constitutional rights* into Spanish and English, and of related books and articles into Portuguese,[15] Italian,[16] Chinese,[17] Japanese,[18] and Korean.[19] The theory of principles is used particularly as a blueprint for the interpretation of fundamental rights in the respective countries' constitutional law. Alexy's theory of principles aspires to become one of the major general theories of law in a global perspective. The legitimacy of this aspiration is the focus of the following reflections. Given the theoretical aspirations of the theory of principles, the aforementioned doctrinal objections, that are already well established, are not the central concern of this article. The article will rather focus on the theoretical

constitutional law, B Schlink, *Abwägung im Verfassungsrecht* (Berlin, Duncker & Humblot, 1976) 128–43; M Jestaedt, *Grundrechtsentfaltung im Gesetz. Studien zur Interdependenz von Grundrechtsdogmatik und Rechtsgewinnungstheorie* (Tübingen, Mohr Siebeck, 1999) 206–60; R Poscher, *Grundrechte als Abwehrrechte. Reflexive Regelung rechtlich geordneter Freiheit* (Tübingen, Mohr Siebeck, 2003) 73–84, 99ff; W Cremer, *Freiheitsgrundrechte. Funktionen und Strukturen* (Tübingen, Mohr Siebeck, 2003) 218–27.

[14] For the German doctrine, see R Poscher, 'Die Funktionenordnung des Grundgesetzes' in W Hoffmann-Riem et al (eds), *Grundlagen des Verwaltungsrechts. Methoden, Maßstäbe, Aufgaben* (Munich, CH Beck, 2006) 493–532.

[15] R Alexy, 'Constitutional rights, Balancing, and Rationality' (2003) 16 *Ratio Juris* 131.

[16] R Alexy, 'Kollision und Abwägung als Grundprobleme der Grundrechtsdogmatik' (2001) 6 *World Constitutional Law Review* 181; R Alexy, 'Grundrechte, Abwägung und Rationalität' (2002) 7 *Ars Interpretandi. Yearbook of Legal Hermeneutics* 113; R Alexy, 'The Weight Formula' (B Brożek and SL Paulson trans) in J Stelmach et al (eds), *Studies in the Philosophy of Law. Frontiers of the Economic Analysis of Law* (Krakow, Jagiellonian University Press, 2007) 9–27; R Alexy, *The Argument from Injustice: A Reply to Legal Positivism* (BL Paulson and SL Paulson trans, Oxford, Oxford University Press, 2010).

[17] R Alexy, 'Grundrechte als subjective Rechte und als objektive Normen' (1990) 29 *Der Staat* 49; R Alexy, 'Rights, Legal Reasoning and Rational Discourse' (1992) 5 *Ratio Juris* 143; R Alexy, 'Grundrechte im demokratischen Verfassungsstaat' in A Aarnio et al (eds), *Justice, Morality and Society. A Tribute to Aleksander Peczenik on the Occasion of his 60th Birthday. 16 November 1997* (Lund, Juristförlaget, 1997) 27.

[18] Alexy, 'Grundrechte als subjective Rechte und als objektive Normen' (n 17); Alexy, 'Grundrechte im demokratischen Verfassungsstaat' (n 17).

[19] Alexy, 'Grundrechte als subjective Rechte und als objektive Normen' (n 17); Alexy, 'The Weight Formula' (n 16); Alexy, *The Argument from Injustice* (n 16).

basis of the theory of principles, since this is the unique feature of the theory of principles as a fundamental rights doctrine: that it is essentially supported by theoretical arguments about the nature of law in general and principles in particular.[20] Though suggestive of unity, the term 'theory of principles' covers a wide array of projects which could be interconnected, but are in fact distinct. One can distinguish between at least five different aspects of the theory of principles:

(1) In the context of Anglo-Saxon discourse, the theory of principles was originally used as an argument at the level of structural theories of law, inquiring into the general characteristics of legal systems and their relation to other normative phenomena, especially in the fields of morals and ethics on the one hand, and politics on the other.[21]
(2) As a project in legal theory or legal logic, the theory of principles stands as a theory not of the structure of a normative order (ie the legal order), but as a theory of the logical structure of individual norms. In this context it advances the thesis that all phenomena in the normative realm can categorically be divided into principles and rules.[22]
(3) Closely connected to the above, but to be differentiated from it, the theory of principles also appears as a methodological theory regarding the categorical distinction between two types of adjudication: adjudication through subsumption in the case of rules, and adjudication through balancing in the case of principles.[23]
(4) Alongside the more formal aspects of logic and adjudication, the theory of principles conceives of itself as a theory of argumentation that examines the significance of principles as the material grounds of legal reasoning. 'Principles are arguments' can be heard from its representatives.[24] Josef Esser's seminal work 'Principle and Norm'[25] can also be best understood as a contribution to a theory of legal argumentation.
(5) Finally, the term 'theory of principles' is connected to a doctrinal thesis concerning fundamental rights. According to this thesis, fundamental rights are optimising requirements and questions concerning fundamental

[20] See K Möller, 'Balancing and the Structure of Constitutional rights' (2007) 5 *International Journal of Constitutional Law* 453, 457–58.

[21] J Raz, 'Legal Principles and the Limits of the Law' (1972) 81 *The Yale Law Journal* 823; RM Dworkin, *Taking Rights Seriously* (Cambridge MA, Harvard University Press, 1977); HLA Hart, *The Concept of Law*, 2nd edn (Oxford, Clarendon Press, 1994) 155–80, 269–72. Their reception in Germany also aims at this context of structural theory, see R Alexy, *The Argument from Injustice* (n 16) 68–82.

[22] Alexy (n 10) 44–47.

[23] Sieckmann (n 9) 18ff; R Alexy, 'On Balancing and Subsumption: A Structural Comparison' (2003) 16 *Ratio Juris* 433. See also K Larenz, *Methodenlehre der Rechtswissenschaft* (Berlin, Springer, 1991) 474–82.

[24] JR Sieckmann, 'Rechtssystem und praktische Vernunft' (1992) 78 *Archiv für Rechts- und Sozialphilosophie* 151; JR Sieckmann, *Modelle des Eigentumsschutzes. Eine Untersuchung zur Eigentumsgarantie des Art. 14 GG* (Baden-Baden, Nomos Verlag, 1998) 38.

[25] J Esser, *Grundsatz und Norm in der richterlichen Fortbildung des Privatrechts* (Tübingen, Mohr Siebeck, 1990).

rights can only be tackled by understanding and balancing them as colliding principles.[26]

I intend to show that the theory of principles in its original form has contributed in a restorative but important way to a theory of adjudication, but that it is also based on mistakes in its norm-theoretical and methodological hyperbole, and wrongly perceives itself as a doctrinal theory of fundamental rights. At all levels of discussion, I will consistently refer to the implication that the theory of principles is a theory of fundamental rights; not only because it is in this field that its reception is most elaborate and widespread,[27] but also because among its adherents the theory of fundamental rights is seen as its paradigm application.

I. The Point of Origin: An Appropriate Critique of the Positivist Theories of Adjudication

The notion of Principle was originally a reaction to a state of discourse in German and Anglo-Saxon legal debates that at times were interconnected but that, in fact, unfolded, to a significant and astonishing extent, parallel to but independently of one another. On both sides of the Atlantic, the theory of principles has its origins in a similar – but time-shifted – development of legal theory, with the German discussion taking the lead. In the German debate at around the end of the nineteenth century, a radical critique of traditional methodological concepts developed as a reaction to the hardening of stances and stylisations of the Jurisprudence of Concepts. This could tie in with the emerging social sciences that were beginning to develop into different disciplines.[28] The concept of judges as 'subsumption machines' was measured against its – stylised[29] – claims and

[26] Alexy (n 10) 47ff.

[27] See the translations of R Alexy, *Theorie der Grundrechte* (Frankfurt, Suhrkamp, 1986) into Spanish or into English, as well as the corresponding works by his students who focus primarily on the dogmatics of constitutional rights: N Jansen, 'Die Abwägung von Grundrechten' (1997) 36 *Der Staat* 27; Sieckmann (n 9); Sieckmann, *Modelle des Eigentumsschutzes* (n 24); M Borowski, *Grundrechte als Prinzipien* (Baden-Baden, Nomos Verlag, 1998); M Borowski, 'Prinzipien als Grundrechtsnormen' (1998) 53 *Zeitschrift für Öffentliches Recht* 307; N Teifke, 'Flexibilität der Menschenwürde? Zur Struktur des Art. 1 Abs. 1 GG' in C Bäcker and S Baufeld (eds), *Objektivität und Flexibilität im Recht* (Stuttgart, Franz Steiner, 2005) 142–56; M Borowski, *Die Glaubens- und Gewissensfreiheit des Grundgesetzes* (Tübingen, Mohr Siebeck, 2006).

[28] R von Jhering, *The Struggle for Law*, 2nd edn (JJ Lalor trans, Chicago IL, Callaghan and Company, 1915); F Adickes, *Zur Lehre von den Rechtsquelle. Insbesondere über die Vernunft und die Natur der Sache als Rechtsquellen und über das Gewohnheitsrecht* (Kassel, Georg H Wigand, 1872) 9–15; R von Jhering, *Scherz und Ernst in der Jurisprudenz. Eine Weihnachtsgabe für das juristische Publikum* (Leipzig, Breitkopf & Härtel, 1884); O von Bülow, *Gesetz und Richteramt* (Berlin, Dunkcer & Humblot, 1885); E Ehrlich, 'Über Lücken im Rechte' (first published 1888) in E Ehrlich, *Recht und Leben* (Berlin, Duncker & Humblot, 1967) 30–169.

[29] The concept served as an ideological moderation of the political aspirations sought by the German bourgeoisie through judicial control under the German monarchies of the time. It had a mainly exoteric political purpose and was not seriously defended on a methodological basis, see R Ogorek, *Richterkönig*

was thus methodologically exposed. In its most radical form, the critique led to the Free Law Movement, which developed a generally sceptical legal agenda that largely rejected the determining power of law and produced alternative programmes for legal practice,[30] often based on the social sciences[31] or on psychological concepts.[32] A central figure in the Free Law Movement was Eugen Ehrlich who was – alongside Rudolf Jhering[33] and François Geny[34] – one of the essential sources of inspiration for early American Legal Realism.[35]

American Legal Realism represented a programme similar to the Free Law Movement. Like this movement, it was a reaction to methodological claims of a conceptual jurisprudence that were stylised and exaggerated by its later enemies, under the banner of formalism.[36] Like the Free Law Movement, the American reaction referred to the indeterminacy of law and, in the more radical forms of Legal Realism, developed into overt legal scepticism.[37]

In the continental European discussion, part of the explosive power embedded in the Free Law Movement was absorbed by the school of the Jurisprudence

oder Subsumtionsautomat? Zur Justiztheorie im 19. Jahrhundert (Frankfurt, Vittorio Klostermann, 1986) 292–325.

[30] For corresponding sociological and psychological approaches in American Legal Realism, see B Leiter, 'American Legal Realism' in WA Edmundson and MP Golding (eds), *The Blackwell Guide to Philosophy of Law and Legal Theory* (Malden, Wiley-Blackwell, 2003) 54–56.

[31] E Ehrlich, *Freie Rechtsfindung und freie Rechtswissenschaft* (Leipzig, Hirschfeld, 1903); E Ehrlich, *Grundlegung der Soziologie des Rechts* (Berlin, Duncker & Humblot, 1913); E Fuchs, 'Was will die Freirechtsschule?' (1929) in AS Foulkes and A Kaufmann (eds), *Gerechtigkeitswissenschaft. Ausgewählte Schriften zur Freirechtslehre* (Karlsruhe, CF Müller, 1965) 21–63; H Kantorowicz, *Rechtswissenschaft und Soziologie. Ausgewählte Schriften zur Wissenschaftslehre* (Karlsruhe, CF Müller, 1962).

[32] G Flavius (pseudonym of H Kantorowicz), *Der Kampf um die Rechtswissenschaft* (first published 1906, Berlin, Berliner Wissenschaftsverlag, 2002) 16–19; H Isay, *Rechtsnorm und Entscheidung* (Berlin, Aalen, 1929) 85–120.

[33] For the influence of von Jhering on the American debate, see RS Summers, 'Rudolf von Jhering's Influence on American Legal Theory' in O Behrends (ed), *Jherings Rechtsdenken* (Göttingen, Vandenhoeck & Ruprecht, 1996) 61–76; N Duxbury, 'Jhering's Philosophy of Authority' (2007) 27 *Oxford Journal of Legal Studies* 23.

[34] F Geny, *Méthode d'interpretation et sources du droit privé positif* (Lausanne, F Pichon et Durand-Auzias, 1899).

[35] See eg R Pound, *Enforcement of Law* (1908) 20 *Green Bag* 401, 406: 'We have a great deal of *freie Rechtsfindung* in America, while disclaiming it in theory'. For a detailed account of the American reception, see D Nelken, 'Pound and Ehrlich on the Living Law' in E Kamenka et al (eds), *Rechtstheorie. Soziologische Jurisprudenz und realistische Theorien des Rechts* (Berlin, Duncker & Humblot, 1986) 175–87; JE Herget and S Wallace, 'The German Free Law Movement as the Source of American Legal Realism' (1987) 73 *Virginia Law Review* 399.

[36] For the observation that formalism was shaped by its critics, see AJ Sebok, *Legal Positivism in American Jurisprudence* (Cambridge, Cambridge University Press, 1998) 57–60; B Tamanaha, *Formalism and Realism on Judging: Beyond the Divide* (Princeton NJ, Princeton University Press, 2009). For the general theory development in the US and the conventional perspective on the formalism-realism debate, see N Duxbury, *Patterns of American jurisprudence* (Oxford, Oxford University Press, 1995) 9–64.

[37] See eg R Pound, *Introduction to the Philosophy of Law*, 24th edn (New Haven CT, Yale University Press, 1982); R Pound, 'Law in Books and Law in Action' (1910) 44 *American Law Review* 12, 23ff; KN Llewellyn, 'A Realistic Jurisprudence: The Next Step' (1930) 30 *Columbia Law Review* 431; J Frank, *Law and the Modern Mind* (New York, Bretano's Publishers, 1930). For the indeterminacy thesis as the basis of American Legal Realism, see B Leiter (n 30) 51ff.

of Interests,[38] which, with its strong emphasis on the purpose of the law, had elements that later also came to bear on the American legal process school.[39] The critical impact of the indeterminacy argument was not absorbed but marginalised in positivist approaches. The marginalisation strategy can also be found in both the continental and the Anglo-Saxon contexts. The theory of adjudication represents the blind-spot not only of Kelsen,[40] but also of Hart[41] in their respective theoretical conceptions. The picture of Kelsen's and Hart's theory of adjudication can be painted with broad brush-strokes without any significant theoretical loss.[42] According to their theories of adjudication, the respective legal requirements have clear positive as well as negative candidates that can be determined according to legal criteria. The remainder of cases tend to be viewed as exceptional phenomena that were to be decided by other means. Judges are considered to be incidentally authorised to decide hard cases according to moral or political criteria.[43]

The positivist model of adjudication led to a time-shifted critical reaction on both sides of the Atlantic, which in both cases drew on the notion of principles. Neither Esser nor Dworkin were convinced by the positivist simplifications which they – positivist in their own way – perceived as a caricature of legal practice. Both exposed the errors of positivist models of adjudication on the basis of the traditional importance of judicial maxims and principles within legal practice.[44] Each theoretically re-established the role of principles in adjudication, that had been rendered theoretically invisible by positivism,[45] but which – as Esser and Dworkin could show – had remained central to the practice of the courts. The enduring

[38] P Heck, *Das Problem der Rechtsgewinnung* (Bad Homburg, Gehlen, 1912); P Heck, *Begriffsbildung und Interessenjurisprudenz* (Tübingen, Mohr Siebeck, 1932).

[39] For the importance of purpose in legal process theory, see B Tamanaha, *Law as Means to an End* (Cambridge, Cambridge University Press, 2006) 102–7.

[40] H Kelsen, 'Legal Formalism and the *Pure Theory of Law*' (first published 1929) in AJ Jacobson and B Schlink (eds), *Weimar: A Jurisprudence of Crisis* (Berkeley CA, University of California Press, 2000) 82–83; H Kelsen, *The Pure Theory of Law* (M Knight trans, Clark NJ, The Lawbook Exchange, 2005) 236–42, 348–56.

[41] Hart (n 21) 173–204.

[42] Hart (n 21) 259, in any case knew about the deficient character of his ideas on adjudication: 'But I certainly wish to confess now that I said far too little in my book about the topic of adjudication and legal reasoning and, in particular, about arguments from what my critics call legal principles. I now agree that it is a defect of this book that principles are touched upon only in passing'. That positivism is not bound to this concept of adjudication is a point that J Gardner, 'Legal Positivism: 5½ Myths' (2011) 46 *American Journal of Jurisprudence* 199, 211, rightly insists upon.

[43] For an attempted reactivation of this aspect of legal positivism – which is regarded as weak even by its adherents – as a theory of normative authorisation, see M Jestaedt, 'Rechtsprechung und Rechtsetzung. Eine deutsche Perspektive' in W Erbguth and J Masing (eds), *Die Bedeutung der Rechtsprechung im System der Rechtsquellen. Europarecht und nationales Recht* (Stuttgart, Richard Boorberg, 2005) 75–79; M Jestaedt, *Das mag in der Theorie richtig sein …: Vom Nutzen der Rechtstheorie für die Rechtspraxis* (Tübingen, Mohr Siebeck, 2006) 43–85.

[44] RM Dworkin, 'The Model of Rules II' in RM Dworkin (ed), *Taking Rights Seriously* (Cambridge MA, Harvard University Press, 1977) 54ff; Esser (n 25) 10ff. For a recent encyclopaedic roundup of the principles of Common Law, see MD Bayles, *Principles of Law: A Normative Analysis* (Dordrecht, Reidel, 1987).

[45] Concerning this development, see JA Ramos Pascua, 'Die Grundlage der rechtlichen Geltung von Prinzipien' in G Orsi (ed), *Prinzipien des Rechts* (Frankfurt, Lang, 1996) 11–13.

merit of the theory of principles is that it insisted on the seriousness and autonomy of legal disagreements[46] with the help of the role of legal principles, and that it rejected the obligatory allusion to a collective self-delusion of legal practice.[47]

The emphasis on the importance of principles for legal practice in the Anglo-Saxon variant was targeted at the relationship between law and morality as conceived by positivism. For Dworkin, the need to consult principles – which at least in some cases were not explicitly codified – in the process of adjudication was an essential pawn against the separation thesis that contested any necessary connection between law and morality. Where could principles that had not been codified come from, if not from morality in the broadest sense?[48]

Positivism generally accepted Dworkin's claim that moral principles play an important role in adjudication, and has wrestled ever since to accommodate Dworkin's criticism in different blends of inclusive or exclusive theories.[49] But it is very much the question of what is proven by the fact that the law relates to moral or philosophical conceptions. Law relates to and borrows from many other discourses and disciplines. It borrows from meteorology when it develops conceptions that it shares with meteorology, from biology when it shares concepts with biology and from mathematics[50] when tax laws require the calculation of taxes. This kind of borrowing from other discourses on the one hand proves a relation but on the other hand is still a matter forming specifically legal standards, since the extra-legal standards are not introduced into the law as such. In the process of adjudication, moral norms are only consulted via principles if they fit into and adapt themselves to positive law, as Dworkin himself has stressed with the dimension of 'fit'.[51] In its interpretation of the constitutional guarantee of human dignity, the Federal Constitutional Court of Germany refers to Kant's phrasing of the categorical imperative to establish a prohibition on the objectification of human beings;[52] however, this doctrinal approach does not absorb Kant's moral philosophy in an unaltered way.

[46] Dworkin's controversial argument first derived from his reflection on principles and later developed into the 'semantic sting'. See RM Dworkin, *Law's Empire* (Cambridge MA, Harvard University Press, 1986) 45–46. See also, T Endicott, 'Are There any Rules?' (2001) 5 *The Journal of Ethics* 199, 209–11.

[47] Heck, *Begriffsbildung und Interessenjurisprudenz* (n 38) 17; Kelsen, 'Legal Formalism and the Pure Theory of Law (1929)' (n 40) 82–83; Kelsen, *The Pure Theory of Law* (n 40) 353ff; Hart (n 21) 176–89.

[48] A short, but interesting abstract about the normative provenance of legal principles in Romanic codifications since the decline of natural law is Ramos Pascua (n 45) 11–13. In the regulations concerning the closure of legal loopholes, the dissociative movement critical towards natural law at first manifests itself in ambivalent allusions to 'common law principles', but, at a later stage, also in self-confident positivist regulations concerning the 'common principles of the positive law'.

[49] An overview of these strategies is offered by Sieckmann (n 9) 178–98, and JL Coleman, *The Practice of Principle* (Oxford, Oxford University Press, 2001) 103–19, both with further bibliographical material.

[50] For this comparison, see H Kantorowicz, *Der Begriff des Rechts* (Göttingen, Vandenhoeck & Ruprecht, 1939) 58ff.

[51] RM Dworkin (n 46) 255–57. The corresponding critique by Sieckmann, 'Rechtssystem und praktische Vernunft' (n 24) 160–63, is based on his theory of validity, not on the theory of principles.

[52] BVerfGE 27, 1 (6) – Mikrozensus; BVerfG, NJW 2006, 757ff.

Legal practice does not simply resort to moral norms, but develops its own legal conceptions through recourse to all kinds of standards and norms outside the law. Thus developed, legal conceptions may resort to or resemble moral and philosophical conceptions of shared concepts whilst still remaining genuinely legal.[53] One of the aims of legal doctrine is precisely to adapt concepts originating in other disciplines, including moral philosophy, to the specifics of a legal system and its history, reflected in its institutions and decisions that in turn reflect the history of the legal system. However, this abolishes the separation between law and morality to about the same extent as recourse to the four basic arithmetical operations in tax law eliminates the separation between law and mathematics.

Insofar as the theory of principles as coined by Alexy postulates an even stronger connection between law and morality than Dworkin, this stronger claim cannot be supported by the use of principles in the law. Alexy basically supports Radbruch's idea that law cannot be radically out of line with the right morality without losing its validity.[54] Instead Dworkin himself has shown that law's borrowings from morality do not result in any standards for the type of morality referred to.[55] Thus, in a tyranny, adjudication may resort to immorality as the law of the tyranny provides itself with corresponding values, maxims, and principles to establish doctrinal structures and build legal precedents. The overreaching postulates of the proponents of the theory of principles do not depend on their notion of principle, but on their notion of law[56] or of normativity,[57] which would require a critique of its own.

[53] For a more elaborate explanation of this idea, see R Poscher, 'The Hand of Midas: When Concepts Turn Legal, or Deflating the Hart-Dworkin Debate' in D von der Pfordten and JC Hage (eds), *Concepts in Law* (Dordrecht, Springer, 2009) 99–116. For a similar argument, see D Priel, 'Farewell to the Exclusive-Inclusive Debate' (2005) 25 *Oxford Studies of Legal Studies* 675.

[54] HJ Koch, 'Zur Methodenlehre des Rechtspositivismus. Das Prinzipienargument' in R Dreier (ed), *Rechtspositivismus und Wertbezug des Rechts* (Stuttgart, Franz Steiner, 1988) 160. For Dworkin's dimension of 'fit', see Dworkin (n 46) 139ff, 102–8 (dealing with Nazi 'law'), 239–60.

[55] RM Dworkin, 'Hard Cases' in RM Dworkin (ed), *Taking Rights Seriously* (Cambridge MA, Harvard University Press, 1977) 102–8.

[56] Alexy, *The Argument from Injustice* (n 16) 76–81, 129–35. Alexy connects the notion of law with moral integrity not only in its claim, but also in its essence. For a critique of Alexy's rationale for this connection, see E Hilgendorf, *Argumentation in der Jurisprudenz. Zur Rezeption von analytischer Philosophie und kritischer Theorie in der Grundlagenforschung der Jurisprudenz* (Berlin, Duncker & Humblot, 1991) 115ff.

[57] Sieckmann (n 9), 100–102. Apart from the efficiency of a norm and its ethical – and relative – standing within the framework of a legal system, Sieckmann asserts another 'absolutely legal' standing. Its theoretical position, however, remains vague, as it is not made clear whether he is talking about a legal standing in its own right, or whether he is merely referring to a relative standing in regard to – right – morality. His elaborations remain nebulous: 'Both constructions are problematic. The acceptance of a legal system "how it ought to be" of its own nature leads to difficult philosophical problems, whether there is a unity of this "ought to" … Furthermore, a definition … of the notion of a legal norm which itself uses the term "legal" is exposed to the accusation of circularity. The second alternative, which is to talk about a moral command of application, easily leads to misunderstandings and into debates about natural law and legal positivism. However, for the purposes of this study we don't need to decide whether we should speak about a maxim that is merely legal or a maxim that is moral as well': ibid, 246 (translated by the author). See also Sieckmann, 'Rechtssystem und praktische Vernunft' (n 24) 246.

The original insistence on the importance of principles by Esser and Dworkin is able to show that the positivistic picture of adjudication does not do justice to the complexity of the enterprise. It can be further established that the law resorts to conceptions developed in other discourses to shape its own conception of concepts it shares with these disciplines. But this does not provide any basis for the much stronger claim put forward by Alexy and his followers that the validity of legal norms depends on their moral merit.

As for the merits of the theory of principles as a theory of fundamental rights, it is important to notice that the theory of principles on both sides of the Atlantic did not develop as a doctrinal theory, but as a reaction to an inadequate theory of adjudication. From the standpoint of its origin, nothing speaks in favour of formulating a theory of principles as a doctrinal theory or even more specifically as a doctrinal theory of fundamental rights. From the point of view of its origin, the theory of principles finds itself at a different level of abstraction: it belongs to the field of a general theory of adjudication and not at the level of a concrete doctrine. Just as subsumption, analogy, or inversion do not provide a doctrinal theory, for example, for tort law, so the idea of principled argumentation does not provide a doctrinal theory for fundamental rights. Principles can be used to form a doctrine, but they are not doctrinal in themselves.

II. The Error of Legal Theory: The Structural Differentiation between Rules and Principles

The logical thesis of the theory of principles essentially states that rules and principles differ in their formal structure. Whereas rules indisputably prescribe certain legal consequences, principles only entail their legal consequences prima facie.[58] This structural difference between the two types of norms is supposed to manifest itself particularly in their collision. In the case of a collision of rules, either exceptions are introduced into one of the rules, or one of the rules is declared null and void. By contrast, the validity of principles is supposed to remain untouched because principles only have a prima facie effect, and in the event of collision they are only substantiated into a definitive rule by means of a balancing procedure that optimises the degree to which the colliding principles can be fulfilled in that particular case.[59] According to this thesis, rules and principles constitute categorically different types of norms.

However, an analysis of how the legal system handles the collision of norms shows that rules and principles are structured identically and differ only in their contingent contents within a uniform normative structure.[60] This becomes especially apparent when we examine how – and how differently – the collision of

[58] Alexy (n 10) 57–59; Sieckmann (n 9) 67–71.

[59] Alexy (n 10) 48–56; Sieckmann (n 9) 68.

[60] Apart from the circle of specific proponents of the theory of principles, this view is prevalent within legal discourse. See P Lerche, *Übermaß und Verfassungsrecht. Zur Bindung des Gesetzgebers an*

norms is tackled. The legal system reacts to collisions of norms with collision rules that vary widely in their content: depending on how they are represented, these collision rules can be depicted as independent rules or as exception clauses integrated into the colliding rules.[61] Thus, these collision rules either lead to the annihilation of one of the colliding norms or are incorporated as exception clauses into one or both of the norms, thus avoiding the collision of norms altogether.[62] Optimisation by balancing is merely one possible content of such an exception clause. In terms of content, optimisation by balancing differs from other exception clauses, much as other exception clauses in turn differ from each other as concerns their contents. However, the different contents of exception clauses leave the structures of the norms untouched. Just as the *lex posterior* principle does not create a structural type of norm, the principle of optimisation by balancing does not create a structural type of norm either.

This can be demonstrated with regard to two norms used by Alexy as examples of principles.[63] Norm N1 authorises the state to take measures to protect its foreign interests. Norm N2 grants citizens freedom of the press.

> N1: If an action endangers foreign interests of the state, this action can be prohibited.
>
> N2: If an action serves to promote the freedom of the press, the state must refrain from prohibiting it.

There is an intersection of circumstances where both norms apply. For this intersection of circumstances, the legal system has to introduce a collision rule that can be incorporated as an exception to the respective norms. This collision rule could, for example, be the *lex posterior* principle (Ka). If norm N1 concerning the protection of the state derives from the time of a military dictatorship and norm N2, from the time after the change to democracy, the *lex posterior* principle might even apply to norms like N1 and N2. This would lead to an interpretation in which N1 is amended by an exception clause, provided that N1 is not diametrically opposed to the new state order and therefore considered invalid.

> N1a: If an action endangers foreign interests of the state *and does not serve to promote the freedom of the press*, this action can be prohibited.
>
> N2a: If an action serves to promote the freedom of the press, the state must refrain from prohibiting it.

die Grundsätze der Verhältnismäßigkeit und der Erforderlichkeit, 2nd edn (Goldbach, Keip, 1999) xxii: 'In my opinion, the differentiation of those two categories is of a merely quantitative nature' (translated by the author); A Marmor, 'The Separation Thesis and the Limits of Interpretation' (1999) 12 *Canadian Journal of Law and Jurisprudence* 135, 135–45ff; B Schilcher, 'Prinzipien und Regeln als Elemente einer Theorie des gebundenen Ermessens' in B Schilcher et al (eds), *Regeln, Prinzipien und Elemente im System des Rechts* (Vienna, Verlag Österreich, 2000) 164, 169; F Reimer, *Verfassungsprinzipien. Ein Normtyp im Grundgesetz* (Berlin, Duncker & Humblot, 2001) 179–82. For the Anglo-Saxon literature, see Hart (n 21) 259ff. For a possible reconstruction of a gradual difference, referring to legal logic, see B Verheij et al, 'An Integrated View on Rules and Principles' (1998) 6 *Artificial Intelligence* 3. For a deconstruction, see P Schlag, 'Rules and Standards' (1985) 33 *UCLA Law Review* 405–30.

[61] Dworkin (n 44) 62.

[62] Alexy (n 10) 48–50.

[63] ibid 103.

However, the interpretation of both regulations could lead to collision rules at the expense of more than one of the norms involved. In this case, the collision rule Ka only needs slight modification, for example with an element of weight. A teleological reduction of N2 might result in the interpretation that N1 should be valid only for important foreign interests. According to this collision rule Kb, we would obtain the following norms:

> N1b: If an action endangers *important* foreign interests of the state, this action can be prohibited.
>
> N2b: If an action serves to promote the freedom of the press *and does not endanger important foreign interests of the state*, the state must refrain from prohibiting it.

Here, too, the assessment of the threat requires the assessment of its weight. But unlike Alexy's law of balancing, this assessment would not relate to any curtailment of the freedom of the press. It needs only to be determined how substantial the endangered foreign interest actually is. No balancing is required.

From collision rule Kb it is only a small step to a collision rule and its corresponding exception clause that is innate in the norms that are defined as principles by the theory of principles. If in a collision rule Kc, instead of 'important' foreign interests the reference is to 'outweighing' foreign interests, two norms are created that require the weighing of importance between the endangered foreign interests and the freedom of the press. These could thus be understood as optimisation requirements in Alexy's sense that could be treated according to his rule of balancing.[64]

> N1c: If an action endangers the *outweighing* foreign interests of the state, this action can be prohibited.
>
> N2c: If an action serves to promote the freedom of the press and does not endanger the *outweighing* foreign interests of the state, the state must refrain from prohibiting it.

The semantic deferral from 'important' to 'outweighing' leaves the structure of the norm untouched. There is no structural difference between norms Nb and Nc, but rather a contingent difference regarding their contents. Both are norms of a conditional type with an exception clause, a type that is ubiquitous in our legal order, with a wide array of different contents.

In the same way, the weighing of relative importance is also found in forms other than the optimisation requirements ontologically defined by the theory of principles. For example, certain doctrines of fundamental rights propose an interpretation of the principle of proportionality that merely demands – apart from the requirement of necessity – a loose plausibility control to ensure that the measure is not grossly disproportionate to the aim pursued by the legislator, to avoid breaking a butterfly on a wheel.[65]

[64] ibid 101–9.

[65] B Pieroth and B Schlink, *Grundrechte. Staatsrecht II*, 21st edn (Heidelberg, CF Müller, 2005) rn 294; Poscher (n 13) 224. For a minimal position, see Schlink (n 13), 76–78, 192–95. On constitutional

N1d: If an action endangers foreign interests of the state *and the danger is not grossly disproportionate to its prohibition*, this action can be prohibited.

N2d: If an action serves to promote the freedom of the press *and either does not endanger foreign interests of the state or its prohibition is grossly disproportionate to the extent of the danger*, the state should refrain from prohibiting it.

One can amuse oneself in developing exception clauses. But norms with different exception clauses, which differ solely in their content, cannot be differentiated on the basis of their norm structure – not even those containing an optimisation requirement.[66] Just as it seems unreasonable to assume an ontological norm type of its own for the *lex posterior* principle or the principle of gross disproportionality, so too, does it make little sense for a principle of proportionality understood as an optimisation requirement.

Since the content of collision rules is contingent, it can also be controversial. The decision as to the correct interpretation of the principle of proportionality, as a prohibition of gross disproportionality or as an optimisation requirement, does not follow from pseudo-ontological differentiations between different kinds of norms, but must be fought out with the help of arguments drawn from constitutional law. In part, the framers of the Basic Law had themselves already introduced collision rules into positive constitutional law, although they are far more complex than those mentioned above. The reservations of statutory powers, for example, can be understood as such collision rules[67] – if they are considered within a framework of colliding fundamental rights.[68] The resolution of a collision case happens in a reflexive way: the framers of the constitution did not resolve this collision case themselves, but left its resolution mainly to the legislator.[69]

Even proponents of the theory of principles no longer deny that principles are in fact optimisation requirements and that optimisation requirements do not belong to a norm category of their own that can be distinguished from rules.[70] However, according to Alexy, this does not present a problem for the theory of principles, but 'simply gives it a sharper focus'.[71] Now – according to Alexy – '[a] distinction is to be made between *commands to be optimised* and *commands to optimise*. Commands to be optimised are the objects of balancing or weighing.

principles, see KE Hain, *Die Grundsätze des Grundgesetzes. Eine Untersuchung zu Art. 79 Abs. 3 GG* (Baden-Baden, Nomos, 1999) 158; Reimer (n 60) 326–48, on constitutional principles as 'level and framework regulations' (translated by the author).

[66] See the rule-like reconstruction of a collision of principles in R Alexy, 'Zum Begriff des Rechtsprinzips' in R Alexy (ed), *Recht, Vernunft, Diskurs* (Frankfurt, Suhrkamp, 1995) 195. See also Sieckmann (n 9) 65; Borowski, *Grundrechte als Prinzipien* (n 5) 76ff.

[67] Borowski, *Grundrechte als Prinzipien* (n 5) 107ff.

[68] For a doctrinal model of fundamental rights which avoids collisions, see Poscher (n 13) 198–203.

[69] For the reflexivity of fundamental rights, see Poscher (n 13).

[70] Sieckmann (n 9) 65ff; Alexy (n 4) 38ff; A Aarnio, 'Taking Rules Seriously' in W Maihofer et al (eds), *Law and the States in Modern Times* (Stuttgart, Franz Steiner, 1990).

[71] Alexy, 'Zur Struktur der Rechtsprinzipien' (n 5) 38. [ed note: see below Chapter 1, p 23].

They can be termed "the ideal 'ought' or 'ideals'".[72] To maintain the ontological distinction between rules and principles, Alexy proposes a distinction between commands to optimise and commands to be optimised.[73] Now, principles are supposed to be the ideal objects of optimisation. According to a logical interpretation of the ideality of principles, this should correspond to an 'infinitely reiterated requirement of validity'.[74]

But whatever one might think of an 'ideal ought' and an 'infinitely reiterated validity imperative' as such, this already awkward rescue attempt fails because the reconstruction of optimisation requirements does not require commands to be optimised, but only non-normative objects of optimisation. Optimisation requires that something be optimised; it does not require that commands should be optimised. According to the theory of principles, the fundamental right to physical integrity and life – Article 2 (2) of the Basic Law – includes the command to optimise physical integrity and health as well as human life. Yet health and life are not commands; they are not normative objects at all, but factual ones. Even a norm that demands the optimisation of the pressure in car tyres according to seasonal circumstances would be an optimisation requirement. In addition, it is equally not the case that the objects of optimisation commands must be normative in character in order to explain the normativity of the optimisation command.[75] Optimisation commands receive their normativity through the obligation to increase an object in relation to legal and factual possibilities, an obligation inherent in the optimisation command itself. As for the objects of optimisation requirements, they need in no way be qualified in a normative sense, as can be seen from the example of tyre pressure. Everything can be optimised, even illness and death, length, width, height, temperature and time. Even the direction of the optimisation is not provided by the command's object, but by the optimisation command which determines, mostly through context, whether the object should be maximised or minimised in relation to the legal and factual possibilities. For a fundamental right that prohibits encroachment on health it is understood that – if it is interpreted as an optimisation requirement – health should be maximised, not minimised in relation to legal and factual possibilities. This might be different in the case of a vermin control regulation, which aims to minimise the health and life of certain species. Neither the optimisation command nor the normative direction of the command results from the 'object of balancing', but from the 'command to optimise'.

[72] ibid.

[73] R Alexy, *On the Structure of Legal Principles* (2000) 13 *Ratio Juris* 294 [ed note: see Chapter 1 for the equivalent text].

[74] JR Sieckmann, 'Zur Analyse von Normkonflikten und Normabwägungen' in G Meggle (ed), *Analyomen 2: Perspektiven der Analytischen Philosophie* (Berlin, Walter de Gruyter, 1997) 349, 352. In principle acknowledging this reconstruction, Alexy, 'Zur Struktur der Rechtsprinzipien' (n 5) 39ff [ed note: see Chapter 1, p 24ff for the translated version].

[75] Though this is how Sieckmann argues. See Sieckmann (n 9) 66.

Furthermore, optimisation requirements are commands in their own right. Normally they do not refer to a command themselves. This becomes clear by contrast with those rare cases where they actually do so. Optimisation requirements can refer to any object. They can also apply to normative objects, but they need not. Even norms can be optimised: the same is true of commands. For example, provisions of penal or tax law that leave gaps for acts that were meant to be criminalised or taxed can be optimised by enacting laws that close these gaps. First, however, the objects of fundamental rights (even when they are understood as optimisation requirements) are mostly not regulations,[76] but empirical conditions or liberties. Second, the regulations to which optimisation requirements may theoretically refer are not to be found in the secretive sphere of the 'ideal ought', nor are they connected to infinitely reiterated validity imperatives. Instead, they are merely real commands, like those of the defective penal or tax code.

Because of their normative structure, optimisation requirements do not have to refer to commands – let alone to an 'ideal ought' or infinitely reiterated validity imperative – nor do fundamental rights usually refer to normative objects, even though the proponents of the theory of principles use them as a paradigm. Even with the supplementary attempt to prove the existence of their ontologically distinct object, the theory of principles is not convincing. The cases examined by the theory of principles are optimisation requirements: not only can it be demonstrated that they are simply rules, but even the proponents of the theory of principles have asserted that this is the case. Insofar as the theory of principles looks for principles as ideal objects within optimisation requirements, their theoretical analyses are flawed.

This does not mean that one cannot distinguish some norms within a legal system, which are somewhat more general, more abstract, or more important than others, and call them principles. But principles in this sense – principles in Esser's sense – are neither always optimisation requirements, nor are they logically distinct from other legal norms. By its own ontological standard, the theory of principles is a theory without an object. The kind of entity the theory is meant to cover – principles that do not have the structure of rule-type norms – does not exist.

III. The Methodological Backslide: The Notion of Rule within the Theory of Principles

The theory of principles has a methodological concern as well. The theory of principles differentiates methodologically between rules and principles. Whereas the concept of subsumption is connected to the notion of 'rule', balancing is

[76] Special cases are fundamental rights which rely in their substance on a normative context, like freedom of contract or property.

methodologically connected to the notion of 'principle'. 'Rules are applied through the *subsumption* of a case under its elements and the deduction of its legal consequences … The application of principles, by contrast, requires a *balancing* of colliding principles'.[77]

> The decisive point in distinguishing rules from principles is that *principles* are norms which require that something be realized to the greatest extent possible given the legal and factual possibilities. Principles are *optimization requirements*, characterized by the fact that they can be satisfied to varying degrees, and that the appropriate degree of satisfaction depends not only on what is factually possible but also on what is legally possible.[78]

Methodologically, there are two forms of adjudication according to the theory of principles: hermeneutically operated subsumption under a clear-cut rule, and the balancing of principles that governs adjudication in all cases not conforming to the ideal of subsumption. From this methodological starting point, principles within a legal system can be identified whenever the subsumption of circumstances under a norm becomes difficult. And who would deny that the subsumption under fundamental rights like 'Arts and sciences, research and teaching shall be free' in Article 5 (3) of the Basic Law or the due process clause in the American constitution is difficult. Therefore, fundamental rights must be principles. *Q.E.D.*

The methodological dubiousness of this deduction results less from the notion of 'principle' as defined by the theory of principles than from its notion of 'rule'. The notion of Rule in the theory of principles is based on a formalist ideal[79] which the theory of principles claims to supersede; however, its own notion of Rule continues to be based on this ideal. This becomes clear when looking at the examples given of the notion of Rule. The rules cited in the theory of principles – the requirement to leave the room at the ringing of a bell, business hours from 7 am to 7 pm, the payment of a poll tax amounting to 1,000 DM[80] – are all so specific that they seem to match the outdated subsumption ideal of conceptual jurisprudence. The rules resulting from the collision of principles are similarly so specific that their application seems possible without any further argumentation or evaluation.

But the application of a legal norm in an abundance of cases under consideration is in principle not restricted to the alternatives of subsumption by mere rule-following in simple cases,[81] or of balancing in the sense of an optimisation requirement in all other cases, regardless of the norm in question. Rather the application of a norm to many of the cases under consideration combines a

[77] Sieckmann (n 9) 18 (translated by the author); Alexy (n 23).

[78] Alexy (n 10) 47ff, footnotes omitted.

[79] For a critical approach to Dworkin's theory of principles on this account, see Koch (n 54) 152ff; as an unfounded interpretation of his notion of rule, it is also refuted by Hart (n 21) 263. See also Endicott (n 46) 211–18.

[80] Alexy (n 10) 49.

[81] For the difference between rule-following and interpretation, see L Wittgenstein, *Philosophical Investigations*, 4th edn (GEM Anscombe, PMS Hacker, and J Schulte trans, Malden, Wiley-Blackwell, 2009) §201.

complex set of techniques of adjudication. These always include subsumption by mere rule-following and sometimes even balancing in the sense of an optimisation requirement, alongside an array of further methods and combinations of all the techniques. For any given norm, adjudication may consist of mere rule-following in easy cases, of more complex analytical considerations when it comes to more complex cases, and of yet more complex argumentations and evaluations in hard cases, where even the balancing of legally protected rights in the sense of an optimisation requirement may play a role. The way in which adjudication proceeds does not depend on the norm to be implemented; rather, it depends on the case to be judged according to the norm.[82] In principle, each norm more or less frequently presents easy cases, where legal practice requires mere subsumption, and more or less frequently gives rise to other cases where further analytical operations, argumentations, evaluations, and possibly even balancing are required. This is true also of the norms used in the theory of principles as paradigmatic examples of the notion of rule. Do schoolchildren really have to leave the room at the ringing of the bell, even if this means exposing them to health risks like extreme temperatures or during a smog alert? Easy cases aside, the application of each law requires a large variety of considerations, one of these being the balancing of arguments, which sometimes takes the form of an optimisation.

From the perspective of a theory of adjudication, the theory of principles turns out to be an attempt to extrapolate two of the many methods used in legal practice – application by mere subsumption in easy cases and optimisation by balancing of legally protected interests – to interpret these as two distinct norms and thus create a distinction, not between different techniques of application, but between different types of norms. However, this idea is flawed for two manifest reasons: first, both techniques considered in the theory of principles are generally used for every norm; thus, according to the theory of principles, each norm is a rule as well as a principle, which in turn does not allow for the subdivision of norms into different classes according to the rule–principle scheme. Despite their claim that 'every norm is either a rule or a principle',[83] proponents of the theory of principles themselves do not succeed in allotting norms unambiguously to one or the other category. Instead, they speak of the 'double aspect of constitutional rights norms',[84] or state that 'in the framework of legal rules, elements of principles are to be found',[85] or revert to a 'complex combination of rules and legal principles'.[86] Second, techniques of adjudication are not confined to the dualism

[82] Vagueness other than ambiguity is a predicate with two variables. A norm is not vague as such, but only in relation to a certain case, a borderline case. To call a norm vague is an ellipsis; spelled out it means that it is a norm for which borderline cases are more frequent than for other norms. For the difference between vagueness and ambiguity, compare L Solan, 'Vagueness and Ambiguity in Legal Interpretation' in VK Bhatia et al (eds), *Vagueness in Normative Texts* (Bern, Peter Lang, 2005) 73–96.

[83] Alexy (n 10) 47ff.

[84] ibid 84–86.

[85] HJ Koch, 'Die normtheoretische Basis der Abwägung' in W Erbguth et al (eds), *Abwägung im Recht* (Cologne, Carl Heymanns, 1996) 9–18 (translated by the author).

[86] L Michael 'Methodenfragen der Abwägungslehre' (2000) 48 *Jahrbuch des öffentlichen Rechts* 169, 176 (translated by the author). For the difficulties already at the origin of the idea, see Dworkin (n 44) 64ff.

of mere subsumption and optimisation by balancing of legally protected interests. Adjudication may require a wide array of further intellectual operations, as in the case of complex norms or cases, that – apart from mere subsumption – *do* require analytical techniques but no balancing operations. According to the schematic framework of the theory of principles, each of these analytical techniques should require a norm type of its own. Furthermore, in the event of a collision of legally protected interests, methods are not confined to processes of optimisation by balancing: gross disproportionality[87] and the idea of minimum positions[88] are competing concepts for the application of the proportionality principle. For all legal practices differing from mere subsumption and optimisation by balancing, individual types of norms would have to be postulated, followed by the assignation of norm types to each of these norms. From the perspective of a theory of adjudication, it is a bizarre categorisation mistake on the part of the theory of principles to ontologise different techniques for the application of norms and consider them different types of norms.[89]

For a theory of principles as a theory of fundamental rights, this means the following: from the fact that fundamental rights are less likely to be the object of mere subsumption, one cannot conclude that they have the character of principles; nor may one conclude that they must be understood as optimisation requirements that can only work in the framework of balancing. Rather, even a doctrine of fundamental rights has at its disposal the entire body of techniques of adjudication and legal argumentation. And this entire body of techniques must be used to display a certain understanding of fundamental rights. In this respect, nothing follows from the categorically mistaken division of the cosmos of norms into rules and principles.

IV. The Systematic Location: The Theory of Argumentation

Another branch of the theory of principles is argumentation theory. In this case, it does not emphasise that principles are norms with a certain logical structure or a certain method of application, but rather norms with a special function within the framework of judicial argumentation. This is essentially what Esser aimed at: he did not see the special function of principles as providing a legal basis for deducing

[87] Pieroth and Schlink (n 65) rn 294; Poscher (n 13) 224.

[88] Schlink (n 13) 76–78, 192–95; Hain (n 65) 158 who, for functional legal reasons, generally claims only a minimum consideration and not an optimisation for constitutional principles. See also Reimer (n 60) 326–48: constitutional principles as 'level and framework regulations' (translated by the author).

[89] See K Günther, *The Sense of Appropriateness: Application Discourses in Morality and Law* (J Farrell trans, Albany, State University of New York Press, 1993) 214–19; the methodical argument also aims at the differentiation of principles and rules with an incompletely or completely stipulated content, as developed by Hain (n 65) 99–106.

legal consequences in particular cases, but in the creation of norms or deductions from norms that only in their turn are directly applicable.[90] By claiming that 'the characterisation of principles as reasons for balancing decisions serves as the principle idea',[91] Jan Sieckmann – a disciple of Alexy – highlights this interpretation of principles.

With this orientation drawn from argumentation theory, the theory of principles returns to its original context: the theory of adjudication. Esser, Dworkin and others rightly pointed out that principles can play an important role in adjudication, especially in difficult cases where legal standards cannot be applied by mere subsumption, as they can in simple cases. These insights, that can hardly be disputed, were radicalised in the theory of principles as coined by Alexy and his disciples.

As a contribution to a theory of legal argumentation, this radicalisation mainly affects the structure of the legal maxims consulted in adjudication. According to Alexy's theory of principles, all legal norms that cannot always be applied by mere subsumption should be considered optimisation requirements. This homogenisation, however, completely denies the diversity of legal principles that play a role in legal argumentation.[92] It is true indeed that some legal principles – like the maxim of the protection of legitimate expectations – can be reconstructed as optimisation requirements. However, this cannot be said of all legal principles. Our legal order includes a number of principles that do not require optimisation, but which are not so unambiguous that they can always be applied by mere subsumption. For example, this is true of one of the most prominent principles not only of civil law. The principle of 'good faith' does not demand optimisation, but simply strict obedience: if something contravenes good faith, there is no room for balancing; nor is there any room for balancing if the opposite is true.[93] Similarly, the principle of equal protection, with its phenomenological comparative perspective, cannot be reduced to an optimisation requirement without losing this specific aspect.[94] Not least, the diversity of legal principles is demonstrated by the principle of proportionality, which, according to the theory of principles, is the paradigm for optimisation requirements: '[p]rinciple theory implies the principle

[90] Esser (n 25) 137.

[91] Sieckmann (n 9) 52 (translated by the author); Sieckmann, 'Rechtssystem und praktische Vernunft' (n 24) 155ff; U Neumann, 'Die Geltung von Regeln, Prinzipien und Elementen' in B Schilcher et al (eds), *Regeln, Prinzipien und Elemente im System des Rechts* (Vienna, Verlag Österreich, 2000) 116ff. Neumann also sees the essential function of principles on the level of the justification of legal decisions.

[92] This can also be said of the inexhaustible wealth of different meanings and facets of the term 'principle' in the philosophical tradition, one of its origins being the Greek 'arché'. For the impressive history of this term, see Reimer (n 60) 146–71, who dismisses the reduction of the term 'principle' to an optimisation requirement already because of terminological reasons, ibid 179.

[93] For this objection with further examples, see O Weinberger, 'Revision des traditionellen Rechtssatzkonzepts' in B Schilcher et al (eds), *Prinzipien und Elemente im System des Rechts* (Vienna, Verlag Österreich, 2000) 64.

[94] A Somek, 'Eine egalitäre Alternative zur Güterabwägung' in B Schilcher et al (eds), *Regeln, Prinzipien und Elemente im System des Rechts* (Vienna, Verlag Österreich, 2000) 113–41.

of proportionality, and the principle of proportionality implies principle theory.'[95] But even the maxim of proportionality need not necessarily be understood as an optimisation requirement. As already noted, the principle of proportionality can be understood not only as an optimisation criterion, but also as a guarantee of a minimal position[96] or as a prohibition of gross disproportionality.[97] Many authors do not see constitutional principles in general as optimisation requirements, but as minimum or framework guarantees.[98] Whatever the exact focus of these controversies, they in any case demonstrate that even the maxim of proportionality does not necessarily have to be interpreted as an optimisation requirement. Optimisation as a method of adjudication lies on a different level from the principles that might be the object thereof. In a given legal order there may be principles that can be applied through optimisation by balancing, but there is no theoretically necessary connection between optimisation by balancing and legal principles. Rather, the claim that a legal principle requires optimisation must be argued by means of legal interpretation. Especially as concerns constitutional rights, their interpretation as optimisation requirements frequently competes with alternative interpretations – a competition that cannot be decided by reference to the universal optimisation character of legal principles.

But the argumentation theoretical claim does not exhaust itself with the homogenisation thesis. In a variation that is as universal as possible, the theory of principles not only aims to reconstruct traditional maxims of law as optimisation requirements, but to reconstruct practical argumentation in general by means of the explanatory scheme of optimisation requirements and the law of balancing. As a general theory of argumentation, the theory of principles does not claim to be the only imaginable form of practical argumentation, but it does claim to be the superior one.[99] This argumentation theoretical variant of the theory of principles is not a specific legal theory, but a universal theory of practical argumentation which claims that the law of balancing is the universal formula for all practical discourse.

According to this variant of the theory of principles as a universal theory of argumentation, all practical arguments – even those that, on the surface, do not indicate an optimisation requirement – can ultimately be traced back to optimisation requirements. In a controversy over the requirement for motorcyclists to wear helmets, the argument for the right to self-determination could directly be construed as an optimisation requirement;[100] but the same is assumed to be true of the counter-argument citing a predictable rise in the number of traffic deaths, which, as a factual prognosis, does not on the surface take the form

[95] Alexy, 'Zur Struktur der Rechtsprinzipien' (n 5) 35 [ed note: see below Chapter 1, p 20].
[96] Schlink (n 13) 76–8, 192–95.
[97] Pieroth and Schlink (n 65) rn 294; Poscher (n 13) 224.
[98] Hain (n 65) 157 and Reimer (n 60) 329–33, 338–48, both providing further bibliography.
[99] Sieckmann (n 9) 155ff.
[100] Concerning such a construction, see K Fischer, *Die Zulässigkeit aufgedrängten staatlichen Schutzes vor Selbstschädigung* (Frankfurt, Peter Lang, 1997) 132–65.

of an optimisation requirement. The proponents of the theory of principles can thus point to the enthymematical character[101] of factual arguments in practical discourses. They rely on Richard Hare for a principle of universalisability, which requires, in order for a moral argument to be complete, that it can specify a general norm which gives normative meaning to the facts referred to in a given moral argument.[102] For the proponents of the theory of principles, this would mean that the argument of fatal accidents must be traced back to an optimisation requirement – eg the requirement to optimise the protection of life relative to factual and judicial possibilities. After tracing all arguments back to appropriate optimisation requirements, all practical issues should be decided according to the law of balancing.

But from Hare's principle of universalisability we can deduce only that factual arguments must be traced back to general norms: we cannot deduce anything about the contents of these norms,[103] nor that they must include an optimisation requirement. For example, neither the norms mentioned by Hare,[104] nor Stephen Toulmin's principle of avoiding unnecessary sufferings[105] include optimisation. Thus, the general thesis of the theory of principles as a universal argumentation theory can only be maintained if norms that do not contain an optimisation requirement can in turn be traced back to optimisation requirements and their balancing. But even the catalogue, not only of formal but also material[106] norms, developed by Alexy for practical argumentation – to which the theory of principles continues to refer[107] – was not developed through a balancing of principles, but through analytical, transcendental or universal pragmatic deliberations.[108] Moreover, as for legal argumentation, it is not apparent for practical argumentation in general that minimal positions, considerations of gross disproportionality or equality, can be reconstructed as optimisation requirements or as a result of optimisation with any systematic or theoretical gain.[109] If, for example, absolute norms that are not subjected to balancing are redefined as absolute principles whose weight is such that they will prevail in any balancing contest,[110] this might contribute to an immunisation of the theory of principles for its own sake; but it does not contribute to

[101] For this discussion, see J Elster et al, *Rationale Argumentation. Ein Grundkurs in Argumentations- und Wissenschaftstheorie* (M Kaiser and G Meggle trans, Berlin, De Gruyter, 1988) 244ff.

[102] RM Hare, *Freedom and Reason* (Oxford, Oxford University Press, 1963) 7–30.

[103] R Alexy, *A Theory of Legal Argumentation: The Theory of Rational Discourse as Theory of Legal Justification* (R Adler and N MacCormick trans, Oxford, Clarendon Press, 1989).

[104] Hare (n 102) 86ff.

[105] SE Toulmin, *The Place of Reason in Ethics* (Cambridge, Cambridge University Press, 1950) 136, 223.

[106] See eg 'rule 2.3' in Alexy (n 103) 240.

[107] Alexy (n 10) 369–387.

[108] For further alternative methods of argumentation, see eg Jansen, 'Die normativen Grundlagen rationalen Abwägens' (n 7) 48–52.

[109] For alternative methods of argumentation, see Jansen, 'Zum Gedanken einer juristischen Strukturtheorie' (n 7).

[110] Sieckmann (n 9) 59; Sieckmann, 'Rechtssystem und praktische Vernunft' (n 24) 156; more reluctant, Alexy (n 10) 110.

a better understanding of practical argumentation. Furthermore, it is not apparent what advantage the balancing of principles should have over other sources of practical knowledge, like moral intuitions, since balancing itself depends on our intuitions as to the relative weight of the colliding principles.[111]

Concerning judicial argumentation, we can add that, within law, optimisations are very often pre-structured by the legislator and cannot be challenged by an act of balancing. The theory of principles tries to counter this argument by redefining the legal obligation to respect legislative acts as a formal principle that is structurally equal to other principles.[112] But legal practice is disfigured when positive law is reduced to an inherent requirement to optimise the legal force of laws which is to be weighed against all other formal and material principles involved in each individual case.

However, a precise description of the role of legal maxims, including those that contain optimisation and the internal logic of optimisation by balancing within the framework of an extensive reconstruction of different methods of adjudication, could be a merit of the theory of principles. As part of a theory of legal argumentation, in turn part of a comprehensive theory of adjudication, the theory of principles would find its systematic designation. However, contrary to the arguments of its proponents, its advantage cannot lie in an 'essential simplification of our understanding of the tasks of legal practice'[113] that reduces legal practice beyond simple cases to the optimisation of principles by balancing.[114] By reducing the diverse methods and instruments of adjudication to the alternative between 'subsumption or balancing', the theory of principles as a theory of legal argumentation falls behind the state of knowledge already attained, to which Alexy himself made an eminent contribution with his dissertation on the theory of legal argumentation.[115] By contrast, simplification along the lines of his theory

[111] A Somek, 'Abwägungsregeln. Ein didaktischer Beitrag zur Grundrechtsdogmatik' in C Hiebaum and P Koller (eds), *Politische Ziele und juristische Argumentation* (Stuttgart, Franz Steiner, 2003) 113ff.

[112] For formal legal principles in general, see Alexy (n 10) 82; Sieckmann, 'Rechtssystem und praktische Vernunft' (n 24) 151; Sieckmann, *Modelle des Eigentumsschutzes* (n 24) 38. For the reconstruction of decision prerogatives by the legislator with the help of formal principles in particular, see M Raabe, *Grundrechte und Erkenntnis. Der Einschätzungsspielraum des Gesetzgebers* (Baden-Baden, Nomos, 1998). Critical with regard to the usefulness of formal principles in reducing losses of certainty, originating from an interpretation of law as derived from the theory of principles, is Hain (n 65) 135–38. For a detailed critique with regard to the legislator's political role see Jestaedt (n 13) 222–60, and Poscher (n 13) 82–84, both with further bibliographical material. The obligatory reference to the general practical discourse on how to overcome these problems within legal discourse on the one hand exposes an inherent circularity, because Alexy (n 103) 355 tries to avoid the uncertainties of general practical discourse by pointing at the restrictions imposed on it by juridical discourse. See also Hain (n 65) 141–57.

[113] HJ Koch, 'Rechtsprinzipien im Bauplanungsrecht. Zur normtheoretischen Basis der planerischen Abwägung' in B Schilcher et al (eds), *Regeln, Prinzipien und Elemente im System des Rechts* (Vienna, Verlag Österreich, 2000) 257 (translated by the author).

[114] Thus, Koch succumbs to a danger he warns of elsewhere: 'Actually, the role of … legal principles when used for solving difficult cases should not be overestimated in … an ecstasy of principles' Koch (n 54) 160 (translated by the author).

[115] Alexy (n 103).

of principles leads to de-differentiation and a degeneration of our understanding of what we are doing when we apply the law.

Fundamental rights can be arguments as well, in the sense that they support value judgements in legal argumentation, which presuppose for example that freedom of speech is basically desirable and not evil as such. Someone who, in a juridical argumentation, bases his statements on the fact that a given application of a norm will enhance freedom of speech without endangering other legal values has an argument because freedom of speech is protected in the constitution. But even from a theory of principles turned into a contribution to a theory of legal argumentation as part of a theory of adjudication, it does not follow that the content of fundamental rights is restricted to principles as balancing requirements. Where fundamental rights not only serve as normative supports for an argument but as a standard for definite confinements, they can unfold in doctrinal forms that are manifestly more ambitious.[116]

V. The Self-Misconception: The Theory of Principles as Legal Doctrine

The development into an argumentation theory reveals where the self-misconception of the theory of principles as a theory of fundamental rights lies. The merits of the theory of principles lie in the field of argumentation theory and it is on this level that it made its first appearance on both sides of the Atlantic. The theory of principles is based on the general methodological level of adjudication, ie the level of legal argumentation. At least this has always been clear to Esser, and for him this constituted the essential element of legal principles.[117] The importance of principles does not lie in replacing doctrine, but in explaining its origins and its necessity. Esser writes of the enrichment maxim, to which he often refers as his paradigm instance of a principle:

> Thus, we require the fixation of all doctrinal elements of contract law and enrichment law and the configuration of those two institutions by virtue of judicial and doctrinal tradition in order to at least be able to comprehend what this "material" principle might stand for.[118]

First, removing the difference between the balancing of principles and other forms of doctrine falls short of the practice of legal argumentation, and thereby also of the role that principles play within the framework of legal argumentation: that is, to establish doctrines. Second, a doctrine which is merely confined to the

[116] There is no shortage of propositions, including a functional pluralist one in C Bumke, *Der Grundrechtsvorbehalt. Untersuchungen über die Begrenzung und Ausgestaltung der Grundrechte* (Baden-Baden, Nomos, 1998) or a monistic one in Poscher (n 13).

[117] Esser (n 25) 79ff.

[118] Esser (n 25) 154 (translated by the author).

balancing of principles can hardly be called a doctrine at all. A doctrine originates by developing normative structures by means of legal argumentation. Such argumentation can encompass different elements such as precedents, traditions, history, genesis, systematic and analytical considerations as well as optimisation by balancing. But the balancing of principles as such is not a doctrine, just as analogy or the consultation of legislative materials is not a doctrine. The balancing of principles is simply one argumentative structure among many which serves to develop a certain doctrine, for example of fundamental rights.[119]

Although optimisation by balancing is involved in the process of legal argumentation, it is intransitive in relation to doctrine. The fact that balancing is involved in legal argumentation does not mean that the outcome of this argumentation is an interpretation that requires balancing. If arguments need to be balanced for the interpretation of the freedom of speech it does not follow that the result must be that content neutrality is only a standard that is open for ad hoc balancing and not absolute. The balancing of arguments on the level of legal argumentation does not mean that doctrine always involves ad hoc, case-by-case balancing. This might be the result of argumentation in some cases,[120] but it does not follow from the fact that arguments need to be weighed and balanced in interpretation and adjudication.

Doctrinal efforts can fail.[121] If, at the end of the day, it was shown that the corpus of fundamental rights does not allow for a structuring effort that goes beyond the advice to balance colliding fundamental rights considering all aspects of the individual case,[122] this might be the result of a failed doctrinal effort. But the interpretation of a set of norms resulting in the advice to make an all-things-considered balancing decision[123] of the individual case is the low point of legal doctrine. This would correspond to a general doctrine of ad hoc, case-by-case balancing for all fundamental rights of the US Constitution.[124] It means that the attempt to develop a structuring, helpful legal doctrine has failed. A theory of fundamental rights with no more to offer than the advice to consider all relevant aspects of the individual case and optimise them by balancing is the least preferable doctrinal theory

[119] Cremer (n 13) 223–27.

[120] For the debate about absolute standard, systemic, or ad hoc balancing in US constitutional law, see KL Karst, 'Legislative Facts in Constitutional Litigation' in PB Kurland (ed), *The Supreme Court Review* (Chicago IL, The University of Chicago Press, 1960) 75–112; TA Aleinikoff, 'Constitutional Law in the Age of Balancing' (1987) 96 *Yale Law Journal* 943–1005.

[121] Positive law can also explicitly demand balancing, as is the case in planning law that can perhaps best be reconstructed as an optimisation requirement. For planning law see eg Koch (n 54).

[122] Sensitivity towards the tendency of the principles' theory to 'Kadijustiz' (ad hoc jurisdiction) is shown by Koch (n 85) 19.

[123] Concisely formulated by H Rossen, 'Grundrechte als Regeln und Prinzipien' in C Grabenwarter et al (eds), *Allgemeinheit der Grundrechte und Vielfalt der Gesellschaft* (Stuttgart, Boorgerg, 1994) 59: 'To infer a decisive singular verdict from an abstract norm has to be justified separately … it can only be impartial when all legal and factual elements of an individual case are exhaustively considered' (translated by the author).

[124] For a general critique of ad hoc and definitional or systemic balancing in US constitutional law see Aleinikoff (n 120).

according to all the criteria established for the performance of legal doctrine – such as offering orientation, teachability and learnability, critical potential, etc.[125] In any case, this surrender of the doctrine of fundamental rights is not predetermined by the logical structure of fundamental rights or by methodological insights into adjudication.[126]

Whether the guarantee of human dignity should be understood as an absolute prohibition that cannot be subjected to balancing or as an optimisation requirement controlled by balancing[127] is not a question of legal logic or methodology, but a doctrinal decision that can be disputed with all the methods of legal argumentation. One of these methods, of course, is the balancing of an abundance of arguments. Likewise, the decision as to whether the term 'general laws' in the German guarantee of the freedom of speech – Article 5 (2) of the Basic Law – should be understood as a balancing or strict content neutrality requirement cannot be made by characterising fundamental rights as principles, which are supposedly always subject to balancing. For each of these doctrinal positions we can – and must – dispute with all available arguments drawn from history, legislative intent, teleology, democratic theory, etc. The theory of principles cannot bring about a decision.[128]

Even courts do not always take the bait of the theory of principles – no matter how attractive the perspective of the theory of principles might be for an activist court – considering the absence of doctrinal limitations that it entails. This is apparent in the rulings of the German Federal Constitutional Court on assemblies of right-wing extremists in which the Court has stressed the content neutrality of state action and not fallen back on balancing.[129] More recently, in the decision concerning the Air Security Act[130] it decided in favour of an absolute protection of human dignity and against weighing human dignity against the interests of those potentially saved by shooting down an airplane in a 9/11-scenario. If a principles theory of fundamental rights wishes to face competing doctrinal proposals, it must do so face to face. It cannot do so from the high ground of legal theory. Instead, it must justify its cause with the whole array of legal argumentation, one fundamental right after the other, explaining why any given fundamental right can best be understood as an optimisation requirement and why fundamental rights cannot be structured any further than simply prescribing balancing in individual cases. In other words, the theory of principles must prove its worth in a house-to-house fight with diverging doctrinal conceptions.

[125] Alexy (n 103) 266.
[126] Möller (n 20) 466–67.
[127] For a point of view drawn from the theory of principles, see N Teifke, 'Flexibilität der Menschenwürde?' (2005) 3 *Archiv für Rechts und Sozialphilosophie* 142.
[128] See eg Hain (n 65) 158. Although he acknowledges a logical differentiation between rules and principles, Hain refuses to interpret constitutional principles as optimisation requirements for functional legal reasons.
[129] BVerfG, NJW 2001, 2075; BVerfGE 111, 147 – Inhaltsbezogenes Versammlungsverbot.
[130] BVerfG, NJW 2006, 751–61.

However, to counter this criticism, the theory of principles could play on its ambiguity as doctrinal and argumentation theory. It could withdraw to the position that it merely wished to indicate that the doctrinal structuring of fundamental rights involves the weighing of legal arguments. Thus, it would not say that fundamental rights must be interpreted as principles, or that the guarantee of human dignity is open to balancing; it would simply note the fact that, in the process of determining whether all or certain fundamental rights have the character of principles or whether the guarantee of human dignity in the Basic Law is absolute or subject to balancing, arguments must be weighed and balanced. This move from the level of doctrine to that of argumentation theory would defuse the criticism advanced here, but from the point of view of the doctrine of fundamental rights it would be a withdrawal to banality.

VI. At the End of the Day

What remains at the end of the day? Does the theory of principles measure up to its aspirations to be a leading general theory of law and to provide a universal blueprint for a doctrinal theory of fundamental rights?

(1) The original argument of principle as put forward by Esser and Dworkin has its merit in rejecting the simplifications of positivist theories of adjudication. It may serve to show that law can resort to moral and ethical concepts. But the connection between law and morals or ethics is far less spectacular than the theory of principles as coined by Alexy and his followers suggests. Specifically, the strong thesis of conformity to the right or basic moral standards as a validity condition of law does not follow from the argument of principle.

(2) Contrary to the general theoretical claim of the theory of principles, principles are not a logical norm type of their own; nor are all principles optimisation requirements. Principles are certain fundamental and, in many cases, somewhat more general norms than others, which play a certain role in adjudication and legal argumentation, but which have no specific logical structures and which do not necessarily have optimisation requirements as their content. The attempt to ontologise principles in the sense of optimisation requirements as a logical norm type of their own is wrong for two reasons: principles are not necessarily optimisation requirements; and both principles and optimisation requirements differ from other norms only gradually and in terms of content. With its general theoretical claim, the theory of principles does not get off the ground.

(3) As a methodological theory which attempts to reduce adjudication to either subsumption by mere rule-following in the case of rules, or optimisation by balancing in the case of principles, the theory of principles falls into the grave it has dug itself with its ontologising of principles and rules. The arsenal of methods and instruments in the process of adjudication is much richer than

the dichotomy suggested by the theory of principles. As a methodological theory, it drastically underestimates the complexity of adjudication.

(4) The designated place of the theory of principles is a theory of legal argumentation. The theory of principles which concentrates on the analysis of arguments that demand optimisation can elucidate how such arguments work. The law of balancing is one of the fruits of this work. But however important the analysis of this specific set of arguments might be, it must be stressed that the scope of the theory of principles as a theory of argumentation is limited. Arguments which draw on optimisation are just one set of arguments among others. The attempt by the theory of principles to reduce every argument to an optimisation requirement leads to further oversimplifications.

(5) As a theory of fundamental rights, the theory of principles misconceives itself. Neither from its mistaken logical standpoint nor from the methodological one that stems from the erroneous ontologising of principles does it follow that fundamental rights must be doctrinally shaped as mere optimisation requirements. Insofar as the theory of principles wishes to emphasise the fact that in the process of constitutional adjudication arguments have to be balanced, it mistakes argumentation for doctrine, or rather, an episode for the whole story. The weighing of arguments in the process of developing a doctrine does not necessarily mean that the doctrine must be one of optimisation by balancing. Argumentation and doctrine are intransitive. Judged as a doctrinal theory, the theory of principles descends to the all-things-considered advice that all relevant interests affected in an individual case should be balanced against each other – a piece of advice that can hardly be supported by doctrinal standards but that cannot be supported by theoretical, logical or methodological arguments either, as has been attempted by adherents of the theory of principles.

Second Round

3

Ideal 'Ought'*

ROBERT ALEXY

A number of objections have been raised against both a principle-based reconstruction of constitutional rights and general 'principles theory' as a system underlying jurisprudential propositions. While these objections differ greatly in essence, they are nevertheless connected more or less closely despite their variations. Against the backdrop of this situation, a classification offers a way forward to avoid losing track. What appears to serve the purpose best is a classification into seven categories or types, ie

(1) objections rooted in norm theory aiming at the existence and structure of principles and how these can be distinguished from rules;
(2) objections informed by argumentation theory pertaining to the question of whether the act of balancing constitutes a rational justification or argumentation;
(3) objections in the context of the legal doctrine on constitutional rights, such as the ones warning of a collapse or decline of constitutional rights due to balancing;
(4) institutional objections which, in turn, fear an inflation of constitutional rights allegedly resulting in the institution of the parliamentary legislative state turning into a juristocracy;
(5) objections based on the theory of legal interpretation inquiring whether and how it may be justified that a principles-based model is indeed a fitting interpretation of a positive-law catalogue of constitutional rights;
(6) objections inspired by validity theory that accuse principles theory of cutting ties with constitution and law and dismantling the tiered structure of the law; and lastly
(7) philosophy-of-science-influenced objections that allege the unsuitability and insufficiency of principles theory for the legal doctrine on constitutional rights.

* Formerly published as R Alexy, 'Ideales Sollen' in L Clérico and JR Sieckmann (eds), *Grundrechte, Prinzipien und Argumentation. Studien zur Rechtstheorie Robert Alexys* (Baden-Baden, Nomos, 2009) 21–38. Translated by Sarah Norman. Copyrights granted by Nomos Publishing.

It would not just be impossible to discuss objections of all these different types; even within individual categories, a selection must be made. I will focus on two objections based on norm theory, and two objections rooted in argumentation theory.

I. Two Objections Based on Norm Theory

A. Ideal 'Ought'

An early objection rooted in norm theory can be summed up as the question of whether or not defining principles as optimisation requirements,[1] a definition that lies at the heart of principles theory, cancels out the equally central distinction between rules and principles.[2] Sieckmann and Aarnio have rightly pointed out that optimisation requirements constitute rules, ie definitive requirements, inasmuch as they definitively call for optimisation, rather than an optimal degree of optimisation to be ascertained as part of a balancing process taking into account specific circumstances.[3] Poscher believes he has identified a 'theoretical (self)refutation' of principles theory.[4] I have attempted to solve this issue by distinguishing between *requirements to be optimised* and *requirements to optimise*.[5] Optimisation requirements *qua* requirements to optimise express a definitive, and in that sense 'real ought'. In turn, principles *qua* requirements to be optimised only comprise an 'ideal'[6] or 'prima facie ought'. Poscher has countered this with the argument that the concept of an ideal 'ought' is unnecessary 'because the reconstruction of optimisation requirements does not require commands to be optimised, but only non-normative objects of optimisation'.[7] According to him, optimisation requirements 'in general'[8] do not refer to normative but to empirical objects, for example life and physical integrity as covered by Article 2 (2) first sentence of the Basic Law. This objection invoking an alleged reconstructive expendability goes hand in

[1] R Alexy, *Theorie der Grundrechte*, 3rd edn (Frankfurt, Suhrkamp, 1996) 75–76.
[2] ibid 45ff.
[3] JR Sieckmann, *Regelmodelle und Prinzipienmodelle des Rechtssystems* (Baden-Baden, Nomos, 1990) 65; A Aarnio, 'Taking Rules Seriously' in W Maihofer and G Sprenger (eds), *Law and the State in Modern Times: ARSP supplement 42* (Stuttgart, Franz Steiner, 1990) 187.
[4] R Poscher, *Grundrechte als Abwehrrechte. Reflexive Regelung rechtlich geordneter Freiheit* (Tübingen, Mohr Siebeck, 2003) 78 (translated by the author).
[5] R Alexy, 'Zur Struktur der Rechtsprinzipien' in B Schilcher et al (eds), *Regeln, Prinzipien und Elemente im System des Rechts* (Vienna, Verlag Österreich, 2000) 31–52 [ed note: see Chapter 1, pp 17–27 for the translated version].
[6] On the notion of the ideal 'ought', see R Alexy, 'Zum Begriff des Rechtsprinzips' in W Krawietz et al (eds), *Rechtstheorie: Argumentation und Hermeneutik in der Jurisprudenz* (Berlin, Duncker & Humblot, 1979) 59–82.
[7] R Poscher, 'Einsichten, Irrtümer und Selbstmissverständnis der Prinzipientheorie' in JR Sieckmann (ed), *Die Prinzipientheorie der Grundrechte* (Baden-Baden, Nomos, 2007) 69 [ed note: see Chapter 2, p 42 for the translated version].
[8] ibid.

hand with an objection claiming ontological obscurity. The ideal 'ought' is said to belong to a 'secretive sphere'.[9] What is more, the connection between optimisation requirements and ideal requirements to be optimised is judged to be an 'already awkward rescue attempt'.[10] This objection culminates in an allegation of non-existence. Poscher holds that the principles theory is unable to prove 'the existence of their ontologically defined object', making it a 'theory without object'.[11]

The ontological objection is the more radical one. If it were true, then the non-necessity objection would also be true, as what does not exist cannot not be unnecessary. It follows that we must first answer the question of whether or not an ideal 'ought' actually exists.

(i) The Existence of an Ideal 'Ought'

An 'ought' represents a thought content that may be expressed by way of the deontic modalities of a requirement, prohibition, or permission, and through the complex modalities of subjective law and competences derived from them with the help of relationalisation and potentialisation.[12] The basic modality is that of a requirement, the simplest normative requirement being captured as follows:

(1) It is required that *p*,

which can be designated using the requirement operator 'O' to signify

(2) O*p*.

Let us assume that O*p* takes on the meaning of

(3) It is required to help those in need.

If (3) were to function as a rule, ie express a definitive or real 'ought', then (3) would demand that help be given in any situation in which someone is in need, regardless of any obligations or rights that might be at odds with this. Conversely, if (3) were to act as a principle, ie express an ideal or prima facie 'ought', then help to be given under (3) would be conditional on disregarding or abstracting from anything which might contradict it. Thus, the ideal 'ought' represents an abstract 'ought', as yet lacking reference to the limited possibilities of the empirical and normative world. Not relating something to the obstructions posed by the world means treating it as if it were standing in for the whole, or for everything which matters. In consequence, the ideal 'ought' might also be dubbed a '*pro tanto*' ought.[13] Yet, any *pro tanto* 'ought' doubles as a prima facie 'ought' provided that the term prima facie

[9] ibid 70.
[10] ibid 69.
[11] ibid 70.
[12] R Alexy, 'Alf Ross' Begriff der Kompetenz' in A Hoyer et al (eds), *Gedächtnisschrift für Jörn Eckert* (Baden-Baden, Nomos, 2008) 55–62.
[13] See SL Hurley, *Natural reasons: Personality and Polity* (Oxford, Oxford University Press, 1989) 130, 261; N Jansen, *Die Struktur der Gerechtigkeit* (Baden-Baden, Nomos, 1998) 101.

'ought' is interpreted in a way which relates it to an 'ought' that emerges when we hone in on a single aspect of a conflict of norms.[14]

The question is whether an ideal 'ought' in the sense just outlined indeed exists. There are two notions underpinning the existence of a norm: a weak and a strong one. According to the weak notion of a norm, the latter exists when it is made up of thought content that may be grasped. This corresponds to a semantic notion of a norm.[15] Now, it is possible to understand what the normative formulation (3) aims to express when it is taken not to express an absolute or definitive requirement to help those in need, but only a general or prima facie requirement. However, the fact that a norm exists in this weak sense, ie that it is conceivable and understandable, is of little consequence in itself. When it comes to taking action and making decisions, only those norms which exist in the strong sense are of interest. This is the case when they are valid, whether it be in a legal, social, or moral sense.[16] It appears conceivable that the general requirement to help those in need is valid in a moral sense. It applies in a moral sense if it can be justified, and there are good reasons to assume that it can be. If this were the case, then this would suffice for the norm to exist in the strong sense of the notion. Furthermore, there is little doubt that general requirements may hold social validity and be duly issued, ie are applicable in a social and legal sense, and that they do precisely that in many cases. Hence, the ideal 'ought' can also exist in the strong sense of the notion. Consequently, the ontological objection can be refuted. The notion of an ideal 'ought' is neither mysterious nor obscure, nor yet empty. There are principles that take on the form of norms which express an ideal 'ought'. From this, it follows that principles theory does indeed have an object – and not just any object, but one of considerable relevance in the realm of norms.

(ii) O_i

This leaves the non-necessity objection to be addressed, which holds that, next to an optimisation requirement and empirical objects of optimisation, norms to be optimised – in the sense of norms that express an ideal 'ought' – are unnecessary. On the surface, this objection appears to be justified, as it is indeed a possibility for the object of a requirement such as (3), ie help for those in need (p), to be made the direct object of optimisation. This would turn

(2) O*p*

into

(4) OOpt *p*.

[14] This notion of a prima facie 'ought' is not purely of epistemic nature. It does not refer to something which only *appears* to be required, but rather to something that is *actually* required but may be relegated to the background once all circumstances have been considered. On this, see J Searle, 'Prima Facie Obligations' in J Raz (ed), *Practical Reasoning* (New York, Oxford University Press, 1978) 81ff; Hurley (n 13) 130ff.

[15] On this, see Alexy (n 1) 42–47.

[16] On this, see R Alexy, *Begriff und Geltung des Rechts*, 4th edn (Freiburg, Karl Alber, 2005) 139–43.

'p', as expressed in (4), would then constitute an empirical, ie non-normative, object of optimisation. However, it would be equally possible to represent the optimisation requirement in such a way as to give the object of optimisation a normative character. This is the case when the requirement to help those in need, ie (2), is made the object of optimisation. This would see the optimisation requirement reconstructed as follows:

(5) O*Opt* Op.

(5) captures the notion that optimisation requirements find themselves on a second level – a meta level – vis-à-vis requirements to be optimised.[17] In this case, the object of optimisation, ie that which is required, encompasses two elements: the optimisation (*Opt*); and the object of optimisation, the norm to be optimised (Op). Both in (4) and (5), the optimisation requirement derives from qualifying the object of the requirement as an optimisation. The only difference is the object of optimisation. The optimisation requirement as such remains a definitive or real requirement in both scenarios.

In fact, the crucial point is that the object of a requirement is not the only aspect that may be qualified. The very modality of a requirement may itself be the subject of qualification.[18] When such a qualification represents an idealisation, then this results in an ideal 'ought'.[19] The idealisation of the modality of the requirement can be expressed using 'O_i'.[20] Here, 'idealisation' equals an abstraction based on contradicting rights and obligations. The fact that (3) should be understood as an ideal 'ought', can be represented as follows:

(6) $O_i p$.

Optimisation requirements *qua* rules and the ideal 'ought', ie the principle as such, are connected through a mutual relationship of implication. The ideal 'ought' implies the optimisation requirement, and vice versa.[21] This mutual relationship

[17] Alexy (n 5) 39.

[18] With this, I revoke the thesis put forward in 1979 that ideal and real 'ought' are a matter of the object of a requirement and do not affect the deontic modalities as such. See Alexy (n 6) 81 (rn 94).

[19] In addition to qualifying the object of a requirement and the deontic modality as outlined here, there is a third option of qualification: that of validity or validity operator. An interesting version of this has been proposed in M Reßing, 'Prinzipien als Normen mit zwei Geltungsebenen. Zur Unterscheidung von Regeln und Prinzipien' (2009) 95 *Archiv für Rechts- und Sozialphilosophie* 28, 28ff. A fourth approach has been suggested by Sieckmann, who gets rid of any indexation and advocates for the reiteration of requirement and validity operators. See JR Sieckmann, *Recht als normatives System. Die Prinzipientheorie des Rechts* (Baden-Baden, Nomos, 2009) 26ff, 51ff.

[20] The indexation proposed here differs fundamentally from the one put forward by Susan Hurley. Hurley is concerned with a specific indexation. Her example is a collision between fairness and friendliness. If fairness $\neg q$ calls for friendliness q, then a contradiction can be avoided by creating a distinct deontic operator for each of the two principles: 'We are in effect operating with as many distinct deontic operators as there are discrete kinds of reason'. Hurley (n 13) 127. Hence, a collision between fairness and friendliness would result in '$O_k\ q$ and $O_j\ \neg q$', which really is not a contradiction. See ibid 130. Conversely, 'O_i' is of an abstract nature and would feature in both the reconstruction of the principle of fairness and in that of the principle of friendliness. The resulting contradiction on an ideal level is necessary for systematic reasons, as will be shown later on.

[21] Alexy (n 5) 39.

of implication can be captured as follows in terms of the relationship between (6) and (5):[22]

(7) $OOpt\ Op \leftrightarrow O_i p$.

This equivalence reveals that the optimisation requirement and the ideal 'ought' are two sides of the same coin.[23] The question remains whether such a model, and consequently the notion of an ideal 'ought', is unnecessary. There is no other way to answer this question than to clarify what $O_i p$ stands for. In this, the first aspect to be clarified needs to be whether $O_i p$ is actually in any way meaningful. If this were not the case, then the ideal 'ought' represented by $O_i p$ could hardly not be unnecessary.

Jan Sieckmann recently put forward the opinion that 'indexing deontic operators' is ill-suited to the reconstruction of 'conflicts of norms that entail balancing'.[24] If this were the case, then the indexed operator would lose its relevance for principles theory. It would no longer be able to play a meaningful role. Sieckmann sees two options. The first would be to abandon the claim that two incompatible indexed requirements be fulfilled at the same time. According to him, this would result in 'no problem from the point of view of the person taking action'.[25] What Sieckmann appears to want to express is that all conflicts of norms that are in need of a solution, ie genuine conflicts of norms, would disappear under this condition. Conversely, he holds that a requirement to 'fulfil all indexed requirements [cannot represent] … an indexed "ought", as it would refer to any form of indexed "ought"'.[26] It seems that the latter should be interpreted to mean that any fulfilment requirement referring to all indexed requirements would remove or cancel out the index itself. However, Sieckmann's alternative fails to grasp the crucial point of an indexation of deontic operators as it is being conducted in this context. According to Sieckmann, what appears to matter is whether or not another, non-indexed requirement can be found behind an indexed requirement, ie whether or not a requirement iteration exists. In the first alternative, he sees 'no problem' with an indexed 'ought', provided that there is no fulfilment requirement behind it. This sounds as though the indexed, ie the ideal 'ought', were nothing unless it were backed up by another 'ought'. Yet this would negate the independent meaning of the ideal 'ought'. Every principle in the form of an ideal 'ought' requires a corresponding solution to the case, meaning a specific 'ought' that corresponds to it. There is

[22] On the relationship between (6) and (4), see below p … Insert the next page of the book at the proofs stage.

[23] Alexy (n 5) 39. Jan Sieckmann has objected to contrasting optimisation requirements and requirements to be optimised by claiming that what needs to be optimised goes beyond requirements, to encompass 'prohibitions, permissions and competences'. Sieckmann (n 19) 23. This can be refuted by pointing out that 'O_i' represents all deontic modalities. The fact that we refer to 'requirements' to be optimised is not just due to simplified language but also due to the fact that all other modalities may be derived from the requirement operator by way of negation, relativisation, or potentialisation.

[24] Sieckmann (n 19) 45 (translated by the author).

[25] ibid (translated by the author).

[26] ibid (translated by the author).

no need for an additional fulfilment requirement in the background. The second alternative presupposes a fulfilment requirement behind every indexed, ie ideal, 'ought'. Interpreting this fulfilment requirement as a definitive fulfilment requirement directly referring to norm content *p* would indeed result in the elimination of the index and thus of the ideal character. Yet again, assuming such a fulfilment requirement disregards the independence of the ideal 'ought' expressed by way of the index. The ideal 'ought' expressed through the indexed requirement operator is a real 'ought', which would imply a specific 'ought' in the event of conflict; this specific 'ought' must, needless to say, still be subject to the options presented by the world as it stands. The abstract ideal 'ought' is a reason for this specific 'ought'. This is precisely what makes the ideal 'ought' suitable for the reconstruction of conflicts of norms that require balancing to find solutions. The following example illustrates this.

The example in question is the *Titanic* Decision of the German Federal Constitutional Court.[27] The satirical magazine *Titanic* had first referred to a paraplegic reserve officer, who had succeeded in being called up for reserve duty military training, as a 'born murderer' (*geborene Mörder*), and in a subsequent issue as a 'cripple' (*Krüppel*). The reserve officer brought an action against *Titanic*, which was ordered to pay 12,000 DM in damages. A subsequent constitutional complaint by *Titanic* was successful with reference to the term 'born murderer', but failed to reach the desired result for the term 'cripple'.

No norm, and hence no principle, may be applied without subsumption.[28] The notion of expression of opinion defines both the protected area of the constitutional right to freedom of expression and the scope of the principle of freedom of expression. This principle can be formulated as either a permissive norm pertaining to constitutional rights or as a prohibitive norm, aimed at the state, pertaining to encroachments on constitutional rights.[29] I shall concentrate on the permissive norm here. It can be expressed as follows:

(8) $\forall x\,(T_1\,x \rightarrow \mathrm{P}_i\,\mathrm{R}x)$.

(8) reads as follows: for all x ($\forall x$), if x is an expression of opinion (T_1), then ($\rightarrow$) its performance or realisation (R) is prima facie constitutionally permitted (P_i).[30] The Federal Constitutional Court rightly classified both the term 'born murderer' and the term 'cripple', in reference to the paraplegic reserve officer, as expressions of opinion (T_1). Let us start with the first term. Inserting '*a*' for the term 'born murderer' leads to:

(9) $T_1\,a$.

[27] BVerfGE 86, 1 – TITANIC/ 'geb. Mörder'.

[28] R Alexy, 'Two or Three?' in M Borowski (ed), *On the Nature of Legal Principles. ARSP-Beiheft 119* (Stuttgart, Franz Steiner, 2010) 9–18.

[29] See Alexy (n 1) 273–78.

[30] The equivalence which connects an optimisation requirement and an ideal 'ought' (7) entails the indexed requirement operator 'O_i' and not the permission operator 'P_i'. There is no reason why 'O_i' should not also be applicable to (8). You would simply have to replace 'P_i' by 'O_i'.

However, based on the underlying pattern of subsumption, the following results from (8) and (9):

(10) $P_i\ Ra$.

(10) says: there is a prima facie permission (P_i) to call the reserve officer a 'born murderer' (*Ra*). What is remarkable about (10) is that (10) is both specific and ideal in nature, which is expressed by way of the index.

The principle of freedom of expression as formulated in (8) collides with the general right to free development of one's personality guaranteed under Article 2 (1) of the Basic Law in conjunction with Article 1 (1) of the Basic Law, whose structure is also complex. Here, a rough simplification suffices, which results in a counterpart to the colliding principle of freedom of expression:

(11) $\forall x\ (T_2\, x \rightarrow \neg P_i\ Rx)$

(11) needs to be read as follows: for all *x* ($\forall x$), if *x* is an interference with the right to free development of one's personality (T_2), then ($\rightarrow$) its performance or realisation (*R*) is prima facie constitutionally not permitted ($\neg P_i$). If one inserts the term 'born murderer' (*a*) for T_2:

(12) $T_2\ a$,

then, again pursuant to the underlying pattern of subsumption, this leads to:

(13) $\neg P_i\ Ra$.

However, this results in a contradiction at the level of specific legal 'ought' judgements: with both (13) and (10) applicable, the following applies:

(14) $P_i\ Ra \wedge \neg P_i\ Ra$.

This raises the question of whether this contradiction is indicative of the fact that reconstructing ideal 'oughts' by way of indexed deontic operators is inadequate or even pointless. The answer is no.

That said, some statements by Sieckmann suggest otherwise. He holds that if 'weighing up [is to] represent a process of rational justification of norms', then this may 'not result in logical contradictions'.[31] Sieckmann demonstrates this using an example that also pertains to a collision between freedom of expression and the right to free development of one's personality. His argument for why 'a contradiction is unacceptable' is telling.[32] He deems such a contradiction unacceptable 'because a contradictory system of norms falls short of its guiding function'.[33] Yet this very claim misses the crucial point. The 'ideal ought' level is not yet directly concerned with definitive requirements for action but with the reasons for such definitive requirements. It follows that the contradiction expressed by (14) would

[31] Sieckmann (n 19) 42 (translated by the author).
[32] ibid 43 (translated by the author).
[33] ibid (translated by the author).

only prove unacceptable if (14) were indeed concerned with definitive or real 'oughts', which can be formulated as follows using the deontic operator 'P_r' indexed for this purpose:

(15) $P_r\, Ra \wedge \neg P_r\, Ra$.

Yet Sieckmann is of the opinion that the contradiction at the level of the definitive 'ought' (15), which would indeed be unacceptable, is the only possible result if, as is the case here, principles are interpreted as statements or propositions. He sees the reason for this in the alleged fact that any statement always purports a 'definitive validity'.[34] Based on the 'ideal [character] that transcends what is definitively required' of principles as arguments, he holds 'that they cannot be directly represented by statements'.[35] This must be refuted. The sentence that any expression of opinion is categorically or *pro tanto* permitted can be correct and true. Thus, it expresses a normative statement, which – provided that it is correct and true – corresponds to a normative fact. The sentence 'The "ought" behind X is ideal in nature' is true precisely when we ought to fulfil X in an ideal sense.[36] Ideality and propositionality are indeed compatible.

Even the fact that the ideal world coming into contact with the real world can lead to contradictions does not change this. On the contrary, such contradictions are necessary in order explain why principles are able to collide and why they need to be weighed against each other.[37] The contradiction

(14) $P_i\, Ra \wedge \neg P_i\, Ra$

expresses what Sieckmann refers to as a 'practical dilemma'.[38] It results from the initial contact between the ideal level and the real level taking place by way of the subsumptions highlighted above, and it shows what would happen if the ideal were taken as the real, ie if (14) became

(15) $P_r\, Ra \wedge \neg P_r\, Ra$.[39]

Without any barrier to the real, the ideal *does* lead to unacceptable contradictions. This is why barriers are needed. This not only testifies to principles' ability to collide, but also to the fact that they must be balanced. Sieckmann fittingly refers to the postulate of rationality[40] to resolve any collision of principles and hence the

[34] ibid 41 (translated by the author).
[35] ibid 48 (translated by the author).
[36] On this, see R Alexy, 'Probleme der Diskurstheorie' in R Alexy (ed), *Recht, Vernunft, Diskurs* (Frankfurt, Suhrkamp, 1995) 118. If the sentence 'The "ought" behind X is ideal in nature' is true, then one can say that it definitively says that we ought to do something prima facie.
[37] See Searle (n 14) 85: 'the notion of a genuine moral conflict is a notion of a situation where there is no possible world which satisfies all one's obligations'.
[38] Sieckmann (n 19) 49 (translated by the author).
[39] A poet would put it like this: 'Our *thoughts* lie easy next to one another, But *things* will jostle in the space allotted'. Friedrich Schiller, *Wallenstein's Death, Act II, Scene II* (Flora Kimmich trans).
[40] Sieckmann (n 19) 49.

contradiction. This calls for balancing, ie optimisation. It is this necessary link between ideal 'ought' and optimisation which is expressed through the equivalence

(7) $OOpt\ Op \leftrightarrow O_i p$.

The mutual implication shows that the nature of the ideal 'ought' is also echoed in the rules governing rational optimisation. These rules include the law of competing principles[41] and the law of balancing[42] in the form in which it has made its way into the Weight Formula.[43,44] Viewing what has been said on the ideal 'ought' as expressed by 'O_i' against this backdrop leads to the conclusion that such a reconstruction does not just make sense but also holds the advantages of being simple and practical.

(iii) The Normativity of Objects of Balancing

The fact that something makes sense, is simple and practical does not mean that it is not unnecessary. It could be the case that it would be even easier to resolve the issues in connection with principles by focusing on optimisation requirements only and relinquishing the notion of requirements to be optimised, and thus the ideal 'ought' reconstructable through 'O_i'. This is where Poscher is heading with his thesis that, next to optimisation requirements, at least as a rule, only empirical objects such as health or life can constitute objects of optimisation.[45] 'You can optimise anything, including illness and death, length, width, height, temperature, time etc'.[46] What Poscher sees as crucial is that such objects be complemented by an optimisation requirement referring to them. Such an optimisation requirement would take the, already mentioned, form of:

(4) $OOpt\ p$.

If this is meant to say that a collision of constitutional rights does not constitute a collision of norms but merely an issue of preference, then this must be refuted by pointing out that constitutional rights are made up of norms and that, following this, their collision may only adequately be reconstructed as a collision of norms. Any reconstruction in which the very collision does not already incorporate a normative dimension that is revealed in the contradiction of norms would fall short of the normativity of constitutional rights.

One could now assume that the issue of normativity can also be resolved when only optimisation requirements are considered. This would be the case if the

[41] Alexy (n 1) 83–84.
[42] ibid 100.
[43] R Alexy, 'Die Gewichtsformel' in J Jickeli et al (eds), *Gedächtnisschrift für Jürgen Sonnenschein* (Berlin, De Gruyter, 2003) 790.
[44] One might refer to a sort of usage definition or implied definition of the ideal 'ought'. On this, see W Dubislav, *Die Definition*, 4th edn (unchanged reprint of the 3rd edn, 1931) (Hamburg, Felix Meiner, 1981) 39ff.
[45] Poscher (n 7) 69.
[46] ibid (translated by the author).

optimisation requirement were to transfer an 'ought' to the object of balancing which in itself is not normative, for example life or health. Such a transfer does indeed take place. If the 'ought' constitutes an optimisation of health, then health itself is an 'ought'. Nevertheless, this does not substantiate an objection against the thesis of the ideal 'ought'. On the contrary, it backs the thesis up. What is being transferred can only be an ideal 'ought'. The following sentence applies:

(16) $OOpt\ p \rightarrow O_i p$.

(16) expresses that the existence of an optimisation requirement represents a sufficient condition for the existence of an ideal 'ought'.

(iv) The Integrity of the Surrendering Principle

Another indication that the notion of an ideal 'ought' is both adequate and not unnecessary is its power to explain several other phenomena. Of particular relevance is the integrity of the surrendering principle. In the case of the term 'cripple' in the *Titanic* decision, freedom of expression is surrendered. If '*b*' is taken to mean 'cripple', then the following does in fact not apply:

(17) PRb.

However, it would appear that this specific case norm should logically follow from the principle of freedom of expression (8) in connection with the description of the facts

(18) $T_1\ b$

based on the pattern of subsumption. Yet if the conclusion (17) is not applicable, then, *modus tollendo tollens*,[47] at least one premise should not apply either. As there can be no doubt as to the description of facts (18), the non-applicability could only refer to the principle of freedom of expression (8). Both complete and partial non-applicability by way of introducing an exception clause are conceivable. That said, it is characteristic of collisions of principles that the surrendering principle is neither impaired by a complete nor by a partial loss of applicability. This very fact can be explained with the help of the notion of the ideal 'ought'.

(17) PRb

is ambiguous. '*PRb*' can signify an ideal or prima facie permission

(17') $P_i\ Rb$

or a real or definitive permission

[47] Copy editor's note: The rule of logic which states that if a conditional statement ('if p then q') is accepted, and the consequent does not hold (not-q) then the negation of the antecedent (not-p) can be inferred.

(17") $P_r Rb$.

Prior to a weighing up, the principle of freedom of expression (8) can only effect an ideal permission. Only then can it establish a definitive or real permission when it has the upper hand in a balancing process. Its ideal power then translates to a real power. If the principle does not come out on top in a balancing process, it cannot effect a definitive 'ought'. Yet, despite this surrender, it still implies an ideal 'ought'.[48] Consequently, this defeat, when weighed up, does not mean that

(18) $\neg P_i Rb$

applies. Rather, the principle of freedom of expression continues to imply the ideal permission

(17') $P_i Rb$.

While a defeat in the weighing-up process results in

(19) $\neg P_r Rb$,

the negation of (19)

(17") $P_r Rb$

is not implied by the principle of freedom of expression (8) as such, ie before this has been weighed up. It follows that (19) does not threaten the integrity of the principle of freedom of expression (8) by way of *modus tollendo tollens*.

(v) The Ideal 'Ought' and the Construction of Constitutional Rights

Up until this point, the focus has been on the advantages of the notion of an ideal 'ought' from a norm theory point of view. However, its relevance in terms of the legal doctrine on constitutional rights is no less important. This is evident, for example, when the relationship between a constitutional right and the restriction of a constitutional right is retraced. According to the external-theory model, we need to distinguish two entities – namely the right itself, which is neither restricted nor limited in scope, and what remains of a right after a barrier has been introduced, ie a restricted right.[49] The right as such corresponds to the ideal; the restricted right corresponds to the real 'ought'. Conversely, the internal-theory model does not purport two entities – a right and its restriction – but only one: a right with a specific content. In this model, only the real 'ought' is of relevance. Ignoring the ideal dimension also eliminates the element of balancing and replaces it with questions such as 'what the human right in question really is'.[50] Whether

[48] As the contrary principle also continues to imply an ideal 'ought', one can say that the ideal 'ought' is a type of 'ought' that is able to handle contradictions.
[49] Alexy (n 1) 250.
[50] R Dworkin, *Is Democracy Possible Here?* (Princeton NJ, Princeton University Press, 2006) 49.

determining the definitive 'ought' by way of such term definitions is preferable to its determination through balancing depends on the argumentation theory-based question of whether balancing constitutes a rational process. Before going into detail on two aspects of this question, let us take a closer look at another objection rooted in norm theory.

B. The Normative Character of the Ideal 'Ought'

The second objection based on norm theory that will be discussed here does not aim at the existence of an ideal 'ought' or at the way it can be modelled using indexed deontic modalities; instead, it targets the normative character of the ideal 'ought'. Klement, for example, has put forward that, on one hand, a norm is 'the connection of a norm content with an "ought"', and that, on the other hand, 'there is therefore no room for a differentiation between a "definitive" ought" and a "prima facie ought" … at the norm concept level',[51] as 'the "ought" of a norm is always "definitive"'.[52] The first point, ie the thesis that norms are made up of the connection between norm content and an 'ought', must be deemed correct. However, the fact that the 'ought' represents an integral part of norms does not automatically lead to the second conclusion, ie that a distinction between a definitive or real – and an ideal or prima facie – 'ought' should be ruled out. As has been discussed, an ideal 'ought' is also an 'ought'. Further arguments would be needed to exclude the ideal 'ought' from the norm concept.

According to Klement, the crucial argument, which references Esser, is that principles lack a normative quality as they are merely 'preliminary steps on the way … to a norm'.[53] He considers them 'purely elements serving the further thought process, factors in a mathematical operation that ultimately results in a norm'.[54] Klement is of the opinion that they are not 'norms because taken in isolation they do not enable the immediate identification of behaviour which breaches the law'.[55] He believes that categorising principles as norms is tantamount to breaking with the 'standardised norm concept'.[56] This argument can be summarised under the heading of 'preliminary-steps argument'.[57]

In order to assess the meaningfulness of this argument, the question needs to be raised as to what constitutes the crucial characteristic of the concept of a norm. It must be a characteristic that all different types of norms share. As outlined

[51] JH Klement, 'Vom Nutzen einer Theorie, die alles erklärt. Robert Alexys Prinzipientheorie aus der Sicht der Grundrechtsdogmatik' (2008) 63 *JuristenZeitung* 756, 760 (translated by the author).
[52] ibid (translated by the author).
[53] ibid (translated by the author).
[54] ibid (translated by the author).
[55] ibid (translated by the author).
[56] ibid (translated by the author).
[57] On this, see Raz's distinction between 'the deliberative and the executive stages'. J Raz, *Ethics in the Public Domain. Essays in the Morality of law and Politics* (Oxford, Oxford University Press, 1995) 208.

previously, the only suitable candidate for this is the notion of the 'ought'. According to Klement's preliminary-steps argument, only the definitive or real 'ought' has the character of a norm, not the ideal or prima facie 'ought'. If this were to be given credit, then it would lead to an interesting shift in the relationship between the concept of a norm and that of an 'ought'. There would be a shift in scope, as norms without an 'ought' would exist, but an 'ought' without a norm would not. While the 'ought' would remain an essential element of the concept of a norm, it would no longer constitute a sufficient element. Its dominant position would be replaced by the concept of definitiveness.

While there might be reasons to link the concept of a norm with that of definitiveness, there are also reasons not to sever its link with the concept of the 'ought' in both its variations. In many cases, the act of setting norms has resulted in a prima facie 'ought' rather than a definitive 'ought'. For example, 'Every person shall have the right to life and physical integrity', ie Article 2 (2) first sentence, as per the limiting clause Article 2 (2) third sentence: 'These rights may be interfered with only pursuant to a law', does not lay down a definitive 'ought'. Does this mean that Article 2 (2) first sentence lacks a normative character?

A second point is even more relevant. With law being a system of norms, linking definitiveness and the concept of a norm would create a legal system exclusively made up of decisions resulting from decision-making processes that are definitive in essence. Yet in doing so, one would lose sight of the nature of law, which is substantially defined by the fact that it has both a real and an ideal dimension.[58] However, if law is two-dimensional, then it appears adequate to consider both of them to be normative. In turn, this corresponds best to a concept of a norm that encompasses both a real and an ideal 'ought'.

II. Two Arguments Based on Argumentation Theory

The objections rooted in argumentation theory are concerned with whether or not balancing constitutes rational justification or argumentation. This is a crucial question for the principles theory; there would be little point in pursuing the issues of the principles theory in the contexts of the other objections if balancing were indeed a non-process or irrational process. It would see the meaningfulness of the ideal 'ought' fade into insignificance. This discussion being of such utmost importance when debating issues in the context, I have sought to respond to the question of the rationality or – as one could also refer to it – the objectivity of balancing on numerous occasions. The result has been the Weight Formula[59]

[58] R Alexy, 'On the Concept and the Nature of Law' (2008) 21 *Ratio Juris* 281, 292ff. The two-dimensionality extends all the way to encompassing illegality. While principles, considered in isolation, are unable to say what is definitively illegal, they do define what is prima facie illegal.

[59] Alexy (n 43) 790.

and its interpretation as a form of argument of rational practical discourse.[60] Nevertheless, objections have continued to be raised, two of which we will consider in more detail here.

A. Intuitionism

Alexander Somek has countered the law of balancing, which – albeit not quite straightforwardly[61] – comprises the core of the Weight Formula, by accusing it of not reaching beyond a 'formalisation of moral intuitionism'.[62] Jestaedt[63] and Poscher[64] have echoed this critique. Responding to an objection invoking intuitionism first requires a definition of what 'intuitionism' is understood to entail. Two interpretations can be distinguished: a meta-ethical and a methodological one. According to a meta-ethical interpretation,[65] objections invoking intuitionism assert that the degrees of intensity of interference and of abstract weights, as required under the Weight Formula, are nothing more than manifestations of ultimately subjective experiences of evidence. Poscher appears to point in this direction when he refers to that 'balancing itself depends on our intuitions as to the relative weight of the colliding principles'.[66] This may be countered by pointing out that these degrees in essence amount to judgements which assert a claim to correctness to be honoured with arguments, which in turn represent the counterpart to evidences. The rationality of balancing crucially depends on this propositionality.[67]

While it is certainly possible to negate the existence of rational argumentation when it comes to practical correctness, this would have far-reaching consequences for any form of legal argumentation that requires valuations that do not automatically follow from authoritative sources. What is more, this objection no longer aims directly at the rationality of balancing. Consequently, meta-ethical intuitionism-based objections can be countered by pointing to the fact that judgements, rather than experiences of evidence, are of concern here, and that the former are rational to the extent that they enable rational practical discourse.[68]

[60] R Alexy, 'On Balancing and Subsumption. A Structural Comparison' (2003) 16 *Ratio Juris* 448.

[61] See Alexy (n 43) 778–80, 788.

[62] A Somek, *Rechtliches Wissen* (Frankfurt, Suhrkamp, 2006) 135. See also A Somek, 'Abwägungsregeln. Ein didaktischer Beitrag zur Grundrechtsdogmatik' in C Hiebaum and P Koller (eds), *Politische Ziele und juristische Argumentation, ARSP Supplement 92* (Stuttgart, Franz Steiner, 2003) 114 (translated by the author).

[63] M Jestaedt, 'Die Abwägungslehre. ihre Stärken und ihre Schwächen' in O Depenheuer et al (eds), *Staat im Wort. Festschrift für Josef Isensee* (Tübingen, Mohr Siebeck, 2007) 267.

[64] Poscher (n 7) 76.

[65] On this, see R Alexy, *Theorie der juristischen Argumentation. Die Theorie des rationalen Diskurses als Theorie der juristischen Begründung*, 3rd edn (Frankfurt, Suhrkamp, 1996) 58–60.

[66] Poscher (n 7) 76 (translated by the author).

[67] R Alexy, 'Abwägung, Verfassungsgerichtsbarkeit und Repräsentation' in M Becker and R Zimmerling (eds), *Politik und Recht. PVS-Sonderheft 36* (Wiesbaden, VS Verlag, 2006) 254.

[68] ibid.

Rawls has put his stamp on the methodological version of the intuitionism-based objection, and Somek refers back to him.[69] According to Rawls, it suffices to use 'priority rules' when settling colliding principles, rather than weighing-up, to qualify as an intuitionist.[70] Rawls' most important priority rule consists of the strict – or, in his words, 'lexical'[71] – precedence of his First Priority Rule, concerned with liberty, over his Second Priority Rule aimed at social and economic inequalities. It follows that a methodological version of intuitionism directly targets the issue of whether the colliding of liberty with other rights and interests ought to be resolved by reference to strict rules or through the act of balancing. However, this represents a step away from the general issue of whether, and to what extent, balancing constitutes a rational process towards the – related but not identical – question of whether a rule-based model of constitutional rights is more rational than a principle-based model thereof. This question could only be answered by contrasting the costs and benefits of rationality resulting from a rule-based model with those of a principle-based model. For example, a list of the costs associated with Rawls' rule theory would include the waiving of the collision-prone constitutional right to general freedom of action, or that of constitutional social rights.[72] This is not the route this article will go down. It suffices to point out that behind the methodological version of the intuitionism-based objection lies nothing other than the thesis – rooted in general objections claiming irrationalism – that a rule-based model is more rational than a principle-based model. This has been discussed at length in other contexts.[73]

B. Scaling

The second objection rooted in argumentation theory concerns the issue of scaling. The Weight Formula presupposes the possibility of scaling intensities of interference (I_i, I_j), abstract weights (W_i, W_j), and the reliability of epistemic assumptions as to what a specific measure would entail in the event of not realising one but realising the other principle (R_i, R_j).[74] I have proposed a scale which is by no means universal but suits many different scenarios: 'light' (*l*), 'moderate' (*m*), and 'serious' (*s*), corresponding to the geometric sequence of 2^0, 2^1 and 2^2, ie 1, 2 and 4.[75] Riehm considers this an 'ill-suited means of specifying the process of balancing'.[76] His criticism is chiefly aimed at the distinction between discrete values and ranges of

[69] Somek (n 62) 135.
[70] J Rawls, *A Theory of Justice* (Cambridge MA, Harvard University Press, 1971) 34.
[71] ibid 302.
[72] See R Alexy, 'John Rawls' Theorie der Grundfreiheiten' in J Rawls and W Hinsch (eds), *Zur Idee des politischen Liberalismus: John Rawls in der Diskussion* (Frankfurt, Suhrkamp, 1997) 273ff.
[73] See eg Alexy (n 1) 104–25.
[74] Alexy (n 43) 790.
[75] ibid 785.
[76] T Riehm, *Abwägungsentscheidungen in der praktischen Rechtsanwendung. Argumentation – Beweis – Wertung* (Munich, CH Beck, 2006) 66 (translated by the author).

values. According to him, the three values corresponding to 'light', 'moderate' and 'serious', ie 1, 2 and 4, do not really represent specific values, but rather each represent a range or spectrum of values. On a geometric scale, Riehm claims, the value 'light' represented by 2^0, ie 1, corresponds to the range 0 to approximately $2^{0.49}$, ie 1.41; the value 'moderate' represented by 2^1, ie 2, corresponds to the range $2^{0.5}$, ie 1.42, to approximately $2^{1.49}$, ie 2.82; and the value 'serious' represented by 2^2, ie 4, corresponds to the range $2^{1.5}$, ie 2.83, to 4.[77] In Riehm's view, the discrete values 1, 2, 4 do not actually always reflect the '"true" extent' or the '"actual" value' we are trying to represent.[78] Yet he considers that this contradicts the theorem of equivalence relations, which is of fundamental importance to scales,[79] with serious consequences. The Weight Formula, in conjunction with the triadic scale, is said to violate commutativity, ie the rule of $a \cdot b = b \cdot a$, since the value of a light (l) interference with a principle with serious (s) abstract weight need not necessarily be equal to a serious (s) interference with a principle of light (l) abstract weight.[80] Assuming that the three values l, m, and s correspond to ranges, this would indeed be true. For a light interference with principle P_i, using a value towards the lower end of the range for light interferences, eg, 0.1, and a value towards the lower end of the range for serious weights, eg, 2.9, would yield a value of 0.29 in the multiplication required by the Weight Formula for the calculation relating to P_i. Conversely, tapping into the upper range of the respective ranges for P_j, for example using 3.9 for s, and 1.4 for l, would give 5.46. This would see commutativity collapse.

Riehm reinforces his point by claiming that the law of linearity is also contradicted. This states that if $a > b$ and $c > 0$ then $a \cdot c > b \cdot c$. Assuming that l and m represent ranges of values, and interpreting this in such a way that any value from this range could be inserted for l and m, then multiplying l by m should result in a higher value than multiplying m by m. Using values from the upper end of the range for $l \cdot m$ could give values of up to approximately 3.98. Conversely, tapping into the lower end of the range for $m \cdot m$ could give values as low as approximately 2.02.[81] It would follow that $1 \cdot 2$ corresponds to 3.98, and $2 \cdot 2$ to 2.02. The world of mathematics would implode.

This objection can be refuted by pointing out that the problems outlined by Riehm all follow from assumptions made about scalability in law that do not necessarily need to be shared. This concerns questions of how the legal structure is best represented mathematically. A premise of the scaling associated with the Weight Formula is that law, as far as the law itself is concerned, only supports rough, discrete scales, rather than infinitesimal, ie continuous, scales. The reason for this lies in the argumentative nature of law as expressed through the postulate of propositionality. Hence, degrees correspond to propositions or

[77] ibid 67.
[78] ibid.
[79] ibid.
[80] ibid 73.
[81] ibid 73–74.

judgements that require justification. One can only justify what one understands. The sentence '[i]nfringing on the freedom of opinion is easy' can be understood. The same is true of the following sentence, formulated based on a double-triadic scaling: 'Infringing on the freedom of opinion is a serious medium interference'. But what to do with a sentence such as '[i]nfringing on the freedom of opinion is a medium light serious interference'? Anyone contradicting that this sentence is incomprehensible need only move on to a fourth triad enabling propositions such as 'The infringement is a medium light serious light interference'. While there might be psychological mechanisms that would enable us, for example by inserting numbers, to agree with or refute such a sentence, it cannot possibly be the object of rational justification.

This highlights the result clearly. It can be summed up as a discrete value representing a 'true value', and not merely a 'central point in a value range on an actually continuous value scale'.[82] This would see all of the mathematical issues raised by Riehm fall apart. What is more, this result is absolutely compatible with the fact that some cases call for a more granular scale, for example a double-triadic scale.[83] After all, even a double-triadic scale is by no means a 'continuous' scale.

That is not to say that such an increased granularity does not create problems in cases where a more granular scaling is possible for P_i but not for P_j. Yet it appears that there are also solutions for such issues. A very serious (*ss*) infringement on the part of P_i could be contrasted with a simple serious (*s*) infringement for P_j. On a double-triadic scale, it is possible to contrast such a simple serious (*s*) infringement of P_j with a very serious (*ss*) infringement by allocating it the mean value for serious infringements, ie *ms*. P_i has the upper hand due to the value *ss*.

The latter can also be invoked to respond to another of Riehm's objections, in which he claims to have identified a 'covert transition from an ordinal to a cardinal scale'.[84] In this argument, he references the *Titanic* decision I have used as an example. In line with the Federal Constitutional Court, I have classified use of the term 'cripple' in reference to a paraplegic reserve officer as serious. However, Riehm alleges a mere '*relative* weighting', rather than an '*absolute* weighting', as he sees called for by a cardinal scale.[85] He considers this demonstrated by the fact that such 'verbal injuries', as opposed to 'brutal psychological torture', ought to be classified as 'light violations of the right of personality'.[86] It goes without saying that calling someone a 'cripple' is less severe than psychological torture, enabling a straightforward classification on an ordinal scale. Nevertheless, this does not stand in the way of using a cardinal scale. In the given context, the degrading term 'cripple' can qualify as a serious infringement on a double-triadic scale,

[82] ibid 73.
[83] Alexy (n 43) 786–87.
[84] Riehm (n 76) 66 (translated by the author).
[85] ibid (translated by the author).
[86] ibid 66ff (translated by the author).

whilst simultaneously qualifying as a lightly serious (*ls*) infringement within serious infringements, whereas psychological torture is equated with a very serious infringement (*ss*). Having started off on an ordinal scale, this would cardinalise matters. In all this, the 'quantifying benchmark'[87] invoked by Riehm would be the position of the constitution that gives rise to commensurability.[88] Whilst this by no means resolves all scaling issues, it can serve as guidance on how to find such a solution.

[87] ibid 67 (translated by the author).
[88] Alexy (n 43) 781–82.

4

Theory of a Phantom: The Principles Theory's Futile Quest for its Object*

RALF POSCHER

In his *Theory of Constitutional Rights*, Robert Alexy has taken up Ronald Dworkin's distinction between rules and principles and developed it into an all-encompassing principles theory of constitutional rights. In his circle of students, a little principles theory industry has evolved, within which Alexy's approach has been partly reformulated,[1] specified for individual rights,[2] extended from constitutional rights to other areas of law[3] and even elevated to the level of a general theory of law.[4] Alexy himself has fostered this development by continually refining, modifying and sophisticating his principles theory. Under his leadership, the principles theory has developed into a general legal theory, which claims to hold insights for diverse areas of the law, as well as for specific legal questions and for the understanding of law in general thanks to the analysis of both the nature and functional structure of principles.[5]

* Formerly published as R Poscher, 'Theory of a Phantom: The Principles Theory's Futile Quest for its Object' in JA de Oliveira et al (eds), *Alexy's Theory of Law* (Stuttgart, Franz Steiner, 2015) 129–48. Copyrights granted by Franz Steiner Verlag.

[1] See M Borowski, *Grundrechte als Prinzipien. Die Unterscheidung von Prima-Facie Position und definitiver Position als fundamentaler Konstruktionsgrundsatz der Grundrechte*, 2nd edn (Baden-Baden, Nomos, 2007).

[2] See JR Sieckmann, *Modelle des Eigentumsschutzes: Eine Untersuchung zur Eigentumsgarantie des Art. 14 GG* (Baden-Baden, Nomos, 1998); M Borowski, *Die Glaubens- und Gewissensfreiheit des Grundgesetzes* (Tübingen, Mohr Siebeck, 2006).

[3] See JH Park, *Rechtsfindung im Verwaltungsrecht. Grundlegung einer Prinzipientheorie des Verwaltungsrechts als Methode der Verwaltungsrechtsdogmatik* (Berlin, Duncker & Humblot, 1999); J Pietsch, *Das Schrankenregime der EU-Grundrechtecharta. Dogmatik und Bewertung auf der Grundlage einer Prinzipientheorie der Rechte* (Baden-Baden, Nomos, 2005).

[4] Most comprehensively elaborated by JR Sieckmann, *Regelmodelle und Prinzipienmodelle des Rechtssystems* (Baden-Baden, Nomos, 1990); JR Sieckmann, *Recht als normatives System. Die Prinzipientheorie des Rechts* (Baden-Baden, Nomos, 2009).

[5] As to the different aspects of the principles theory see R Poscher, 'Einsichten, Irrtümer und Selbstmissverständnis der Prinzipientheorie' in JR Sieckmann (ed), *Prinzipientheorie der Grundrechte* (Baden-Baden, Nomos, 2007) 59–79; R Poscher, 'Insights, Errors and Self-misconceptions of the Theory of Principles' (2009) 22 Ratio Juris 425–54 [ed note: see above Chapter 2, pp 29–55 for the equivalent text]; R Poscher, 'The Principles Theory: How Many Theories and What is Their Merit?' in M Klatt (ed), *Institutionalized Reason: The Jurisprudence of Robert Alexy* (Oxford, Oxford University Press, 2012) 218–47.

The distinction between rules and principles lies at the heart of the principles theory. For principles theorists, rules and principles are thought to differ in their formal structure. While rules strictly order a certain consequence, principles order a certain consequence only prima facie.[6] The differing structure of these two types of norms is thought to be evident from the way in which they collide with other norms. In the case of rule collision, either one of the rules is amended by an exception, or one of them is declared void; in case of a collision of principles, both principles remain valid, because they have only prima facie validity and therefore need to be optimised and developed into a precise rule by balancing them in each individual case of collision.[7] This norm-theoretical difference is supposed to be accompanied by a methodological one:

> Rules are applied by subsumption of facts under the conditions of a norm in order to deduce the consequence … The application of principles, on the other hand, requires a specific balancing of the colliding principles.[8]

On the level of legal doctrine, the norm-theoretical and methodological theses of the principles theory are combined: legal norms that can be applied by the method of subsumption are qualified as rules and – due to the norm-ontological dualism stipulated by the principles theory – all other norms are principles. As principles they must be interpreted as optimisation requirements for the same norm-theoretical reason. For the principles theory this has a direct impact on the doctrinal understanding of constitutional rights. Since constitutional rights cannot be applied by mere subsumption, they must be qualified as principles in the sense of the principles theory. Accordingly, constitutional rights must be interpreted as optimisation requirements. And this is the doctrinal upshot of the principles theory: the doctrinal interpretation of constitutional rights as optimisation requirements can be deduced already from the norm-theoretical dualism upheld by the principles theory.

The following critique will not focus on the merits of the principles theory as a doctrinal theory of constitutional rights or on its impact in other areas of the law.[9] Rather, it will challenge the central premise of the principles theory: the

[6] R Alexy, *Theorie der Grundrechte* (Frankfurt, Suhrkamp, 1986) 88–90; Sieckmann, *Regelmodelle* (n 4) 67–71.

[7] Alexy (n 6) 77–87; Sieckmann, *Regelmodelle* (n 4) 68.

[8] Sieckmann, *Regelmodelle* (n 4) 18. See also R Alexy, 'On Balancing and Subsumption' (2003) 16 *Ratio Juris* 433, 433–49.

[9] Criticism of the theory's potential as regards the doctrinal development of constitutional rights was already expressed by R Poscher, *Grundrechte als Abwehrrechte. Reflexive Regelung rechtlich geordneter Freiheit* (Tübingen, Mohr Siebeck, 2003) 82–84. See also M Jestaedt, *Grundrechtsentfaltung im Gesetz. Studien zur Interdependenz von Grundrechtsdogmatik und Rechtsgewinnungstheorie* (Tübingen, Mohr Siebeck, 1999) 222–60; W Cremer, *Freiheitsgrundrechte. Funktionen und Strukturen* (Tübingen, Mohr Siebeck, 2003) 218–27; JH Klement, 'Vom Nutzen einer Theorie, die alles erklärt. Robert Alexys Prinzipientheorie aus der Sicht der Grundrechtsdogmatik' (2008) 63 *JuristenZeitung* 756, 760; B Rusteberg, *Der grundrechtliche Gewährleistungsgehalt. Eine veränderte Perspektive auf die Grundrechtsdogmatik durch eine präzise Schutzbereichsbestimmung* (Tübingen, Mohr Siebeck, 2009) 158–66.

very existence of principles in the sense of the principles theory. Of course, their existence is not sufficient for the principles theory, but without it, the theory must collapse and with it the theoretical imposition of a constitutional rights doctrine.

The principles theory presupposes the existence of legal principles. At first sight, this seems a fairly unsuspicious assumption, since legal principles have formed part of the inventory of our legal universe for ages. But when the principles theory refers to legal principles, it does not refer to the rich diversity of traditional legal principles like the standard of the reasonable man, good faith, unjustified enrichment, equality and the like. When the principles theory talks about principles, it refers to the theoretical dualism mentioned above, according to which there are only two kinds of norms: rules that allow for precise subsumption[10] and principles, which are to be found in the sphere of an 'ideal ought', and which express themselves in the form of optimisation requirements in the sphere of the 'real ought'. So, the concept of a principle in the sense of the principles theory should not be confused with the traditional concept of a legal principle, connected neither to a normative dualism, nor to the idea of an 'ideal ought', nor yet to a monism of optimisation. Due to the confusion between 'principles' in the sense of the principles theory and 'principles' in the traditional sense, it is rarely noticed how demanding the principles theory's concept of a principle really is. For the principles theory, it is not sufficient to refer to the existence of principles in the traditional sense. Instead, it must prove the existence of principles in its own special understanding, ie as a distinct normative entity that differs from other legal norms in terms of its structure and not only due to a more or less abstract content or a greater or lesser importance. Even within the principles theory, there is controversy over what principles are supposed to be, how they should be described and how they need to be theoretically reconstructed. It is a remarkable fact in itself that the central object of the principles theory is so hotly disputed by its own adherents.[11] This dispute is not over the refinement of the theory; adherents, too, contest each other's construction of principles in their special sense and thus the object of their own theory.

Initially, Robert Alexy equated principles in the sense of the principles theory with optimisation requirements. In his foundational *Theory of Constitutional Rights*, the central passage on 'principles as optimisation requirements' is still written with this equation in mind:

> The decisive point in distinguishing rules from principles is that *principles* are norms which require that something be realized to the greatest extent possible given the legal and factual possibilities. Principles are *optimisation requirements*, characterized by the fact that they can be satisfied to varying degrees, and that the appropriate degree of satisfaction depends not only on what is factually possible but also on what is legally possible … By contrast, *rules* are norms which are always either fulfilled or not.[12]

[10] As to criticism of the principles theory's notion of a rule, see Poscher, 'Einsichten' (n 5) 70–73; Poscher, 'Insights' (n 5) 438–41.

[11] See the renewed criticism of Alexy's notion of a principle by Sieckmann, *Recht als normatives System* (n 4) 22–23.

[12] R Alexy, *A Theory of Constitutional Rights* (Oxford, Oxford University Press, 2002) 47–48.

In the beginning, principles were just optimisation requirements. And this was the very point of Alexy's conception of principles, namely that it specified Dworkin's idea of a 'prima facie ought' as an optimisation requirement.[13] Optimisation in this sense requires the relativisation of the consequence of a norm in accordance with the factual and legal possibilities,[14] which, in turn, specifies Dworkin's dimension of weight. This specifying reconstruction of Dworkin's principles as optimisation requirements was the analytical achievement of the early principles theory.

But it did not take long for adherents of the principles theory themselves to see that in fact, optimisation requirements present all the features of rules in the sense of the principles theory. Like any other requirement, they can be strictly and completely obeyed by performing the required optimisation. If a legal norm requires truck drivers to optimise tyre pressure for the sake of fuel consumption and safety purposes, truck drivers are strictly obliged to perform the required optimisation. Jan Sieckmann, a student of Alexy, thus states 'that the problem remains that the optimisation requirements … show just the features that are characteristic for rules, ie strict validity and definite satisfiability'.[15] The insight that optimisation requirements are not structurally distinct from other norms, however, is a problem only for the principle's theory. On the basis of a traditional understanding of principles, which sees only gradual differences between legal principles and other types of legal norms, the insight would not come as a surprise. It would merely corroborate the traditional view by showing that the traditional understanding of principles also applies to legal principles that can be reconstructed as optimisation requirements.

The loss of optimisation requirements as candidates for the conception of principles caused the principles theory to slide into a precarious situation: it was threatened with losing its very object. It comes as no surprise that adherents of the principles theory engaged in serious theoretical efforts to provide a concept of principles that could support the theoretical dualism they were claiming. For Robert Alexy, however, the discovery that optimisation requirements are not principles was no reason to revise the principles theory, but to 'simply give[] [them] a sharper focus'.[16] Ever since, Alexy has maintained that principles are an 'ideal ought'.[17]

With regard to rescue attempts like these, it does not seem too far-fetched to object that they only serve the purpose of creating a theoretical artefact to replace the object of the principles theory with the realisation of the rule-like character of optimisation requirements.[18] In two of his more recent publications, Alexy has

[13] ibid 57–59.

[14] ibid 47–48.

[15] Sieckmann, *Regelmodelle* (n 4) 65.

[16] R Alexy, 'Zur Struktur der Rechtsprinzipien' in B Schilcher et al (eds), *Regeln, Prinzipien und Elemente im System des Rechts* (Vienna, Verlag Österreich, 2000) 31, 38–39 [ed note: see above Chapter 1, p 23].

[17] ibid.

[18] Poscher, 'Einsichten' (n 5) 10–12; Poscher, 'Insights' (n 5) 436–38; Poscher, 'The Principles Theory' (n 5) 229–35.

responded to this line of critique and defended his conception of principles as an 'ideal ought'.[19] The critique he faced is twofold: first, that the supposition of an 'ideal ought' is superfluous; second, that there is no 'ideal ought' in legal systems. And as Alexy has correctly remarked: 'The ontological objection is the more radical one. If it were true, then the non-necessity objection would also be true, as what does not exist cannot not be unnecessary'.[20]

In what follows, I first want to scrutinise Alexy's reply to the objection of superfluity. This is not for dramaturgical reasons only – superfluity follows from non-existence – but also on strategic grounds. While most adherents of the principles theory agree on why they need their theoretically demanding concept of principles – namely to explain the functioning and normative qualities of optimisation requirements – almost every theorist has his own thesis about what principles are supposed to be and how they differ from optimisation requirements.[21] Almost half a dozen different conceptions are on offer. The development of the principles theory nourishes the suspicion that critique is confronted with a Hydra-like phenomenon. For each candidate of the principles concept rejected by critique, two new ones are advanced.[22] Due not only to the general problem of negative proofs of existence, but also to the promiscuity of the principles theory's conception of principles, the superfluity critique is more suitable for confronting the polyphonic choir of principles theorists. Just as a defender of the laws of mechanics can leave open the existence of angels if he does not need them to explain macro-physical phenomena, a critic of the principles theory can leave open the existence of principles as 'ideal ought'[23] or 'pro tanto ought'[24] or infinitely 'reiterated requirements of validity'[25] or 'norms with two levels of validity'.[26] If it can be shown that the normative phenomena that the principles theory tries to explain can be perfectly well explained by the idea of optimisation requirements, there is no need to worry about a mysterious conception of principles, since even by their own standards optimisation requirements are not principles (anymore). If the superfluity thesis can be defended, the existence theses become uninteresting, even offered by the dozen. It would be as if principles theorists insisted that angels have wings or wear white nightgowns: nothing would follow from it.

[19] R Alexy, 'Ideales Sollen' in L Clérico and JR Sieckmann (eds), *Grundrechte, Prinzipien und Argumentation* (Baden-Baden, Nomos, 2009) 21–22 [ed note: see above Chapter 3, pp 60–61].

[20] ibid.

[21] For an overview, see Borowski, *Grundrechte als Prinzipien* (n 1) 68–105.

[22] For a new sprout see M Reßing, 'Prinzipien als Normen mit zwei Geltungsebenen' (2009) 95 *Archiv für Rechts- und Sozialphilosophie* 28, 28–48.

[23] Alexy (n 16) 38–39 [ed note: see above Chapter 1, pp 23–24]; Alexy (n 19).

[24] N Jansen, *Die Struktur der Gerechtigkeit* (Baden-Baden, Nomos, 1998) 101.

[25] JR Sieckmann, 'Prinzipien, Ideales Sollen und normative Argumente' (2011) 97 *Archiv für Rechts- und Sozialphilosophie*, 178, 178, 190–92; JR Sieckmann, 'Zur Analyse von Normkonflikten und Normabwägungen' in G Meggle (ed), *Analyomen 2: Proceedings of the 2nd Conference 'Perspectives in Analytical Philosophy'*, vol 3 (Berlin, Walter de Gruyter, 1994) 349–52.

[26] Reßing (n 22) 46–48.

In the first section below, I will explain the objection that principles in the sense of the principles theory are theoretically superfluous, and defend this objection against Alexy's reply. In the second section, I will discuss the existence objection only with regard to the 'ideal ought', which Alexy himself equates with principles. The third section will explain why principles theorists are not satisfied by the discovery that at least some principles can be reconstructed as optimisation requirements. In the short final section, I will again stress that the critique of the principles theory is not aimed at legal principles in the traditional sense; I will also explain why our traditional – gradualist – understanding of legal principles is very sensible compared to the theoretically overcharged and misconceived concept of the principles theory.

I. The Objection of Superfluity

If optimisation requirements are not principles in the sense of the principles theory, then such principles have to be found elsewhere. It would, however, be of no help to the principles theory to completely detach its conception of principles from optimisation requirements, since the doctrinal payoff of the principles theory is that all sorts of norms can be interpreted as optimisation requirements due to their quality as principles, and that all legal conflicts involving principles have to be solved by a balancing with the aim of optimisation. The intimate connection between principles and optimisation requirements is as vital to the principles theory as the structural distinction between rules and principles itself. Doctrinal suggestions like understanding constitutional rights as optimisation requirements could no longer be deduced from the norm-theoretical dichotomy of rules and principles if principles were associated with something other than optimisation requirements. So, it comes as no surprise that Alexy now finds principles inside optimisation requirements. Optimisation requirements are not principles, but, according to Alexy, principles do the work within optimisation requirements. For Alexy, we should distinguish between '*commands to be optimised* and *commands to optimise*. Commands to be optimised are the objects of balancing or weighing. They can be termed "the ideal 'ought'" or "ideals"'.[27] So now, principles are not optimisation requirements as such, but rather the 'ideal ought' that forms the object of the optimisation. Therefore, optimisation requirements are a special kind of rules that incorporate a principle. Although in the sphere of the 'real ought' optimisation requirements have the mundane character of rules only, they are connected to the sphere of the 'ideal ought' by their special object, ie by principles.

The critique of this reconstruction of principles as the objects of optimisation requirements mainly claims that such reconstruction misrepresents the objects of

[27] Alexy (n 16) 38–39 [ed note: see above Chapter 1, pp 23–24]; Alexy (n 19).

optimisation requirements. According to the reconstruction suggested by Alexy, the objects of optimisation requirements are themselves normative in character – even of an ideal normative character, namely an 'ideal ought'. This reconstruction, however, misses the fact that the object of optimisation requirements is generally not another norm but rather of an empirical nature. Optimisation requirements generally do not demand to optimise norms but rather aim at factual circumstances. Optimisation requirements are generally not reflexive in the sense of being norms requiring the optimisation of other norms – let alone 'ideal oughts'. For instance, a requirement to optimise the freedom of speech requires optimising the empirical possibilities of expression; it does not require optimising another norm that guarantees the freedom of speech. Optimisation requirements generally aim at the improvement factual circumstances, and not reflexively at the adjustment of other norms. They demand freedom of speech, not an improvement of the norms that refer to the freedom of speech. Accordingly, a repressive state does not follow the requirement to optimise the freedom of speech by signing ever more international conventions on the freedom of speech in order to optimise the guarantee of constitutional rights by international obligations, but only by actually abandoning censorship.

Contrary to some principles theorists, the objects of optimisation requirements need not have a normative character if we want to explain the normativity of optimisation requirements either.[28] Such normativity is already established by the requirement to enhance a certain object relative to the given legal and factual possibilities. The normativity of optimisation requirements follows from the mere requirement to optimise. There is no need to presuppose a requirement to be optimised as the object of optimisation. All kinds of objects can be optimised: tyre pressure, health, freedom of speech – optimisation requirements do not depend on normative objects. The direction of an optimisation requirement is usually determined by the context. The context determines whether the object of an optimisation requirement is supposed to be maximised or minimised relative to the legal and factual possibilities. If understood as an optimisation requirement, the constitutional right to physical integrity demands that infringements on physical integrity are minimised relative to the legal and factual possibilities and not maximised. In public administration, the requirement to optimise the rate of employment must be understood as a requirement to maximise employment relative to the legal and factual possibilities.

The insight that optimisation requirements are themselves normative but generally not aimed at a normative object becomes evident in comparison with rare cases in which this is different. Optimisation requirements can have any kind of object. They can also have norms as their object. Norms can be optimised as well, ie when it comes to closing tax loopholes. But optimisation requirements of this sort are a rather rare exception in legal systems. Constitutional rights, which

[28] As claimed by Sieckmann, *Regelmodelle* (n 4) 66.

the principles theory takes as a paradigm for optimisation requirements, do not aim at the optimisation of norms[29] even if they are understood as optimisation requirements. They aim at empirical objects or circumstances.

Confronted with this critique, Alexy now concedes: '[o]n the surface, this objection appears to be justified, as it is indeed a possibility for the object of a requirement such as (3), ie help for those in need (*p*), to be made the direct object of optimisation. This would turn.

(2) O*p*

into

(4) O*Opt p*'.[30]

In this quote, O*p* in (2) is to be read as a formalisation of the proposition that it is required that *p*,[31] which can be expressed in different sentences. In (4) O*Opt p* is supposed to stand for the proposition that it is required to optimise the object of *p*.

Though Alexy's concession of the initial plausibility of the superfluity objection is to be welcomed, it must be stressed that (4) makes use of a misleading notation. In (2) *p* – in accordance with standard notations – stands as a variable for a proposition. In the example that Alexy himself gives, *p* stands for the proposition that people in need should receive aid. With respect to this example, O*p* should be read as: it is required that people in need receive aid. In (4) the expression *Opt* takes the place of an operator, even though *Opt* merely qualifies the content of the proposition *p*.[32] In the example, *Opt p* stands for the requirement that aid for people in need is to be optimised. *Opt* qualifies the object required – in the example, it is not just aid for the people in need that is required, but the optimisation of said aid. The qualification clarifies that the proposition *Opt p* is distinct from *p* in having the optimisation of the object of *p* as its content. But this would be more precisely expressed by the indexical p_{opt}. Regardless of Alexy's notational idiosyncrasy, it

[29] This might be different for constitutional rights whose object is largely dependent on normative configuration.

[30] Alexy (n 19) 24. [ed note: see above Chapter 3, p 62].

[31] This formalisation is in line with deontic standard logic as established by Jan Henrik von Wright, who introduced the expression 'OA' as an abbreviation for the proposition that the action described by 'A' is required. See GH von Wright, 'Deontic Logic' (1951) 60 *Mind* 1, 4. Based on von Wright's initial conception of a logic of action, in which the operator 'O' was exclusively applied to actions, numerous scholars have developed the deontic standard logic as it is known today. Analogous to predicate logic, deontic standard logic provides for a propositional interpretation of variables and operators, see AN Prior, *Formal Logic* (Oxford, Oxford University Press, 1962); AR Anderson, 'The Formal Analysis of Normative Systems' in N Rescher (ed), *The Logic of Decision and Action* (Pittsburgh PA, University of Pittsburgh Press, 1967) 147–213. Later, von Wright himself adopted this view. For instance, see GH von Wright, *A New System of Deontic Logic: Logical Studies* (London, Routledge and Keagan Paul Ltd, 1964) 58–75; GH von Wright, *An Essay in Deontic Logic and the General Theory of Action* (Amsterdam, North Holland Publishing, 1968). Accordingly, by applying the conventions of deontic standard logic, the operator 'O' has to be read as an abbreviation for the proposition 'that it is required' and '*p*' has to be read as an abbreviation for any proposition 'that *p*'.

[32] Also, '*Opt*' cannot be read as the predicate of an variable *p* that stands for an individual, since this would violate the rule of consistent notation, because in (2), '*p*' stands for a proposition.

should be noted that *Opt* is a qualification of the proposition *p* and not a deontic logical operator – like eg the 'ought'-operator '*O*'. The freedom of notational design does not give freedom regarding the substance of the issue.

To refute the plausible objection, Alexy replies to it in two steps: first, he attempts to show that the profane reconstruction of optimisation requirements is not the only possible one. He contends that a reconstruction based on an 'ideal ought' is also possible. Second, he tries to show that the reconstruction based on an 'ideal ought' is not only possible but actually necessary to explain certain features of optimisation requirements. Below, both of these theses – the possibility thesis and the necessity thesis – will be refuted. Optimisation requirements cannot be adequately reconstructed by relying on normative entities as their objects, nor is such a reconstruction necessary to explain their features.

A. The Possibility Thesis

Alongside the profane way of reconstructing optimisation requirements as

O*Opt p*

for Alexy 'it would be equally possible to represent the optimisation requirement in such a way as to give the object of optimisation a normative character. This is the case when the requirement to help those in need, ie (2), is made the object of optimisation. This would see the optimisation requirement reconstructed as follows:

(5) O*Opt* O*p*'.[33]

Alexy's possibility thesis is ambiguous. On the one hand, it can be understood in a reconstructive way. As a reconstructive thesis, it says that any optimisation requirement (O*Opt p*) can be reconstructed as a requirement to optimise another requirement. On the other hand, it can be understood as a constructive thesis according to which – irrespective of optimisation requirements that have a factual object – we can construct optimisation requirements that, in a reflexive sense, have another requirement as their object of optimisation. As a reconstructive thesis, however, Alexy's possibility thesis is simply wrong; as a constructive thesis it is trivial and of no interest for the optimisation requirements in which the principles theory is interested.

(i) Reconstructive Reading

When Alexy talks about the 'ideal ought', he consistently refers only to optimisation requirements that have factual objects of optimisation like aid for people in need. None of his own examples deals with optimisation requirements that

[33] Alexy (n 19) 24. [ed note: see above Chapter 3, p 63].

require the optimisation of norms. When he now talks about the possibility of reconstructing optimisation requirements he seems to think that a requirement to optimise a factual object can be reconstructed as the requirement to optimise a normative object. For him, this interpretation is strongly supported by the fact that the requirement to aid people in need, understood as an 'ideal ought', is equivalent to the following optimisation requirement:

O*Opt* O*p*.[34]

But even if *p* has the same propositional content, the reconstruction proposed by Alexy is not equivalent to the optimisation requirement that he intends to reconstruct:

O*Opt* O*p* ≠ O*Opt* *p*.

This can easily be demonstrated by putting a random proposition in the place of *p*. The requirement to optimise health (O*Opt* *p*) is a different optimisation requirement than the requirement to optimise health-related norms (O*Opt* O*p*). Health can be optimised by medical treatments or fitness programmes; the requirement to stay or to become healthy might be optimised by a system of sanctions like higher health insurance premiums or less sophisticated medical treatments – but the requirement to live healthily cannot be optimised by massages or workouts. The optimisation of a requirement is totally different from the optimisation of factual circumstances. Confusing the two will lead to category mistakes.

This is also true of Alexy's own example. Alexy takes the requirement to help people in need as a starting point. Alexy first concedes that 'it is indeed a possibility for the object of a requirement such as (3), ie help for those in need (*p*), to be made the direct object of optimisation. This would turn

(2) O*p*

into

(4) O*Opt* *p*'.[35]

But according to Alexy it would also be possible that 'the requirement to help those in need, ie (2), [becomes] the object of the optimisation. This would see the optimisation requirement reconstructed as follows:

(5) O*Opt* O*p*'.[36]

The simple requirement to optimise aid for people in need (O*Opt* *p*), though, has a very different content from the reflexive requirement to optimise the requirement to aid people in need (O*Opt* O*p*). Aid for people in need can be optimised by distributing tents and food supplies. By contrast, the requirement to aid people

[34] ibid 25. [ed note: see above Chapter 3, p 63].
[35] ibid.
[36] ibid.

in need might be optimised by introducing or increasing a penalty for omitting to help people in need or extending the scope of the respective norm. The simple optimisation requirement is different from the reflexive requirement.

This difference is further underlined by the different legal and factual possibilities that are of importance for the different objects of optimisation. Aid for people in need may find its legal boundaries in the property rights of third parties and its factual boundaries in the material resources at hand. The legal and factual boundaries for the optimisation of the requirement to provide aid are of a very different kind: legally speaking, they might be found in proportionality requirements for sanctions against omissions; factually, they might be found in limited surveillance capacities of the state. As a reconstructive thesis, Alexy's possibility theorem is so obviously wrong that the principle of charity speaks against a reconstructive interpretation of Alexy's defence – despite the many arguments for such a reading in his text.

For the sake of completeness, it should be mentioned that a notational manoeuvre that Alexy employs in his reply does not change anything in substance. Alexy tries to shift the 'ideal ought' to the deontic operator. He attempts to abandon his previous thesis that the normative quality of the object of optimisation itself produces principles as well as an 'ideal ought'. 'With this, I revoke the thesis put forward in 1979 that ideal and real "ought" are a matter of the object of a requirement and do not affect the deontic modalities as such'.[37] He now contends that the crucial point is the fact,

> [t]hat not only the object of a requirement can be qualified. Also the modalities of a requirement themselves can be subject to qualification. If the qualification is an idealization, this leads to an ideal ought. The idealization of the modality of the requirement can be expressed by 'O_i'. 'Idealization' thus means that the ought does not relate to conflicting rights and duties.[38]

$O_i p$

shall then be the expression for the 'ideal ought'. This is supposed to lead to the mutual implication

'$OOpt\ Op \leftrightarrow O_i p$'[39]

O_i, however, is not a normative operator that expresses an ideal ought; nor does $O_i p$ – as defined by Alexy – correspond to $OOpt\ Op$; nor would an $O_i p$ that corresponds to $OOpt\ Op$ affect the optimisation requirements that the principles theory is concerned with.

A norm that requires *p* regardless of the legal or factual possibilities has the form *Op* – there is no need for an index. A requirement of *p* that is independent of contrary legal obligations is not equivalent to *OOpt Op*: first, because *OOpt Op*

[37] ibid.
[38] ibid.
[39] ibid.

has a different object, namely *Opt* O*p*; second, because the optimisation (*Opt*) just expresses the relativisation to the legal and factual possibilities. If O*Opt* O*p* and O_i were equivalent, then *Opt* O would merely be contracted to the index '${}_i$'. But the expression *Opt* O is part of the proposition *Opt* O*p*. The object of the requirement O*Opt* O*p* is not *p*, but the optimisation of the requirement of *p* (*Opt* O*p*). The index '${}_i$' is only a different way of expressing *Opt* O*p*. Just as *Opt* is a qualification of the proposition *p*,[40] *Opt* O qualifies the object of the proposition *p*. *Opt* O*p* stands for the proposition that the requirement of the object of the proposition *p* shall be optimised. Contrary to what Alexy's notation O_i suggests, *Opt* O is not an index of the normative operator 'O'. If '${}_i$' were to stand for *Opt* O, then the proposition *p* could be qualified by an index p_i. It remains Alexy's secret how this misleading notational suggestion could give birth to an 'ideal ought' that is different from O*Opt* O*p*, which, according to Alexy's newest twist, does not have a principle or an 'ideal ought' as its object. And last, but not least, it should be remembered that the whole notational manoeuvre deals with the reflexive requirement O*Opt* O*p*, which – as shown above – does not affect the optimisation requirements of non-normative objects that the principles theory and Alexy are exclusively concerned with in their examples and other writings.

(ii) Constructive Reading

While the reconstructive reading of Alexy's possibility thesis is obviously false, the opposite is true of its constructive reading: it is obviously right, but also so trivial that nothing follows from it for any of the questions that the principles theory is concerned with. If the possibility thesis merely aims to show that, irrespective of the actual requirements that Alexy discusses, like the requirement to give aid to people in need, it is possible to construct requirements that do not aim at aid for people in need, but at the optimisation of laws penalising failure to assist people in danger, there is nothing to object to. As already shown, normative objects can be optimised as well. But these reflexive requirements do not contribute to an understanding or explanation of non- reflexive optimisation requirements. They are just requirements with a different object. In our legal order, they are an exception. Accordingly, in Alexy's explanation of principles, we do not find any concrete example of such reflexive optimisation requirements, let alone one from an existing legal system. Constitutional rights in particular, which represent the main area of application for the principles theory, are not norms that require the optimisation of other norms. In their interpretation according to the principles theory, they are norms that require the state to optimise its non- interference, not norms that demand the optimisation of the norms of constitutional liberties. They aim at factual, not normative objects.

[40] ibid 24. [ed note: see above Chapter 3, p 62].

In its constructive reading, the possibility thesis only explains that the character of a norm as an optimisation requirement does not depend on the object of optimisation: it is not only empirical objects and factual circumstances that can be optimised, but also norms. Thereby, the possibility thesis only corroborates the idea that optimisation requirements do not have to be related to normative objects, let alone 'ideal oughts'. There is no need to draw on principles of the kind that Alexy equates with an 'ideal ought' in order to explain the features of optimisation requirements.

B. The Necessity Thesis

Even Alexy's thesis that optimisation requirements can be reconstructed by means of an 'ideal ought' fails. The reconstruction he proposes does not lead to a reconstruction of the optimisation requirements he claims to reconstruct. Rather, it leads to optimisation requirements that are hardly relevant to actual legal orders and that do not in any way explain the connection in which an 'ideal ought' is supposed to figure in those kinds of optimisation requirements that the principles theory is concerned with.

But even though Alexy's explanation of optimisation requirements via an 'ideal ought' is based on norm-logical errors and only confuses their understanding, there would be some merit in searching for further normative entities were Alexy's second thesis to hold, namely that optimisation requirements cannot be fully understood without presupposing some form of principle – whatever its nature. The almost feverish search for new constructions of principles besides, beyond, or within the idea of optimisation requirements might then make scientific sense. If there were something about optimisation requirements that we did not understand or were not able to explain, this might be due to the fact that we still lack insight into a special kind of normative entity that Alexy might not have fully grasped with his 'ideal ought', but for which the concept of principles could serve as a kind of placeholder.

Alexy's argument for why optimisation requirements are not sufficient to explain constitutional rights understood as optimisation requirements is

> that constitutional rights are made up of norms and that, following this, their collision may only adequately be reconstructed as a collision of norms ... One could now assume that the issue of normativity can also be resolved when only optimisation requirements are considered.[41]

But Alexy thinks that this would be wrong. Alexy believes that optimisation requirements as such fail to explain two things: first, the normativity of constitutional

[41] ibid 30. [ed note: see above Chapter 3, p 68].

rights if they are understood – as the principles theory would have it – as optimisation requirements; and, second, the way in which the collision of optimisation requirements can be dealt with.

(i) The Normativity Argument

As concerns Alexy's formulation, it should be clarified that constitutional rights do not 'consist of' norms: they *are* norms. Insofar as the formulation is supposed to suggest that constitutional rights have a normative object, since they are described as consisting of norms, it must be rejected. The constitutional right of physical integrity requires the state to abstain from intrusions. It is a norm, but does not have a norm as its object. Its objects are actions of the state that intrude upon the physical integrity of the bearers of constitutional rights. Such intrusions by the state are not norms, but factual actions. Norms can only appear as intrusions upon constitutional rights insofar as they empower the government to intrude upon the physical integrity of its citizens. So, ultimately, the object of the requirement to abstain from intrusion is not normative but factual in nature.

This also answers the question concerning the normativity of constitutional rights. Constitutional rights are normative because they require abstention from infringements – not because they relate to some other kind of requirement. If constitutional rights are understood as optimisation requirements, they simply have – according to Alexy's notation – the form:

OOpt p.

p represents refraining from infringement on constitutional rights – in the case of the right to personal integrity, refraining from physical mistreatment. The normative operator 'O' is not only sufficient to explain the normativity of this optimisation requirement; it is also the only adequate expression of the requirement. Duplicating the normative operator would not only be redundant; it would also give constitutional rights an object that does not adequately represent them. Article 2 (2) of the Basic Law does not require optimisation of the requirement to refrain from intrusions upon physical integrity, but aims for the direct opposite of such factual intrusions. There is no need for further normative entities to explain the normativity of optimisation requirements.

But those optimisation requirements that have a norm as their object also receive their normativity solely from the normative operator relating to the optimisation, and not from the normative operator of the requirement that has to be optimised. This can easily be seen when the normative operator is replaced by a descriptive one. If it is required that '*p*' is replaced by 'it is a fact that *p*', the whole expression becomes descriptive, even though the object (*p*) may be normative. The proposition that the optimisation of a requirement *p* is a fact is descriptive. The normativity of the object of optimisation has no influence on the normativity of the expression as a whole.

The normativity of optimisation requirements is not in any way obscure. As with any other norm, the normativity just follows from the normative operator which relates to the optimisation of an object – be it factual or normative.

(ii) The Collision Argument

The explanation of collisions between optimisation requirements does not depend on a redoubling of their normativity either. Collisions of norms are coordinated by collision rules. These collision rules can be integrated into the norms to be coordinated, as is done by the principles theory with regard to optimisation requirements, by relativising the requirement to the legal and factual possibilities on the basis of balancing. The content of the collision rule is contingent, though, and leaves the logical structure of the norms untouched. Norms with collision clauses are in no way mysterious. They can be construed and applied like any other norm. There is no need for an 'ideal ought' in order to understand them. This can easily be demonstrated by reference to two norms that Alexy himself presents as examples of principles.[42] A norm N1 empowers the government to take measures to protect its foreign interests. A norm N2 guarantees the freedom of the press.

> N1: If an action endangers foreign interests of the state, this action can be prohibited.
>
> N2: If an action serves to promote the freedom of the press, the state must refrain from prohibiting it.

There is an overlap of scenarios in which both norms apply. For these scenarios, the legal system must introduce a conflict rule that can be incorporated as an exception to both norms. The content of the collision rule is a totally contingent matter. A traditional collision rule would be the *lex posterior* principle (C_a). If norm N1 concerning the protection of state interests stems from a period of military dictatorship and norm N2 from the time after the state became a democracy, the *lex posterior* principle might even apply to norms like N1 and N2. This would lead to an interpretation in which N1 is amended by an exception clause, provided that N1 is not diametrically opposed to the new state order and therefore considered invalid. This would give us:

> N1a: If an action endangers foreign interests of the state *and does not serve to promote the freedom of the press*, this action can be prohibited.
>
> N2a: If an action serves to promote the freedom of the press, the state must refrain from prohibiting it.

By inserting the collision element, the normative structure of the colliding norms remains untouched. What is more, the collision rule does not give the norms a

[42] Alexy (n 6) 147.

reflexive character in the sense that they are not only requirements themselves, but have a requirement as their object. Their structure is still

Op

not

O *Op*.

Nothing changes when the collision rule incorporates an element of weight. For instance, a teleological reduction might result in the interpretation that N1 is only valid for *important* foreign relations. According to this collision rule 'C_b', we would obtain the following norms:

> N1b: If an action endangers *important* foreign interests of the state, this action can be prohibited.
>
> N2b: If an action serves to promote the freedom of the press *and does not endanger important foreign interests of the state*, the state must refrain from prohibiting it.

Like optimisation requirements, $N1_b$ and $N2_b$ require the balancing of interests. The only difference from optimisation requirements lies in the fact that in this case the balancing is not relative to another interest. It must only be established that the foreign relations are of importance. As before, the structure of the norms is not changed by the collision rule. There is nothing about norms $N1_b$ and $N2_b$ which requires us to refer to an 'ideal ought' or any other phenomenon like infinitely 'reiterated requirements of validity' in order to understand their content.

From a collision rule C_b it is only a short step to a collision rule that relies on the idea of optimisation. If a collision rule C_c does not rely on important foreign relations, but on the question of whether the affected relations outweigh the freedom of the press, two norms are created that make it necessary to balance the relative importance of the endangered foreign relations and the freedom of the press. These norms could thus be understood as optimisation requirements as defined by Alexy, and can be treated in accordance with his rule of balancing.[43]

> N1c: If an action endangers the *outweighing* foreign interests of the state, this action can be prohibited.
>
> N2c: If an action serves to promote the freedom of the press and does not endanger the *outweighing* foreign interests of the state, the state must refrain from prohibiting it.

The semantic shift from 'important' to 'outweighing' leaves the structure of the norms untouched – just like other collision rules. The norms' object remains factual and does not become normative. Even if the collision rule demands a relative balancing in the form of an optimisation process, neither of the norms present any features requiring the presupposition of an 'ideal ought' or any other normative entity. The optimisation requirements neither have the structure that Alexy

[43] ibid 145–54.

thinks they have, nor do they present norm-structural features that could set them apart from norms with integrated 'collision clauses'. For a theory of constitutional rights that suggests solving constitutional rights issues by the process of optimising, a reconstruction of constitutional rights as optimisation requirements should be perfectly sufficient. There is no need for principles that are not identical to optimisation requirements.

II. The Existence Objection

So, what are principles theorists talking about when they talk about principles? What is meant by the mysterious talk about an 'ideal ought'? What Alexy tries to reconstruct as an 'ideal ought' in his principles theory are unconditional norm formulations, as in N1 and N2, that are not explicitly relativised to their legal and factual possibilities by collision rules. The requirement to aid people in need could also be understood as a rule in the sense of the principles theory. As a consequence, aid would have to be supplied to people in need regardless of the costs and risks to those providing the aid.[44] For principles theorists, such a literal interpretation seems implausible. In order to provide a plausible meaning for such unconditional norm formulations, principles theorists understand the respective norms as an 'ideal ought', as an unconditional 'ought' in the realm of the ideal. In an ideal world, such norms would satisfy their unconditional formulations, because they would not have to be relativised with regard to the legal and factual possibilities. In the realm of the ideal they are principles. In the realm of the real, so the idea goes, principles would become optimisation requirements.

The effort of the principles theory to do justice to the wording of a norm formulation is honourable. The distinction and the dialectics between an ideal and a 'real ought', however, are an unnecessary and unnecessarily complicated interpretation of a norm formulation, which has the further disadvantage of illegitimately limiting interpretative options. Norm formulations like N1 and N2 or the unconditional requirement to provide aid are abbreviated and elliptic expressions of more complex norms, which have to be developed by the classic means of legal interpretation and construction.[45] The legal interpretations of the abridged and elliptic norm formulations will then lead to the collision clauses, which determine the norms' relations to other legal norms and the legal system as a whole.

Unlike the interpretation of unconditional norm formulations in the sense of an 'ideal ought', which reduces them to principles in the sense of the principles theory and thus always to optimisation requirements, collision rules that arise from classic legal interpretations of unconditional norm formulations can take on

[44] Alexy (n 19) 23. [ed note: see above Chapter 3, p 61].

[45] See Rusteberg (n 9) 158–66, who shows that, in determining the scope of constitutional rights, the classic methods of legal interpretation are diluted by the principles theory.

the most diverse forms and are not restricted – as the little examples with norms N1 and N2 show – to one specific kind of collision clause.

Even where the collision rule amounts to some kind of proportionality test, it is not determined which interpretation of the proportionality principle should be applied – even though the principles theory seems to think that it can take the proportionality principle hostage: 'The principles theory implies the principle of proportionality and the latter implies the former'.[46] The proportionality principle, though, does not have to be understood in the sense of an optimisation requirement. Beyond the Pareto-optimum necessity requirement, it can also be understood as a guarantee of a minimum position[47] or as a prohibition against gross disproportionality[48] or in the sense of an equal-weight model along the lines of Bruce Chapman's suggestion.[49] Accordingly, most authors generally do not understand constitutional principles as optimisation requirements, but rather as minimum guarantees or as a framework guarantee.[50] The interpretation of the abbreviated and elliptic norm formulations, especially as regards constitutional law, is no question for which the purported distinction between rules and principles in the sense of the principles theory can be of any help. It is a contingent matter which collision rule will coordinate N1 and N2. It is even a contingent matter whether an unconditionally formulated norm is modified by a collision rule at all. For the guarantee of human dignity in Article 1 (1) of the Basic Law, the opposite was undisputed for a long time.[51]

The 'ideal ought' that Alexy proposes does not relate to norms, but to abbreviated and elliptic norm formulations, which should not be stylised into an 'ideal ought', but merely interpreted in the way that laws have always been interpreted. Just as the descriptive formulation 'Arts and sciences, research and teaching shall be free' in Article 5 (3) of the Basic Law must be interpreted, in the first instance, not as a factual statement but as a norm and then as a subjective right against government intrusions, which can only be limited on the basis of colliding constitutional norms. But as little as the interpretation of the descriptive formulation in Article 5 (3) first sentence of the Basic Law requires the presupposition of some kind of 'factual ought', it *does* require the presupposition of an 'ideal ought' for the interpretation of unconditionally formulated norms. In both cases, it only takes the legal interpretation and construction of a concrete norm formulation in its respective context. By presupposing principles in the sense of an 'ideal ought', the principles theory hypostatises abbreviated and elliptic norm formulations.

[46] Alexy (n 16) 35 [ed note: see above Chapter 1, p 20].

[47] B Schlink, *Abwägung im Verfassungsrecht* (Berlin, Duncker & Humblot, 1976) 76–78, 192–95.

[48] B Pieroth and B Schlink, *Grundrechte. Staatsrecht II*, 26th edn (Heidelberg, CF Müller, 2010) rn 304; Poscher (n 9) 224.

[49] B Chapman, 'Preference, Pluralism, and Proportionality' (2010) 60 *University of Toronto Law Journal* 177.

[50] KE Hain, *Die Grundsätze des Grundgesetzes. Eine Untersuchung zu Art. 79 Abs. 3 GG* (Baden-Baden, Nomos, 1999) 157; F Reimer, *Verfassungsprinzipien. Ein Normtyp im Grundgesetz* (Berlin, Duncker & Humblot, 2001) 329–33, 338–48, each with further references.

[51] See R Poscher, 'Die Würde des Menschen ist unantastbar' (2004) 59 *JuristenZeitung* 756 for further references.

III. Why Optimisation Requirements do not Suffice for the Principles Theory

The only object that can reasonably be equated with principles in the sense of the principles theory are the objects that Alexy originally equated them with: optimisation requirements. In all practical applications of the principles theory, it tries to support an interpretation of legal norms as optimisation requirements and to operationalise the optimisation by its law of balancing. Why does it not suffice for the principles theory to be a theory of optimisation requirements? Why can it not, as it did originally, equate its principles with optimisation requirements and refrain from its strained attempts to postulate principles besides optimisation requirements – an issue highly contested even among its own adherents?[52] Why can the principles theory not simply be the theory of optimisation requirements?

The answer lies in the strategic function of the dualism postulated between rules and principles within the project of the principles theory.[53] Were the principles theory right in its claim that all norms can be theoretically subdivided into rules on the one hand and principles on the other, and were principles to be understood as optimisation requirements which in turn have to be applied by the law of balancing, then the theoretical qualification of a norm as a principle would always be accompanied by a specific doctrinal approach demanded by the underlying theory – namely optimisation by balancing. If all other norms are rules and therefore do not pose any serious application problems, then for theoretical reasons all serious issues of adjudication and application of law would have to be solved by optimisation via balancing. Norms that are not applicable via simple subsumption are principles, or at least have a principle element, and must therefore be applied by optimisation and balancing. Due to the postulated normative dualism, all contested issues of legal interpretation could supposedly be decided via legal theory. For example, the guarantee of human dignity in Article 1 (1) of the Basic Law is not a norm that lends itself to mere subsumption; according to the strategy of the principles theory, it must be a principle. Principles necessarily imply an understanding as optimisation requirements. Thus, Article 1 (1) of the Basic Law has to be understood as a requirement to optimise human dignity and can therefore be subject to balancing.[54] Positions of the courts and legal scholars that insist on the strictness of the guarantee of human dignity in the Basic Law can thus be regarded as refuted by means of legal theory. If, however, principles were

[52] With regard to the internal quarrels about the principle concept, Borowski (n 1) 105 worries: '[a]lthough the ongoing specification of the principles theory has to be appreciated from a theoretical point of view, it must not be ignored that a crucial advantage of the principles theory is its intuitive plausibility and this plausibility being endangered by increasing the theory's complexity'.

[53] See also K Möller, 'Balancing and the Structure of Constitutional Rights' (2007) 5 *International Journal of Constitutional Law* 453, 457–58.

[54] For an interpretation of Human Dignity based on the principles theory see N Teifke, 'Flexibilität der Menschenwürde? Zur Struktur des Art. 1 Abs. 1 GG' (2005) 103 *Archiv für Rechts- und Sozialphilosophie* 142.

just optimisation requirements, then principles would be rules in the sense of the principles theory. If principles were rules, the whole normative dualism on which the principles theory is founded falls apart. Then we would only have norms with different contents and different interpretations and constructions. Their content could no longer be determined by their theoretical qualification as a principle. It would no longer be possible to determine via legal theory whether the guarantee of human dignity in the Basic Law is subject to balancing or an absolute guarantee. This would not mean that no argument can be made for an optimisation doctrine as such; but this argument would have to draw on traditional legal methods and could not rely on some kind of norm-theoretical dualism. The doctrine of constitutional rights could not be reduced to the idea of optimisation and balancing as proposed by the principles theory. Doctrinal arguments would have to be presented in support of the view that an interpretation of constitutional rights as optimisation requirements should prevail despite the numerous doctrinal counter-arguments already advanced.

In this text, however, the question is not which interpretation of constitutional rights should prevail. The issue is rather to show the strategic function of normative dualism as proposed by the principles theory. If the principles theory were satisfied with being a theory of optimisation requirements, it would have to give up its argumentative strategy, ie putting forward a theoretical argument with the aim of supporting a concrete doctrinal approach. The principles theory would become just one doctrinal theory among others and many of the criteria that were suggested (by, amongst others, Alexy himself)[55] for assessing the quality of doctrinal theories would militate against it.[56] Regarding the argumentative strategy of the principles theory, everything seems to depend on the purported norm-theoretical difference between optimisation requirements and principles. This might explain why its supporters come up with ever-new suggestions which are supposed to uphold the difference, and which are increasingly difficult to track for the non-initiate. They try to stabilise the illusion of a difference between principles and optimisation requirements – despite all the external and internal arguments against each of these approaches.

IV. The Traditional Notion of Principle Re-Established

There are no principles in the sense of the principles theory that are distinct from optimisation requirements and that are of any relevance to the explanation of optimisation requirements. Measured by its own criteria, the principles theory is a theory without an object, the theory of a phantom. This, however, does not

[55] R Alexy, *Theorie der juristischen Argumentation. Die Theorie des rationalen Diskurses als Theorie der juristischen Begründung*, 3rd edn (Frankfurt, Suhrkamp, 1996) 326.

[56] For more extensive elaborations on this aspect, see Poscher (n 9) 81–82, 101–13.

mean that the talk about legal principles in the traditional sense has no object, or that there are no principles in the traditional sense. Quite the opposite, there are far more principles than the principles theory – which reduces principles to optimisation requirements – allows.[57] It might be true that some legal principles – eg the principle of the protection of legitimate expectations – could be reconstructed in the sense of optimisation requirements. But this does not hold true for every legal principle. The principle of good faith does not require optimisation, but simply compliance: if something violates the principles of good faith, no balancing is required anymore.[58] Equally, the principle of equality, with its phenomenologically comparative perspective, cannot be forced onto the Procrustean bed of optimisation requirements without losing its specificity.[59] And even the principle of proportionality can be interpreted in many other ways than as an optimisation requirement – consider pro-rata optimality, minimum guarantee, protection against gross disproportionality, etc.[60] And it might have to be interpreted differently in different legal contexts.

The world of legal principles is much richer and more colourful than the principles theory wishes to make us believe with its narrow understanding of principles as optimisation requirements. Contrary to the principles theory, it becomes apparent that the difference between legal principles and other norms is not of a structural, but rather of a gradual nature.[61] Norms can be called legal principles if they are of specific importance,[62] especially if their impact is not restricted to a certain area of law. There is no reason not to single out legal norms presenting

[57] This also holds true for the rich variety of meanings and facets of the concept of principle in the philosophical tradition, with one of the origins being the Greek idea of '*Arché*'. For information on the impressive history of the concept, see Reimer (n 50) 146–71, who straightaway rejects the idea of reducing the concept of principle to mere 'balancing' on grounds of the conceptual history, see ibid 179.

[58] On this objection, see O Weinberger, 'Revision des traditionellen Rechtssatzkonzepts' in B Schilcher et al (eds), *Regeln, Prinzipien und Elemente im System des Rechts* (Vienna, Verlag Österreich, 2000) 64 with more examples.

[59] See A Somek, 'Eine egalitäre Alternative zur Güterabwägung' in B Schilcher et al (eds), *Regeln, Prinzipien und Elemente im System des Rechts* (Vienna, Verlag Österreich, 2000) 193–220.

[60] For some of the relevant literature, see above footnotes nn 47–50.

[61] This conception is in line with most scholars that do not follow Alexy's lead. For instance, see P Lerche, *Übermaß und Verfassungsrecht. Zur Bindung des Gesetzgebers an die Grundsätze der Verhältnismäßigkeit und der Erforderlichkeit* (Cologne, Heymann, 1961) XXII: 'distinctions between these two categories of quantitative nature only'; B Schilcher, 'Prinzipien und Regeln als Elemente einer Theorie des gebundenen Ermessens' in B Schilcher et al (eds), *Regeln, Prinzipien und Elemente im System des Rechts* (Viena, Verlag Österreich, 2000) 164, 169; Reimer (n 50) 179–82. In the Anglo-American literature this point of view was expressed by HLA Hart, *The Concept of Law*, 2nd edn (Oxford, Clarendon Press, 1994) 259–60; A Marmor, 'The Separation Thesis and the Limits of Interpretation' (1999) 12 *The Canadian Journal of Law and Jurisprudence* 135, 145–46; MS Moore, 'Legal Principle Revisited' in MS Moore (ed), Educating Oneself in Public (Oxford, Oxford University Press, 2000) 225; M Bódig, 'Rules, Principles, and the Problem of the Limits of Legal Reasoning' in M Borowski (ed), *On the Nature of Legal Principles* (Stuttgart/Baden-Baden, Franz Steiner/Nomos, 2010) 131. For a reconstruction of the gradual difference based on legal logics, see B Verheij et al, 'An Integrated View on Rules and Principles' (1998) 6 *Artificial Intelligence and Law* 3–26. For a deconstructive reading of the distinction, see PJ Schlag, 'Rules and Standards' (1985) 33 *UCLA Law Review* 379, 405–30.

[62] J Esser, *Grundsatz und Norm in der richterlichen Fortbildung des Privatrechts*, 4th edn (Tübingen, Mohr Siebeck, 1990) 154.

these features by calling them legal principles. This does not mean, however, that all other norms can be applied by mere subsumption and that only legal principles are in need of legal construction. For almost all norms, there are borderline cases in which a need for construction arises and many legal norms employ abstract concepts that are not always applicable by mere subsumption. The difference between legal principles and other norms is a merely gradual one and it can be found in the dimensions of the norm's need for concretisation and its relevance to the legal system as a whole.

V. Concluding Remarks

Alexy's renewed attempt to defend the normative dualism of the principles theory by modifying and elaborating upon his specific concept of principles as 'ideal oughts' is not convincing. Quite the opposite: his new considerations make it even more apparent how misguided he is to insist on a conception of principles that belong to an 'ideal ought' and are not identical with optimisation requirements. His argumentation becomes entangled in obvious mistakes, or trivialities at best, which are of no value for the attempt to explain the normative phenomena that the principles theory is concerned with. Instead of losing themselves in idiosyncratic debates over phantoms, circling around non-existent normative objects, supporters of the principles theory should rather understand and, for the sake of honesty, call their theory by its correct name: a theory of optimisation requirements. Insofar as principles theorists approach doctrinal issues,[63] they provide suggestions that form part of an optimisation doctrine, which should be evaluated with respect to the specific fields in which the suggestions are made. But, if duly understood as a contribution to specific doctrinal debates, an optimisation doctrine cannot be defended from the high road of a legal theory. Instead, optimisation doctrines must convince with doctrinal arguments.

[63] For other aspects of the principles theory (eg argumentation theory), see Poscher, 'Einsichten' (n 5) 73–77; Poscher, 'Insights' (n 5) 441–45; Poscher, 'The Principles Theory' (n 5) 238–42.

Third Round

5

Ideal 'Ought' and Optimisation*

ROBERT ALEXY**

The basis of principles theory is the norm-theoretic distinction between rules and principles. In the *Theory of Constitutional Rights* I define principles as *optimisation requirements*. As such, they require 'that something be realized to the greatest extent possible given the legal and factual possibilities'.[1] Rules aside, the legal possibilities are determined essentially by opposing principles. For this reason, principles, each taken alone, always comprise merely prima facie requirements. The determination of the appropriate degree of satisfaction of one principle relative to the requirements of other principles is brought about by means of balancing. Thus, balancing is the specific form of the application of principles. By contrast, rules are norms that require something determinate. They are *definitive requirements*. Their form of application is subsumption.

Against the definition of principles as optimisation requirements, Aulis Aarnio and Jan-Reinard Sieckmann raised, more than 20 years ago, the objection that the concept of optimisation requirement is ill-suited for distinguishing between rules and principles. The obligation to optimise has a definitive character. It can only either be fulfilled or not fulfilled, and its complete fulfilment is always obligatory.[2] Aarnio puts this point as follows: '[e]ither one does or one does not optimise. For example, in the case of conflict between two value principles, the principles must be brought together in the optimum manner, and only in the optimum manner'.[3] They are right. Optimisation requirements are rules. In my reply, 15 years ago, I introduced the distinction between optimisation requirements and requirements to be optimised. Drawing on this distinction, I classified optimisation requirements

* Formerly published as R Alexy, 'Ideal "Ought" and Optimization' in R Alexy (ed), *Law's Ideal Dimension* (Oxford, Oxford University Press, 2021) 190–204. Copyrights granted by Oxford University Press and reproduced with permission of the Licensor through PLSclear.

** I should like to thank Stanley L Paulson for suggestions and advice on matters of English style. The author kindly acknowledges the financial support of a research grant on *The Role of Proportionality in Constitutional Adjudication* (15-23955S) awarded by the Grant Agency of the Czech Republic.

[1] R Alexy, *A Theory of Constitutional Rights* (J Rivers trans, Oxford, Oxford University Press, 2002) 47.

[2] JR Sieckmann, *Regelmodelle und Prinzipienmodelle des Rechtssystems* (Baden-Baden, Nomos, 1990) 65.

[3] A Aarnio, 'Taking Rules Seriously' (1990) 42 *Archives for Philosophy of Law and Social Philosophy* 180, 187.

as rules and requirements to be optimised as principles. The first is clear and true, but the second leads to problems and is, therefore, in need of explication. The basis of this explication will be the thesis that principles express an 'ideal "ought"',[4] a thesis found in this article and, indeed, in my very first article on principles theory, stemming from 1979.[5] It is of the greatest importance for principles theory that there exists a necessary connection between optimisation requirements and the ideal 'ought'. To say it in the words I used in my reply to Aarnio and Sieckmann: 'The ideal "ought" implies the optimisation requirement and vice versa. These are two sides of the same coin'.[6]

Poscher, in 2007, raised the objection that principles *qua* ideal 'ought' are not necessary.[7] The 'interpretation of principles as optimisation requirements does not require that requirements actually be optimised but only that they constitute non-normative objects of optimisation'.[8] This non-necessity thesis is connected with a non-existence thesis, which maintains that 'principles that do not have the structure of rules' do 'not exist'.[9] I have attempted to refute the non-existence thesis as well as the non-necessity thesis by means of an index model of the ideal 'ought', published in 2009.[10] This model, too, has been criticised by Poscher[11] and also by Sieckmann.[12] Poscher's critique stems from a point of view outside principles theory, whereas Sieckmann's critique comes from a point of view within principles theory. My reply to both begins with a presentation of the index model.

I. The Index Model of the Ideal 'Ought'

The basis of the index model is the distinction between two kinds of deontic modalities. Those of the first group concern the ideal 'ought'. They are expressed, for instance, in the following way:

(1) $O_i\, p$.

[4] R Alexy, 'On the Structure of Legal Principles' (2000) 13 *Ratio Juris* 294, 300 [ed note: see above Chapter 1, p 23 for the equivalent text].

[5] R Alexy, 'Zum Begriff des Rechtsprinzips' (1979) 1 *Rechtstheorie* 59.

[6] ibid 301.

[7] R Poscher, 'Einsichten, Irrtümer und Selbstmissverständnis der Prinzipientheorie' in JR Sieckmann (ed), *Die Prinzipientheorie der Grundrechte. Studien zur Grundrechtstheorie Robert Alexys* (Baden-Baden, Nomos, 2007) 69 [ed note: see above Chapter 2, p 42 for the translated version].

[8] R Poscher, 'The Principles Theory: How many Theories and What is their Merit?' in M Klatt (ed), *Institutionalized Reason: The Jurisprudence of Robert Alexy* (Oxford, Oxford University Press, 2012) 233.

[9] ibid 235.

[10] R Alexy, 'Ideales Sollen' in L Clérico and JR Sieckmann (eds), *Grundrechte, Prinzipien und Argumentation. Studien zur Rechtstheorie Robert Alexys* (Baden-Baden, Nomos, 2009) 21–38 [ed note: see above Chapter 3, pp 59–77 for the translated version].

[11] R Poscher, 'Theorie eines Phantoms: Die erfolglose Suche der Prinzipientheorie nach ihrem Gegenstand' (2010) 1 *Rechtswissenschaft* 349 [ed note: see above Chapter 4, p 79 for the translated version].

[12] JR Sieckmann, 'Prinzipien, ideales Sollen und normative Argumente' (2011) 97 *Archiv für Rechts-und Sozialphilosphie* 178.

To be sure, the other deontic modalities can also be indexed in this way, that is to say, $F_i\,p$ and $P_i\,p$ are possible as well. The modalities of the second group concern the real 'ought'. They are expressed as follows:

(2) $O_r\,p$.

The other deontic modalities can also be indexed in this way.

The ideal 'ought', expressed by '$O_i\,p$', is an 'ought' that abstracts from any countervailing 'ought', be it a right or a duty. This abstraction means that it is not yet related to limited possibilities of the normative world.[13] In this sense, it expresses an ideal. This abstraction from countervailing reasons implies that the ideal 'ought' is only a prima facie[14] or *pro tanto* 'ought'.[15] By contrast, the real 'ought', expressed by 'O_r', is a definitive 'ought' or an 'ought', all things considered. In this way, '$O_i p$' and '$O_r p$' count as a formal reconstruction of the distinction between rules and principles.

This formal reconstruction would be of little value if the index model offered no more than a new notation. This, however, is not the case. The notation presented is the basis for two rules that express in a formal way an insight of principles theory that is so fundamental that one might speak of them as the two 'basic axioms of principles theory'. They run, formulated with the help of the possibility operator '$\Diamond$', as follows:

(3) $\Diamond\ (O_i\,p\ \&\ O_i\,\neg p)$

(4) $\neg\ \Diamond\ (O_r\,p\ \&\ O_r\,\neg p)$.

The formulation at (3) – we can call it 'axiom 1' or the 'first axiom' – states that a contradiction of norms at the ideal level is possible in the sense that both norms retain their validity. The formulation at (4) – we can call it 'axiom 2' or the second axiom – states that a contradiction of norms at the real level is not possible in the sense that both norms retain their validity. This makes explicit the different structures for resolving conflicts of principles and of rules. Competing principles and their implications in concrete cases remain valid even if they are outweighed by another principle. That is, the competition is resolved by means of the dimension of weight, not by means of the dimension of validity. By contrast, a conflict of rules is resolved by means of the dimension of validity in that one of the conflicting rules is declared to be completely invalid or in that an exception clause is read into it,[16] which is to declare it as partially invalid.[17] It is of greatest importance that both the conflict that arises in connection with the ideal 'ought' and the conflict that arises

[13] The optimisation relative to the factual possibilities concerns not limitation but extension.

[14] See Alexy (n 1) 57–59.

[15] See SL Hurley, *Natural Reasons: Personality and Polity* (Oxford, Oxford University Press, 1989) 130.

[16] See Alexy (n 1) 49–50.

[17] See C Kallmeyer, *Ideales Sollen. Eine Analyse der Prinzipienkonstruktion* (Baden-Baden, Nomos, 2016) 156–62.

in connection with the real 'ought' are conflicts of norms. Thus, we arrive at an initial intermediate result. The ideal 'ought' and, with it, principles, exists if there exist conflicts of norms that arise in connection with the ideal 'ought', and principles are necessary if the solution of these conflicts can be adequately understood only on the basis of the first axiom.

II. The Law of Competing Principles

Along with the two axioms, there are two laws that are constitutive for principles theory: the law of competing principles and the law of balancing, which is further elaborated by the weight formula. In order to answer the question of whether there exist conflicts of norms in the context of the ideal 'ought', it is as well to have a look at the law of competing principles. For this law, two concepts are constitutive. The first is the relation of precedence. This relation is symbolised by '**P**'. The second is the condition of precedence. It is symbolised by '*C*'. The result of each application of the weight formula can be expressed on the basis of these two concepts. The standard form is:

(5) $(P_i \mathbf{P} P_j)\ C$.

This formula expresses a conditional relation of precedence. It is to be read as follows: 'Principle P_i takes precedence over principle P_j under the condition C'. The decisive point is that this conditional relation of precedence implies a rule. Precisely this implication is expressed by the law of competing principles, which runs as follows:

> If principle P_i takes precedence over principle P_j in circumstances C: $(P_i \mathbf{P} P_j)\ C$, and if P_i gives rise to legal consequences Q in circumstances C, then a valid rule applies, which has C as its *protasis* and Q as its *apodosis*: $C \rightarrow Q$.[18]

In order to illustrate this, it might be useful to turn to a case. The case in question is a decision of the German Federal Constitutional Court that concerns the classic conflict between freedom of expression and personality rights.[19] Specifically, the case concerned a paraplegic reserve officer who had successfully carried out his responsibilities, having been called to active duty. A widely published satirical magazine, *Titanic*, described him first as a 'born murderer' and in a later edition as a 'cripple'. The Düsseldorf Higher Regional Court of Appeal ruled against *Titanic* in an action brought by the officer and ordered the magazine to pay damages in the amount of DM 12,000. In its constitutional complaint, appealing against this decision, the *Titanic* was successful insofar as the Constitutional Court's decision related to damages for the description 'born murderer'. As far as the description 'cripple' was concerned, the constitutional complaint was rejected. Only the first point shall be considered in what follows.

[18] Alexy (n 1) 54.
[19] BVerfGE 86, 1 – TITANIC/'geb. Mörder'.

Principles can be more or less abstract. The most abstract version of the principle of freedom of expression is the requirement of a state of affairs[20] in which freedom of expression is realised to the greatest extent possible. One can call principles of this kind 'principles at the highest level of abstraction'.[21] At this level, principles are closest to values.[22] Where constitutional rights are concerned, principles have the character of constitutional permissive norms as well as the character of constitutional prohibitions of interferences.[23] Here only the permissive norm addressed to the *Titanic* shall be considered. It can be expressed as follows:

(6) $\forall x\,(S_1 x \rightarrow P_i Rx)$.

(6) may be read as follows: for all x ($\forall x$), if x is an expression of opinion (S_1), then ($\rightarrow$) its performance or realisation (R) is prima facie constitutionally permitted (P_i). The Federal Constitutional Court has justifiably classified the description of the paraplegic reserve officer as a 'born murderer' and as a 'cripple' as an expression of opinion. Letting 'a' stand for the description 'born murderer' yields

(7) $S_1 a$.

From (6) and (7), one arrives at

(8) $P_i Ra$.

(8) follows logically, according to the basic scheme of subsumption, from (6) and (7). (8) states: it is prima facie permitted that the paraplegic reserve officer is described as a 'born murderer'. The special feature of (8) is that it has a concrete as well as an ideal character, expressed by the index.

The principle of freedom of expression (6) collides in our case with the personality right. This principle has a complex structure. A gross simplification will suffice here. It leads to a counterpart to the competing principle of freedom of expression:

(9) $\forall x\,(S_2 x \rightarrow \neg P_i Rx)$.

(9) may be read as follows: for all x ($\forall x$), if x is an interference with the personality right (S_2), then ($\rightarrow$) its performance or realisation (R) is prima facie constitutionally not permitted ($\neg P_i$); that is, it is forbidden. If one classifies the description of the paraplegic reserve officer as a 'born murderer' as an interference with the personality right (S_2), expressed as (10):

(10) $S_2 a$,

then

(11) $\neg P_i Ra$

[20] See Alexy (n 1) 92.
[21] ibid 354.
[22] ibid 92–3.
[23] ibid 196–200.

follows logically, again according to the basic scheme of subsumption, from (9) and (10). This, however, means that the application of the two principles to the *Titanic* case leads to a contradiction between two concrete instances of the ideal 'ought'. According to the first axiom, this contradiction is possible without any loss of validity. But this does not mean that this contradiction does not exist. It exists, for the two rights colliding in the *Titanic* case are both valid – that is, both exist – and it is therefore incumbent on me to explain what a collision of rights is. It is a collision or conflict not of empirical entities,[24] but of norms – more exactly, of norms that have the character of principles. The collision consists of a contradiction, which has to be resolved by balancing according to the third sub-principle of proportionality. To be sure, establishing a collision is only the first step in the balancing process. The second axiom shows that the collision must be resolved if one is going to arrive at the level of the real or definitive 'ought'. That is, the ideal contradiction cannot be transformed into a real contradiction. If such a transformation were possible, the law would lose its power to regulate human behaviour. For this reason, only one of the two contradictory instances of the ideal 'ought' – in our case either the permission to describe the paraplegic reserve officer as a 'born murderer', as expressed in (8) $P_i\ Ra$, or the prohibition from doing so, as expressed in (11) $\neg P_i\ Ra$ – can pass to the level of the real 'ought'. This selection is regulated by the two basic laws of principles theory, the law of competing principles and the law of balancing, the latter in the form familiar from the weight formula.

The law of competing principles says what it means to transform an ideal or prima facie 'ought' to a real or definitive 'ought'. The weight formula establishes the criteria for this transformation. In order to demonstrate how, according to the law of competing principles, the transformation is performed, the principle of freedom of expression, as formulated above in (6), shall be given the short notation P_1, whereas the personality right (9) is designated as P_2. Now, the Federal Constitutional Court, with respect to the description of the paraplegic reserve officer as a 'born murderer', gives precedence to freedom of expression owing to the satirical context. The condition 'description of a paraplegic reserve officer as a "born murderer" in a satirical context' stands for the variable '*C*' in the law of competing principles, where it expresses the condition of preference. The condition in our case just mentioned shall be designated by 'C_1'. This yields the following preferential statement:

(12) $(P_1\ \mathbf{P}\ P_2)\ C_1$.

The point of the law of competing principles is that this preferential statement (12) implies a rule that has C_1 as its *protasis* and the legal consequences to which P_1

[24] Collisions or conflicts of rights cannot be explained at a purely descriptive or empirical level. At a purely empirical level, only causal effects are possible. That *p* causes *q* does not represent, as such, a conflict. A drill that penetrates into a wall produces, indeed, a drilled hole, but this is not a case of a conflict between the drill and the wall. See R Alexy, 'Jörn Ipsens Konstruktion der Grundrechte' (2013) 52 *Der Staat* 87, 91.

gives rise in our case – that is, the permission of the description 'born murderer' – as its *apodosis*. It is of the utmost importance that this permission is no longer an ideal permission. It is a real or definitive permission, which can be noted as 'P_r', for it derives from the solution to the collision of the two principles by the establishing of the conditional relation of precedence expressed by (12). In this way, (8), that is, $P_i\ Ra$, is transformed into

(13) $P_r\ Ra$.

This transition from the ideal level to the real level would not be possible if principles did not exist, for it is not possible to derive something from something that does not exist. Without understanding, first, what a conflict of prima facie or ideal obligations is, and, second, how it is resolved by a transformation of the ideal 'ought' into a real 'ought' by means of a conditional relation of precedence, one cannot understand what balancing is. This suffices to establish the existence and necessity of principles *qua* ideal 'ought'.

To be sure, all this is necessary but not yet sufficient for understanding or constructing balancing. A complete understanding is not possible without the second law of principles theory, the law of balancing.

III. The Weight Formula

The law of balancing, which is identical to the third sub-principle of the principle of proportionality, the principle of proportionality in the narrower sense, states:

> The greater the degree of non-satisfaction of, or detriment to, one principle, the greater must be the importance of satisfying the other.[25]

Nearly everywhere in constitutional adjudication, the law of balancing is found in various different formulations. It expresses the essence of balancing and is of great practical importance. If, however, one wishes to achieve a precise and complete analysis of the structure of balancing, the law of balancing has to be elaborated further. The result of such a further elaboration is the weight formula.[26] It runs as follows:

$$W_{i,j} = \frac{I_i \cdot W_i \cdot R_i}{I_j \cdot W_j \cdot R_j}$$

[25] Alexy (n 1) 102.

[26] R Alexy, 'The Weight Formula' (B Brożek and SL Paulson trans) in J Stelmach et al (eds), *Studies in the Philosophy of Law. Frontiers of the Economic Analysis of Law* (Krakow, Jagiellonian University Press, 2007) 25.

'$W_{i,j}$' represents the concrete weight of the principle P_i relative to the colliding principle P_j. The weight formula defines this concrete weight as the quotient of three factors standing, so to speak, on each side of balancing. I_i and I_j are of special importance. 'I_i' stands for the intensity of interference with P_i. 'I_j' represents the importance of satisfying the colliding principle. I_j, too, can be understood as intensity of interference, that is, as the intensity of interference with P_j through non-interference with P_i. 'W_i' and 'W_j' stand for the abstract weights of the colliding principles P_i and P_j. When the abstract weights are equal, which is often the case in collisions between constitutional rights, they cancel each other out. 'R_i' and 'R_j' represent two factors that have received ever-greater attention in recent discussions on constitutional rights. They refer to the reliability of the empirical and normative assumptions concerning the question of how intensive the interference with P_i is, and how intensive the interference with P_j would be if the interference with P_i were omitted.

IV. Law of Competing Principles and Law of Balancing

The weight formula stands in the centre of the debate over principles theory. Nevertheless, it will not be discussed here.[27] Only its relation to the law of competing principles shall be considered. This relation is a justification relation. The weight formula makes explicit the form of the justification of the preferential statement $(P_i \mathbf{P} P_j)\ C$, which makes possible the transition from the ideal to the real 'ought'. Three preferential relations are possible: (1) P_i takes precedence over P_j, (2) P_j takes precedence over P_i, and (3) neither takes precedence over the other. To these three precedence possibilities there correspond three possible concrete weights: (1) $W_{i,j}$ can be greater than 1, (2) it can be less then 1, and (3) it can be 1. If it is greater than 1, P_i takes precedence over P_j; if it is less then 1, P_j takes precedence over P_i; and if it is 1, a stalemate exists. In this case, neither does P_i take precedence over P_j nor does P_j take precedence over P_i. This means that the state, in particular the legislator, has discretion. This can be described by three rules which that be called the 'connection rules':

(14) (a) $W_{i,j} > 1 \rightarrow (P_i \mathbf{P} P_j)\ C$

(b) $W_{i,j} < 1 \rightarrow (P_j \mathbf{P} P_i)\ C$

(c) $W_{i,j} = 1 \rightarrow \neg\ (P_i \mathbf{P} P_j)\ C\ \&\ \neg\ (P_j \mathbf{P} P_i)\ C$ (stalemate).

The connection rules show that the connection between the law of competing principles and the weight formula, and thus the connection to the law of balancing, is as close as possible. This, in turn, means that there exists an intrinsic connection

[27] ibid 20–27.

between the two axioms and the two laws of principles theory. They form a system. Without the ideal 'ought', the system would be uncompleted. This is the core of the proof of the existence of principles as well as the proof of their necessity.

V. A Fundamental Equivalence

On the basis of the two axioms and the two laws, a fundamental equivalence can be formulated:

(15) $O_r\ Opt\ p \leftrightarrow O_i\ p$.

'$O_i\ p$' represents the ideal 'ought'. It says that it is ideally or prima facie obligatory that *p*. '$O_r\ Opt\ p$' expresses an optimisation requirement. The obligation to optimise is a definitive or real obligation. Therefore, it starts with 'O_r'. The subject of this real obligation is not the *complete realisation* of *p*, as in the case of the ideal 'ought', but only the *optimisation* of *p*.

In my article on the ideal 'ought' in 2009, I formalised the equivalence between the ideal 'ought' and the optimisation requirement in the following way:

(16) $O\ OptO\ p \leftrightarrow O_i\ p$.[28]

The subject of optimisation, however, is the same as the subject of the ideal 'ought', and this is a state of affairs in the broadest sense, represented by *p*. In the earlier article on the ideal 'ought', I said that optimisation requirements can be expressed by

(17) $OOpt\ p$

as well as by

(18) $OOpt\ Op$.[29]

This must be corrected. Only the first formalisation (17) is adequate. On this point, Poscher's critique[30] is correct. A second correction of the old formula is that 'O' at the beginning of the equivalence is replaced by 'O_r'. These two corrections of the fundamental equivalence do not mean, however, that the central thesis of my reply to Aarnio and Sieckmann in 2000 – which says that the ideal 'ought' implies the optimisation requirement and vice versa[31] – has to be corrected. On the contrary, embedded in the system of the two axioms and the two laws of principles theory, this thesis of mine is corroborated.

[28] Alexy (n 10) 25.
[29] ibid 24.
[30] Poscher (n 11) 359.
[31] Alexy (n 5) 301.

VI. Poscher's Argument from Identity

One of Poscher's main arguments for his thesis that 'principles that do not have the character of rules [do] not exist'[32] is his argument from identity. The argument claims that an analysis of 'collision[s] between norms shows … that rules and principles are structured identically and differ only in their contingent contents within a single normative structure'.[33] The reason for this, Poscher continues, is that, first, all norms have the structure of rules and that, second, only the content of those 'exception clauses'[34] that solve the conflict is different. As a means of demonstrating this, he uses the following example:

> $N1_c$: If an action endangers *outweighing* foreign interests of the state, this action is to be prohibited.
>
> $N2_c$: If an action serves the press *and does not endanger outweighing foreign interests of the state*, the state should refrain from prohibitions.[35]

The exception clauses in these two norms refer, without question, to balancing, and the two norms have, indeed, the character of rules. But this is no problem for principles theory. Principles theory incorporates this with its concept of 'double aspect constitutional-rights norms'.[36] Double aspect constitutional-rights norms are constitutional-rights norms that have a limitation clause 'referring to competing principles'.[37] This is exactly the type of norm to which Poscher refers with $N1_c$ and $N2_c$. He misses the point, however, when he maintains that the step from a norm with an exemption clause that does not require balancing to a norm with an exemption clause that *does* require balancing is 'only a small step'.[38] It is in fact a great step, indeed, a leap from subsumption to balancing.[39] It is impossible to grasp the nature of a limiting clause that refers to balancing and, with it, the structure of the rule that contains it, without having recourse to the concept of collision between principles or rights. Collisions of principles, however, can exist only if principles exist. Optimisation requirements do not suffice to reconstruct collisions between principles or rights, for optimisation requirements as such cannot collide. Only the ideal 'ought', connected with them by the fundamental equation, can do this. In short, Poscher's attempt to reconstruct collisions between constitutional rights exclusively at the level of rules is doomed to fail.[40]

[32] Poscher (n 8) 235.
[33] ibid 230.
[34] ibid.
[35] ibid 231 [ed note: see above Chapter 2, p 40].
[36] Alexy (n 1) 85 (translation amended).
[37] ibid.
[38] Poscher (n 8) 231.
[39] R Alexy, 'Comments and Responses' in M Klatt (ed), *Institutionalized Reason: The Jurisprudence of Robert Alexy* (Oxford, Oxford University Press, 2012) 343.
[40] To this, an argument might be added that refers to the construction of constitutional rights. I shall not, however, discuss this here. See ibid 345 and Alexy (n 10) 31–32.

VII. Sieckmann's Reiterated Validity Obligations

By contrast with Poscher, Sieckmann defends the thesis that principles express an ideal 'ought'.[41] Nevertheless, he radically criticises the index model defended here. His critique culminates in the thesis that 'the Alexyian conception … seems to be a principles theory without principles'.[42] Thus, he arrives from a point of view inside principles theory at the same result as Poscher from a point of view outside principles theory.

Sieckmann's critique is based on two theses. The first says that principles *qua* ideal 'ought' have to be constructed as infinitely reiterated validity obligations.[43] The second thesis claims that for the distinction between rules and principles, one has to substitute the distinction between normative propositions and normative arguments.[44] I will begin with the argument of infinite reiteration.

The starting point of the thesis of infinite reiteration of validity obligations is plausible. The analysis of the *Titanic* decision presented above can well be interpreted in the sense that principles require the validity of certain norms. In our case the norms in question are that the description of the paraplegic reserve officer as a 'born murderer' is permitted (8), and that the description of the paraplegic reserve officer as a 'born murderer' is prohibited (11). For this reason, the idea of a validity obligation presents one possibility for reconstructing the normative impact of principles. And Sieckmann is also right when he says that 'the "ought" that is contained in validity obligations'[45] cannot, on the one hand, be definitely valid, for this would preclude the possibility of 'colliding principles also claiming validity',[46] but this 'ought' must, on the other hand, 'possess some form of validity'.[47] That is to say, that validity obligations must have a validity that is neither definitively valid nor non-valid. In my first critique of Sieckmann's reiteration thesis, published in 2000, I characterised this thesis as a 'middle course',[48] that is, as an attempt to establish some kind of validity between definitive validity and lack of validity. The ideal 'ought' of the index model can be understood just in this sense. And I agreed with Sieckmann up to this point. But I did not agree with his thesis that infinitely reiterated validity obligations count as an adequate construction of the special validity of principles.

[41] Sieckmann (n 12) 180.

[42] JR Sieckmann, 'Zur Prinzipientheorie Robert Alexys. Gemeinsamkeiten und Differenzen' in M Klatt (ed), *Prinzipientheorie und Theorie der Abwägung* (Tübingen, Mohr Siebeck, 2013) 273. Here, and in what follows, the quotations from Sieckmann's German-language articles are translated into English by the author.

[43] Sieckmann (n 12) 183–92.

[44] Sieckmann (n 42) 274.

[45] Sieckmann (n 12) 190.

[46] ibid.

[47] ibid.

[48] Alexy (n 5) 302.

The reiteration model begins with the thesis that validity obligations have the following structure:

(19) 'O VAL_{DEF}N'.[49]

In the *Titanic* case, a validity obligation of this structure would require that it be definitively valid that all expressions of opinion are permitted. Now, Sieckmann's formula 'O VAL_{DEF}N' can express neither a definitive obligation nor a non-obligation if it is supposed to express an ideal 'ought'. And here the problem begins. Sieckmann attempts to make the middle course explicit by means of reiteration. With this, the first validity obligation is, at a second level, transformed into a validity obligation that requires that 'it shall be definitively valid that it shall be definitively valid that all expressions of opinion are permitted'.[50] At this second level, the problem of definitiveness arises again, which results from the fact that a definitive 'ought' is never an ideal 'ought'. Sieckmann's 'solution'[51] consists in adding a third level to the second one: 'It shall be definitively valid that it shall be definitively valid that it shall be definitively valid that all expressions of opinion are permitted'.[52] And this has to be continued infinitely. Sieckmann's formal reconstruction of all of this looks like this:

(20) '(1) O VAL_{DEF} N

(2) O VAL_{DEF} O VAL_{DEF} N

(3) O VAL_{DEF} O VAL_{DEF} O VAL_{DEF} N,

and so on'.[53]

In my first objection, I classified this as a 'continuous oscillation' that 'describes in a relatively complicated way the notion that principles stand somewhere between definitive validity and non-obligation',[54] and I argued that this is not enough to 'serve as an explanation of the character of principles'.[55]

Sieckmann has replied that this objection fails, for it is based on an incomplete description of the model of infinite reiteration. It separates the different levels on which definitive validity stands on the one side and non-obligation on the other. With this, 'the infinite structure of reiterated validity obligations and the possibilities of argumentation resulting from it are not seen'.[56] I answer here that I *do* see the infinite structure, but I do not see that it adds anything to the understanding of the structure of principles. Sieckmann points in his reply to 'possibilities of

[49] Sieckmann (n 12) 190.
[50] ibid.
[51] ibid.
[52] ibid.
[53] ibid.
[54] Alexy (n 5) 303.
[55] ibid.
[56] Sieckmann (n 12) 193.

argumentation resulting from' the infinite structure. This leads to his second thesis, which says that for the distinction between rules and principles one has to substitute the distinction between normative propositions and normative arguments.[57]

Sieckmann's thesis is that the index model of the ideal 'ought' 'does not allow the construction of reasons with the character of principles that can justify definitive balancing judgements'.[58] His reason for this is that the ideal 'ought' expressed by 'O_i *p*' is an 'ought' that abstracts from any countervailing 'ought'. This abstraction implies that it is only a prima facie or *pro tanto* 'ought'. Sieckmann maintains that it is impossible to 'construct reasons for balancing'[59] on this basis. This is said to result from the necessity or 'including counter reasons in balancing'.[60] Now, I completely agree with Sieckmann that counter reasons must be included in balancing. Balancing without competing reasons would not be balancing. But I contest the thesis that the abstract character of the ideal 'ought' in the index model precludes the inclusion of the competing ideal norms in balancing. Quite the opposite is the case.

The *Titanic* case can once again serve as an example. If one applies the two abstract principles of freedom of expression and protection of personality, formalised above as (6) and (9), to the case, one acquires two concrete ideal norms, (8) and (11), that contradict each other. In the index model, with this contradiction, which is, according to axiom 1, possible, balancing begins and it begins in order to select, as required by axiom 2, one of the two concrete norms[61] for the level of the real 'ought'. All of this is carried out by applying the two laws of principles theory, the law of competing principles and the law of balancing, the latter as explicated by the weight formula. Thus, the colliding reasons are closely and systematically connected.

The basis of Sieckmann's critique is his concept of argument. According to Sieckmann, 'the relation between balancing reasons and balancing results is not a logical inference, but has the structure of a normative demand'.[62] Balancing reasons demand that the norm in question is acknowledged as definitively valid. With this, they do not concern the correctness or truth of a judgement or proposition, but require the performance of an action, so, for Sieckmann, the 'determination of a balancing result is an action'.[63]

I agree with Sieckmann that the institutional or authoritative striking of a balance, as performed by judges, is an action. But if this action is to be rational, it must be preceded by a judgement in form of a proposition. In the *Titanic* case, this judgement can take the following form: 'The freedom of expression has a higher concrete weight than the personality right as far as the description of the

[57] Sieckmann (n 42) 274.
[58] Sieckmann (n 12) 183.
[59] ibid 184.
[60] ibid.
[61] The possibility of a stalemate, see (14)(c), shall not be considered here.
[62] Sieckmann (n 12) 188.
[63] ibid.

paraplegic reserve officer as a "born murderer" in a satirical context is concerned'. This is a proposition that raises a claim to correctness, a claim that has to be justified in legal discourse. In the *Theory of Legal Argumentation*, I defined the concept of argument as follows: 'an argument consists of the propositions belonging to a single argument form which are adduced in support of a further proposition'.[64] This is an expression of the propositionality thesis. Sieckmann defends a pragmatically orientated non-propositionality thesis.[65] I agree with Sieckmann that the pragmatic dimension of argumentation must be taken seriously. Discourse theory attempts to make the pragmatic dimension explicit by means of a system of rules and forms of general practical and legal discourse. But this does not imply that propositions, which can be true or false, correct or incorrect, thereby lose their central role. On the contrary, discursive rationality presupposes propositionality.

[64] R Alexy, *A Theory of Legal Argumentation. The Theory of Rational Discourse as Theory of Legal Justification* (R Adler and N MacCormick trans, Oxford, Clarendon Press, 1989) 92.

[65] Sieckmann (n 12) 195.

6

Resuscitation of a Phantom? On Robert Alexy's Latest Attempt to Save His Concept of Principle*

RALF POSCHER

The goal of my critique is not so much to deconstruct an idiosyncratic norm-theoretical ontology but rather to break the spell that this misguided but in some parts of the world very influential theoretical position casts over the interpretation of constitutional rights as optimisation requirements.

This is a longstanding debate that began some 15 years ago with a chapter in my habilitation in which I criticised both the doctrinal merits and the theoretical foundations of the principles theory, namely, their peculiar dichotomy of principles and rules.[1] Now is my turn in round three of our exchange. However, before I evaluate Robert Alexy's latest attempt to make sense of his non-gradualist notion of principle, I wish to do three things.

First of all, I want to assure the reader that the debate, though longstanding, is not personal. I have always been an admirer of Robert Alexy's work. When I was a student, his book on legal argumentation made a considerable impression on me, not just for its substance but also for its interdisciplinary approach and analytical clarity. It reintroduced an analytical style into the German legal debate, which was otherwise often cluttered with rhetorical posturing and strong opinionising. Robert Alexy's work was and still is an inspiration for those who seek a rigorous approach to legal theory.

Second, I wish to clarify what our disagreement is *not* about or what is not the aim of my critique in the theatre of legal theory.

Third, I wish to briefly recapitulate rounds one and two, since I neither presume nor expect persons with no special interest in idiosyncratic theoretical debates to be familiar with them.

* Formerly published as R Poscher, 'Resuscitation of a Phantom? On Robert Alexy's Latest Attempt to Save His Concept of Principle' (2020) 33 *Ratio Juris* 134. Copyrights granted by John Wiley & Sons and Copyright Clearance Center.

[1] R Poscher, *Grundrechte als Abwehrrechte. Reflexive Regelung rechtlich geordneter Freiheit* (Tübingen, Mohr Siebeck, 2003) 72–84.

Only then will the stage be set for round three: Here, I will try to give a fair account of Robert Alexy's latest move, a paper in late 2017 that opened this round in response to my previous critique in round two. I will then address this latest attempt to salvage the principles theory's peculiar notion of principle. Since the assessment turns out to be negative, the last part of this article is dedicated to the question of why Robert Alexy and his followers are so committed to their special notion of principle and do not settle for optimisation requirements. What – aside from the obvious fact that they are heavily invested in their specific notion of principle – drives them to cling to a notion that proves to be theoretically indefensible?

I. What the Disagreement is not About

Having cleared up the first point at the outset, it is of considerable importance to offer a preliminary clarification of what our argument is not about. This clarification is twofold: first, it concerns the peculiar notion of principle that is contested; second, it aims to avoid the possible misconception that the critique of Alexy's peculiar notion of principle also concerns optimisation requirements – which it does not.

A. Legal Principles

Framing our debate as one about the existence of legal principles simpliciter gives rise to an ambiguity that may create a gross misunderstanding. I am not arguing against the existence of legal principles. In fact, I am much more open to legal principles than Robert Alexy is. Not only do I think that there are many legal principles; I also think that these principles have many different types of content. I also agree that there may be some principles whose content consists of optimisation requirements. However, I doubt that *all* legal principles have only this type of content, and I doubt that they form an ontologically separate class of norms that is categorically distinguishable from some supposedly clear-cut rules.[2]

I think that there are principles of equality or fairness, for example, whose content differs from optimisation requirements and that these principles, like optimisation requirements, are only gradually – in their level of abstractness and importance – distinguishable from the other, more concrete types of norms that the principles theory likes to call rules. My argument is not directed against the idea of legal principles but only against the – in my view – misguided way in which the principles theory tries to hypostatise principles with a specific but

[2] See K Möller, Balancing and the Structure of Constitutional Rights' (2007) 5 *International Journal of Constitutional Law* 453, 455, 458–61 for a similar critique.

theoretically contingent content into an ontologically distinct type of norm. I thus side with the gradualist understanding of the distinction between legal rules and principles espoused by just about everyone else who has ever concerned herself with legal principles[3] – except Dworkin in an early phase of his battle against legal positivism[4] and the Alexy school.

B. Optimisation Requirements

Furthermore, our disagreement is not about optimisation requirements. I, like Robert Alexy, think that there can be norms that require the optimisation of two or more opposing values or interests or – more generally – objects. An example is an optimisation requirement for truck tyres that requires, on the one hand, the optimisation of air pressure to ensure road safety and, on the other hand, the optimisation of mileage per gallon for environmental reasons. An even more mundane example might be the requirement to optimise the number of small balls and larger cubes contained in an irregularly shaped vessel.

We do not even disagree that constitutional rights could also be interpreted as optimisation requirements. I – and most of my German colleagues, for that matter – think that this is a bad doctrinal idea. However, this, too, is not the crux of our theoretical disagreement.

The reason that I bother to take issue with Robert Alexy's peculiar dichotomy of principles and rules at all stems from the specific connection that he and his students and followers try to establish between their purported theoretical dichotomy of legal norms and the interpretation of constitutional rights as optimisation requirements. The connection does not stem from their concept of principle alone, but from its dichotomic opposition to their concepts of rules and the methodological distinction that goes along with this opposition. Alexy first introduces the idea that constitutional rights are best understood as optimisation requirements inductively by reconstructing some decisions of the German Federal Constitutional Court that have recourse to balancing as proof that constitutional rights are at least sometimes treated as principles.[5] Since principles – at that stage of the

[3] HLA Hart, *The Concept of Law*, 3rd edn (Oxford, Oxford University Press, 2012) 260; A Marmor, 'The Separation Thesis and the Limits of Interpretation' (1999) 12 *The Canadian Journal of Law and Jurisprudence* 135, 145–46; MS Moore, 'Legal Principles Revisited' in MS Moore (ed), *Educating Oneself in Public: Critical Essays in Jurisprudence* (Oxford, Oxford University Press, 2000); J Raz, 'Legal Principles and the Limits of Law' (1972) 81 *Yale Law Journal* 838; F Schauer, 'Prescriptions in Three Dimensions' (1997) 82 *Iowa Law Review* 911; B Verheij et al, 'An Integrated View on Rules and Principles' (1998) 6 *Artificial Intelligence and Law* 3. For further references, see R Poscher, 'Theory of a Phantom: The Principles Theory's Futile Quest for Its Object' (2015) in JA de Oliveira et al (eds), *Alexy's Theory of Law* (Stuttgart, Franz Steiner, 2015) 147 [ed note: see above Chapter 4, p 99 for the equivalent text].

[4] RM Dworkin, 'The Model of Rules I' in RM Dworkin (ed), *Taking Rights Seriously* (London, Duckworth, 1977) 14–45.

[5] See M Kumm, 'Constitutional Rights as Principles: On the Structure and Domain of Constitutional Justice: A Review Essay on *A Theory of Constitutional Rights* by Robert Alexy' (2004) 2 *International*

theory – were equated with optimisation requirements, at least *some* constitutional rights are to be understood as optimisation requirements. That there remain hardly any alternatives to qualifying constitutional rights as optimisation requirements follows not so much from this inductive analysis, as from the principles theory concept of a rule, which is the only alternative qualification that the dichotomy offers. The principles theory concept of rule is tied to the methodological idea of subsumption. Rules are norms that allow for the mere subsumption of a case. The examples provided are thus clear-cut norms: the command to leave the room at the ringing of a bell,[6] or business hours from 7am to 7pm.[7] The norms that the principles theory has in mind seem to provide only for easy cases. Should hard cases arise, however, norms turn into principles, which have to be balanced.[8] Since constitutional rights rarely allow for simple subsumption and are obviously prone to hard cases, they cannot be mere rules but have to be principles.

> There are, of course, many cases that can be solved simply by means of subsumption. Hard cases, however, are defined by the fact that there are reasons both for and against any resolution under consideration. Most of these collisions of reasons have to be resolved by means of balancing. This general reason for the ubiquity of balancing is reinforced by a reason based on the structure of the constitutional state. If the constitution guarantees constitutional rights, then many or even all legal decisions restricting the freedom of individuals have to be understood as interferences with constitutional rights. Interferences with constitutional rights are admissible, however, only if they are justified, and they are justified only if they are proportional. Proportionality judgments, however, presuppose balancing.[9]

In short, the logic of the principles theory with respect to the interpretation of constitutional rights runs as follows: principles, as opposed to rules, are norms that do not lend themselves to being readily applied to concrete cases by mere subsumption but rather involve balancing. Constitutional rights norms are usually so abstract and far-reaching that they cannot readily be applied to concrete cases by mere subsumption but require balancing. Thus, they must be principles according to the principles theory's dichotomy of norms. Moreover, since, according to the principles theory, principles must be interpreted as optimisation requirements,

Journal of Constitutional Law 574, 574–75, highlighting the ambivalence between the reconstructive and the structural and prescriptive character of the principles theory.

[6] R Alexy, *A Theory of Constitutional Rights* (J Rivers trans, Oxford, Oxford University Press, 2002) 49.

[7] ibid.

[8] For a critique of the flawed idea of basing an ontology of norms on the distinction between hard and easy cases and of Alexy's formalist notion of rules, see R Poscher, 'Insights, Errors, and Self-Misconceptions of the Theory of Principles' (2009) 22 *Ratio Juris* 425, 438–41 [ed note: see above Chapter 2, pp 43–46 for the equivalent text]; R Poscher, 'The Principles Theory: How Many Theories and What Is Their Merit?' in M Klatt (ed), *Institutionalized Reason: The Jurisprudence of Robert Alexy* (Oxford, Oxford University Press, 2012) 229–35. On the hermeneutic specificities of easy cases, see R Poscher, 'Interpretation and Rule-Following in Law: The Complexity of Easy Cases' in M Araszkiewicz et al (eds), *Problems of Normativity, Rules and Rule-Following* (Cham, Springer, 2015) 281–93.

[9] R Alexy, 'On Balancing and Subsumption: A Structural Comparison' (2003) 16 *Ratio Juris* 433, 436.

it follows from the ontology of legal norms promoted by Alexy and his followers that constitutional rights must be understood as optimisation requirements.

It is this logic that makes the principles theory dangerous and that motivates my attempt to prevent its proponents from getting away with their theoretical idiosyncrasies. This line of argument, while not threatening to legal cultures with strong and autonomous constitutional and constitutional rights traditions – eg, the United States, where nobody seriously considers interpreting the constitutional amendments with the help of the principles theory; Germany, where the Alexy school is anything but mainstream; and Great Britain, which in fear that the principles theory would be adopted by the European courts voted for Brexit – does real damage in many Asian and South American legal cultures that do not have such strong traditions. These cultures are vulnerable to a theory that seemingly offers both a doctrinal interpretation of constitutional rights so flexible that it allows for almost any kind of political projection, on the one hand, and norm-ontological claims that seem to support this constitutional rights doctrine on unassailable grounds of legal theory, on the other. Though the theoretical implications are often poorly understood, the norm-ontological claims seem to make allegiance to an optimisation doctrine for constitutional rights (which they support for other reasons) ironclad from a theoretical perspective. According to legal practitioners in the federal judiciary of Brazil, the principles theory has real-life effects in their legal system. Judges do not waste their time deciphering complex social legislation but rather rely on balancing constitutional principles and deciding cases on the basis of their own personal whims.[10] It is exactly for these doctrinal reasons that the principles theory is much criticised in the German literature.[11] The principles theory does not deliberately aim at such perversions, but it does lend itself to them, and it offers far fewer defences against them than alternative doctrinal approaches.

Thus, I do not engage with the principles theory because I regard it as a particularly fruitful task: engaging negatively in round after round of arguments against a theory that I consider mistaken is not my ideal form of academic research. However, I feel a sense of duty to break the theoretical spell of the principles theory. By exposing its underlying fundamental misconception, I wish to clarify first and foremost that no one is forced by purported theoretical insights to interpret constitutional rights as optimisation requirements. This is one doctrinal choice among many others, and a bad one for that matter – but that is not the subject of our theoretical debate.

[10] For a detailed account, see F Santos de Morais, *Ponderação e Arbitrariedade: A Inadequada Recepção de Alexy pelo STF* (Salvador, Juspodivm, 2018).

[11] H Dreier, 'Vorbemerkungen vor Artikel 1 GG' in H Dreier (ed), *Grundgesetz-Kommentar, vol 1* (Tübingen, Mohr Siebeck, 2013) rn 79; M Jestaedt, *Grundrechtsentfaltung im Gesetz. Studien zur Interdependenz von Grundrechtsdogmatik und Rechtsgewinnungstheorie* (Tübingen, Mohr Siebeck, 1999) 212–23; and R Poscher (n 1) 81–84 – each with further references.

II. The Story So Far

With these preliminaries out of the way, we can briefly recapitulate the argument over the principles theory's peculiar notion of legal principle as a categorically distinct type of legal norm in a purported ontological dichotomy of rules and principles.

A. Principles as Optimisation Requirements

Initially, Robert Alexy equated principles as understood by the principles theory with optimisation requirements:

> The decisive point in distinguishing rules from principles is that *principles* are norms which require that something be realized to the greatest extent possible given the legal and factual possibilities. Principles are *optimisation requirements*, characterized by the fact that they can be satisfied to varying degrees, and that the appropriate degree of satisfaction depends not only on what is factually possible but also on what is legally possible. By contrast, *rules* are norms which are always either fulfilled or not.[12]

There is much to say about the rule element of this distinction, too.[13] However, the notion of legal principle at this stage of development of the principles theory was clear: a legal principle is a norm that requires the optimisation of a value, an interest, or more generally an object with respect not only to factual but also to normative circumstances. Of particular interest here are normative circumstances that involve a plurality of (competing) optimisation requirements. In order to resolve the conflict that arises due to the competition among the optimisation requirements – especially when two or more constitutional rights are involved – the proportionality principle and the weight formula are applied.[14]

B. Optimisation Requirements as Rules

However, it did not take long for adherents of the principles theory themselves to see that, in fact, optimisation requirements have all the features of rules as defined by the theory itself. As in the case of any other requirement, strict and complete obedience can be achieved if the required optimisation is performed. To return to the example of tyre pressure: if truck drivers must optimise tyre pressure for the sake of fuel efficiency, on the one hand, and safety, on the other, they are strictly obliged to perform the required optimisation. The stringency of optimisation requirements can also be illustrated with the example of the vessel filled with small

[12] Alexy (n 6) 47–48, footnotes omitted.

[13] For a critical account, see Poscher, 'Insights' (n 8) 438–41; Poscher, 'The Principles Theory' (n 8) 229–35.

[14] Alexy (n 6) 66–69, 408.

balls and larger cubes. If the vessel can hold a maximum of either 100 balls or 50 cubes, the optimal balance of balls and cubes derived from Alexy's weight formula would be 50 balls and 25 cubes, since this represents an equal degree of realisation of the respective maximum values. In such cases, optimisation requirements even provide numerically exact values. Jan Sieckmann, a student of Alexy, thus stated 'that the problem remains that the optimisation requirements … show just the features that are characteristic of rules, ie strict validity and definite satisfiability'.[15]

The insight that optimisation requirements are not structurally distinct from other norms, however, is a problem only for the principles theory. Under a traditional understanding of principles, which sees only gradual differences between legal principles and other types of legal norms, this insight would come as no surprise. It would merely corroborate the traditional view by showing that its understanding of principles also applies to legal principles whose content is an optimisation requirement.

C. Principles as Ideal 'Oughts'

Robert Alexy never doubted the soundness of Jan Sieckmann's argument. He was thus forced to abandon his initial concept of principles as optimisation requirements. With one side of the purported dichotomy breaking down, one might have expected Alexy to make do with optimisation requirements and the interpretation of constitutional rights as optimisation requirements. Yet for him, the discovery that optimisation requirements are rules did not lead him to revise his view of the dichotomy and the nature of principles, but to 'simply give[] [them] a sharper focus'.[16] Ever since, Alexy has maintained that principles are not optimisation requirements but an 'ideal ought'.

D. Critique: Superfluity of Ideal 'Oughts'

Since then, the nebulous notion of an ideal 'ought' – and its relevance for explaining optimisation requirements – has been the focus of my critique.[17] What are we to make of this ideal 'ought', and what function is it supposed to fulfil besides and beyond that of optimisation requirements? I contend that there is no need for an 'ideal ought' in addition to optimisation requirements; that Alexy's emphasis on ideal 'oughts' is merely an ad hoc stipulation to save his theory. Optimisation requirements are all there is to optimisation requirements and are all we need.

[15] JR Sieckmann, *Regelmodelle und Prinzipienmodelle des Rechtssystems* (Baden-Baden, Nomos, 1990) 65.

[16] R Alexy, 'Zur Struktur der Rechtsprinzipien' in B Schilcher et al (eds), *Regeln, Prinzipien und Elemente im System des Rechts* (Vienna, Verlag Österreich, 2000) 38–39 [ed note: see above Chapter 1, p 23].

[17] Poscher, 'Insights' (n 8) 433–41; Poscher, 'The Principles Theory' (n 8) 229–38; Poscher (n 3) 133–43.

E. Reply: Principles as Requirements to be Optimised

Robert Alexy took his time but eventually reacted to this line of critique.[18] He elaborated on his notion of ideal 'ought' by incorporating it into optimisation requirements, which are rules in his sense of the term. Optimisation requirements are not principles; instead, according to Alexy, principles do their work within optimisation requirements. We should distinguish 'between *commands to be optimised* and *commands to optimise*. Commands to be optimised are the objects of balancing or weighing. They can be termed "the ideal 'ought' or 'ideals"".[19] So now, principles are not optimisation requirements per se; rather, they are the 'ideal ought' that forms the object of the optimisation. Therefore, optimisation requirements are a special kind of rules that incorporate a principle.

Before I move on to my critique of this attempt to save Alexy's unconventional idea of principles from collapsing, we should take note that it leads to a significant change in the structure of the principles theory's ontology of norms. Before, there were rules on the one hand and principles on the other. Now there are only two different types of rules: first, rules that the principles theory previously thought of as rules; and second, rules that have a specific content, namely, an incorporated ideal 'ought' that is also a principle but that does not affect the rule character of the rule within which it is incorporated.

Even at first glance, this theory of two types of rules has lost much of the initial clarity of the distinction between rules and principles. Furthermore, the notion of an ideal 'ought' that is also a principle within a rule is much more difficult to understand – especially since it does not affect the nature of optimisation requirements as rules. We thought we understood the meaning of the rule that we must optimise the number of small balls and larger cubes contained in a vessel or the amount of tyre pressure to ensure both safety and gas mileage without seeking refuge in an ideal 'ought' that is also a principle within the rule. What started out as a seemingly clear-cut distinction between rules and principles turned into something that, on the face of it, looks rather stilted.

However, stilted or not, this is how Robert Alexy now defines principles: ideal 'oughts' nested within rules that do not affect the latter's nature as rules. Does this demotion of the once proud and independent principles to parasitic ideal 'oughts' within rules work? Does it make sense to understand principles as requirements to be optimised within optimisation requirements?

[18] R Alexy, 'Ideales Sollen' in L Clérico and JR Sieckmann (eds), *Grundrechte, Prinzipien und Argumentation. Studien zur Rechtstheorie Robert Alexys* (Baden-Baden, Nomos, 2009) 22, 30–33 [ed note: see above Chapter 3, pp 60, 69–70].

[19] Alexy (n 16) 38–39 [ed note: see above Chapter 1, p 23].; R Alexy, 'Ideales Sollen und Optimierung' in F Salinger et al (eds), *Rechtsstaatliches Strafrecht. Festschrift für Ulfrid Neumann zum 70. Geburtstag* (Heidelberg, CF Müller, 2017) 17–30 [ed note: see Chapter 5, pp 103–116 for the translated version].

F. Response: Factual Character of the Object of Optimisation

In my response to Robert Alexy's reply, I contended that it does not make sense. This is because, contrary to Alexy's suggestion, the objects of optimisation requirements are – at least typically – not norms but factual conditions. It is easy to see why Alexy wanted them to be norms: he needs a place for his ideal 'ought'. If he wants to place the ideal 'ought' within optimisation requirements as their object, then the object of the optimisation requirement must have a normative, not a factual, character. However little we understand of what ideal 'oughts' are supposed to be, one thing is certain: they are some kind of norm.

However, the objects of optimisation requirements are typically not norms. Take, for instance, one of Alexy's examples: the principle of helping people in need. According to Alexy, 'the requirement to aid people in need becomes the object of the optimisation. The optimisation requirement then takes the following form:

(5) O*Opt* O*p*'.[20]

The content of the simple requirement to optimise aid for people in need (O*Opt p*), though, is very different from that of the reflexive requirement to optimise the requirement to aid people in need (O*Opt* O*p*). Aid for people in need can be optimised by distributing tents and food supplies. In contrast, the requirement to aid people in need could be optimised by introducing or increasing a penalty for omitting to help people in need or by extending the scope of the relevant norm. The simple optimisation requirement is different from the reflexive requirement. This difference is further underlined by the different legal and factual possibilities that are of importance to the different objects of optimisation. Aid for people in need may find its legal boundaries in the property rights of third parties and its factual boundaries in the material resources at hand. The legal and factual boundaries for the optimisation of the requirement to provide aid are very different: legally speaking, they might be found in proportionality requirements for sanctions against omissions; factually, they might be found in the limited surveillance capacities of the state.

As the example shows, normative objects can also be optimised. However, these reflexive requirements do not contribute to an understanding or explanation of non-reflexive optimisation requirements. They are merely requirements with a different object. In our legal order, they are – insofar as they exist at all – an exception. We could, for example, imagine a constitutional provision that requires the legislature to optimise tax laws concerning the prevention of tax evasion and loopholes. However, constitutional rights, in particular, which represent the main area of application of the principles theory, are not norms that require the optimisation of other norms. According to the principles theory, they are norms that require the state to optimise its non-interference with the factual exercise of freedoms – of

[20] Alexy (n 18) 24 [ed note: see above Chapter 3, p 63].

assembly, of speech, of movement, etc – not norms that demand the optimisation of the norms of fundamental liberties. They aim at factual, not normative, objects.

In a paper published in 2017 in German, Robert Alexy conceded that his attempt to clarify his notion of 'ideal ought' via requirements to be optimised was misguided: 'This has to be corrected … On this point, Poscher's critique is correct'.[21]

Before we enter the third and current round of our dispute, let us again pause for a moment and take note of where we stand. For the second time, the *spiritus rector* of the principles theory has had to concede that what he thought was a principle in his peculiar, untraditional sense proved not to be a principle after all. Let us further note that some of Alexy's most prominent developments, such as the 'weight formula', pertain not to principles but to optimisation requirements. Again, even at first glance, his original position identifying principles as optimisation requirements seems to have been right. Where he went wrong was simply in claiming that optimisation requirements are rules in his contorted taxonomy. However, this is an issue with the taxonomy, not with optimisation requirements. Optimisation requirements do not need misguided taxonomies or ideal 'oughts'. They are plain and simple norms with a specific content that can be so general and important that some of them qualify as legal principles in the traditional sense. Everything else seems simply to be a convoluted attempt to save a theoretical dichotomy that is not worth saving.

III. The Third Round

We enter the third round! I did not expect Robert Alexy to end our dispute over the theoretical viability of the central concept of his principles theory with the concession: 'On this point, Poscher's critique is correct'. Now, Alexy[22] has attempted to defend what he calls an 'index model of the ideal ought' and thus an index model of principles. The new defence of his special concept of principle rests on a formal and a substantive argument. I will deal with them both in turn.

A. The Formal Argument

Alexy's formal argument relies on two new deontic operators. They are unique in that they figure neither in standard nor in currently known, nonstandard systems of deontic logic.[23] However, that is the fun of doing logic: you can come up with any operator you like if it serves to formalise our way of thinking. So, fundamentally, there is nothing wrong with inventing new deontic operators.

[21] Alexy (n 19) 25.

[22] ibid 18–19.

[23] For a good overview, see R Hilpinen and P McNamara, 'Deontic Logic: A Historical Survey and Introduction' in D Gabby et al (eds), *Handbook of Deontic Logic and Normative Systems* (London, College Publications, 2013) 3–136.

The two operators Alexy invents are O_i and O_r. The index '$_i$' modifies the standard operator 'O' for 'ought' into an 'ideal ought'; the index '$_r$' modifies the standard operator 'O' for 'ought' into a 'real ought'. Whether the invention of new deontic operators is helpful or a superfluous complication with respect to every other known deontological system should be judged by what they stand for and what work they do.

As for the real 'ought', things are straightforward and simple. The 'real ought' simply stands for our everyday 'ought' and the 'ought' used in any other deontological system. The case of the 'ideal ought' is much less straightforward. It is supposed to be an 'ought' that abstracts from all opposing reasons, an 'ought' for which the principle of noncontradiction is not supposed to hold, since – in the deontological system of 'ideal oughts' – an 'ideal ought' of *p* and an 'ideal ought' of non-*p* can coexist.[24]

Formally, there is no objection to this logical system of 'ideal oughts'. However, the question is: what does it do that cannot be done by optimisation requirements in which the normative operator is just an ordinary or – in Alexy's indexed terminology – a 'real ought'?

The case of a contradiction between 'ideal oughts', the possibility of 'oughts' with contradictory objects, is handled just as easily by optimisation requirements. A requirement to optimise *p* and non-*p* is not a logical contradiction. A logical contradiction would lie only in the obligations to optimise *p* and not to optimise *p*.

$$(OOpt\,p \land OOpt \neg p) \rightarrow \neg\bot$$

$$(OOpt\,p \land \neg OOpt\,p) \rightarrow \bot$$

The obligation to optimise the darkness and lightness, ie non-darkness, of paint for a room can be fulfilled by choosing a lighter or darker shade of grey. As regards opposing objects of optimisation, optimisation requirements behave just like 'ideal oughts': they do not contradict one another.

Alexy himself sees this no differently. He insists on the 'fundamental equivalence'[25] of optimisation requirements and 'ideal oughts'.

'$O_r\,Opt\,p \leftrightarrow O_i\,p$'[26]

Logical equivalence means that two logical expressions have the same truth-value in any expression. They can be substituted for one another in every expression with no consequence to its truth-value. Examples of logical equivalences are:

$$\neg\neg p \leftrightarrow p$$

$$p \land q \leftrightarrow q \land p$$

[24] Alexy (n 19) 19.
[25] ibid 24.
[26] ibid.

So, we could use a logical notation that uses the expression 'non-non-*p*' to say '*p*' or '*p* v *p*' to say '*p*', but that does not change the fact that we are simply talking about '*p*'.

In the same fashion, Alexy can introduce his 'ideal ought', which is equivalent to the corresponding optimisation requirement, but equivalence – and especially fundamental equivalence – means that we can dispense with it as well. O_i adds nothing to our formal logical apparatus, and it adds nothing to our understanding of norms beyond what could be expressed, in standard deontological systems, with the standard, non-indexed 'ought' or, in our informal legal language, with optimisation requirements. Alexy's proposed formalisation does nothing to show that anything other than our ordinary 'ought' is necessary or even helpful for understanding optimisation requirements. The transformation of optimisation requirements into a new deontic operator may be formally permissible,[27] since there are virtually no limits to the inventions of new ingredients in systems of deontic logic, but it proves a superfluous addition.

B. The Substantive Argument

Alongside this ill-fated attempt at formalisation, Alexy offers another substantive argument for why his notion of 'ideal ought' and principle is necessary. He contends that optimisation requirements cannot be understood without recourse to the collision of principles.[28] However, what is there not to understand when faced with the norm requiring us to optimise the number of small balls and larger cubes contained in an irregularly shaped vessel? Using Alexy's weight formula or degrees of maximum realisation, we can even provide exact numbers. We would not even know what was meant if we were to understand it as the requirement to optimise the 'ideal ought' of balls and cubes. The same is true of the norm on tyre pressure: we understand perfectly well that we must optimise tyre pressure to ensure fuel efficiency and safety, but it would only confuse us to be told to optimise the 'ideal ought' of fuel efficiency and the 'ideal ought' of safety. It is confusing for much the same reasons as mentioned above. We do not want to optimise 'ideal oughts' of balls, cubes, fuel efficiency, or safety, but the things themselves.

However, maybe Alexy is on to something here, and he is after something like this – and this is my own speculation; there is nothing in his texts to suggest this: the command to optimise does not indicate the direction of optimisation. Simply knowing the object of optimisation does not tell us whether to push it in the direction of its minimisation or in the direction of its maximisation. Maybe the idea is that there must be something normative in the object of optimisation – an 'ideal ought' – that tells us whether it is to be minimised or maximised relative to

[27] For a critique of Alexy's previous notation of optimisation requirements, see Poscher (n 3) 135–36.
[28] Alexy (n 19) 26.

the legal and factual possibilities. For example, fuel efficiency, health, and life are connected to an ideal of fuel efficiency, health, and life, indicating that we have to maximise them.

That cannot be true, however, since we can easily think of – ethically perverted but theoretically possible – norms with the same objects but the opposite direction of optimisation. The US Navy celebrates its new laser weapons employed on warships not only for their precision and firing rate but also for their cost efficiency, which is sometimes calculated in 'cost per kill'.[29] It is probably not too far-fetched to imagine a norm of the US military for their arms contractors that obliges them to optimise the cost-per-kill ratio. The contractors will understand that they must look for ways to minimise survivors, and thus human life, and costs at the same time.

The direction of optimisation requirements is not conveyed by their objects but by the context of the norm, which reveals its purpose and thus the appropriate direction. The direction of the optimisation is independent of its object. It is a qualification not of the object of optimisation but of the command to optimise. Optimisation requirements are ambiguous concerning minimisation or maximisation relative to the legal and factual possibilities and – like most ambiguities – can be disambiguated through their context. Optimisation requirements could also make their direction explicit by demanding either minimisation or maximisation relative to the legal and factual possibilities or – if I may say so – by an index: Opt_{max} and Opt_{min}.

So even with a little help from a friend, principles in the form of 'ideal oughts' are in no way necessary or even helpful in understanding optimisation requirements. On the contrary, the postulation of principles in the form of indexed 'ideal oughts' inside optimisation requirements still misleads us into thinking that the objects of optimisation requirements are norms, which Alexy has already conceded they are not.

C. Optimisation Requirements are All We Need

Optimisation requirements are all we need to understand everything there is to know about the norms that Alexy calls principles. An optimisation requirement is a norm like any other that is distinct not for some kind of norm-ontological status within a purported dichotomy of rules and principles, but for its content. The upshot of this destruction of the ontological dichotomy of rules and principles is that the question of whether or not a norm has an optimisation requirement as its content is one of legal interpretation, not of theoretical categorisation. Highly abstract norms, such as many constitutional rights, are not optimisation requirements for

[29] For a critical account, see JE Walsh, 'Inadequacy of Cost per "Kill" as Measure of Effectiveness' (1957) 5(6) *Operations Research* 750.

theoretical reasons. Rather, the question of whether or not it is sensible to regard them as optimisation requirements or to interpret them – or at least some of them – as 'trumps' in Ronald Dworkin's sense[30] or 'shields', as Fredrick Schauer[31] suggests, or even differently on a case-by-case basis according to classic hermeneutical canons, is one of legal interpretation, doctrinal construction, and, ultimately, constitutional theory and political morality.[32] These interpretative, doctrinal, and substantive theoretical and philosophical questions are neither contributed to, let alone decided by, the flawed norm-theoretical distinction between principles and rules that Alexy still defends with ever more idiosyncratic arguments.

There is no theoretical reason to understand the guarantee of human dignity in the Basic Law as a mere optimisation requirement, and there are many historical, systematic, and teleological arguments against such an interpretation.[33] The resuscitation of the phantom has failed. On the theoretical side, this is all I wish to demonstrate, since it opens the debate – especially the debate about constitutional rights – to interpretative, doctrinal, and substantive philosophical arguments and alternatives that the principles theory tries to exclude by norm-theoretical means.

IV. Optimisation Requirements

The following points are now settled: first, there are no principles as defined by the principles theory; rather, there are optimisation requirements. Second, optimisation requirements can be one type of principle in the classical, gradualist sense when they pertain to objects of high generality, abstraction, and importance. However, they can also be more like rules in this gradualist sense. They can even have the character of strict rules and can even provide numerically exact outcomes, as in the example of the optimisation of the number of small balls and larger cubes contained in a vessel. Third, whether a norm has an optimisation requirement as its content is a question of legal hermeneutics, not one of legal theory. Fourth, principles theory is a misnomer. The principles theory is actually concerned with optimisation requirements, and it should be rebranded as what it is: a theory of optimisation requirements.

However, maybe there is something special about optimisation requirements. And, indeed, that is Robert Alexy's view. He regards optimisation requirements as unique because they depend on balancing.[34] So, maybe as a theory of optimisation

[30] Dworkin (n 3) xxi, 365–68.

[31] Schauer (n 3) 428–29.

[32] For a defence of a substantively modified interpretation of constitutional rights as optimisation requirements on the bases of political justice, see Kumm (n 5) 589–95; with a more pluralist bent, M Kumm, 'Political Liberalism and the Structure of Rights: On the Place and Limits of the Proportionality Requirement' in G Pavlakos (ed), *Law, Rights and Discourse: The Legal Philosophy of Robert Alexy* (Oxford, Hart Publishing, 2007) 165–69.

[33] Möller (n 2) 465–67; Kumm (n 5) 590 thus regards Alexy's account as 'incomplete' because it does not integrate the prioritising of certain rights in the balancing procedure.

[34] Alexy (n 19) 26.

requirements, Alexy's theory can support the uniqueness of its object? Instead of a dichotomy of rules and principles, we would have a dichotomy of optimisation requirements, on the one hand, and norms with a different content, on the other, with only the optimisation requirement in need of balancing.

A. Multiple Ways of Balancing

In previous articles, I have tried to show that there is nothing unique about balancing in the context of optimisation requirements that cannot be found in other norms.[35] There can be rules for norm collisions that do not rely on optimisation but simply on the weighing of one of the protected interests against a certain fixed threshold of importance; there can be rules for norm collisions that rely not on an optimising weighing procedure but on a procedure that excludes only obvious disproportionalities – an interpretation of the proportionality principle that is quite prominent in the German literature.[36] Although I still think that these examples of alternative collision rules are a good way of showing the non-uniqueness of optimisation requirements, Alexy was never convinced.[37] I will therefore not repeat the illustration here. Instead, I will try to make the same point in a different way using Alexy's weight formula, which in his view is the most precise analysis of the balancing operation that he regards as the core of optimisation requirements.

Alexy's weight formula combines three aspects of two opposing optimisation requirements:[38]

$$W_{i,j} = \frac{I_i \cdot W_i \cdot R_i}{I_j \cdot W_j \cdot R_j}$$

The formula relies on the quotient of the weight or importance of the objects of the opposing optimisation requirements (W_i, W_j), the intensity of the interference with a constitutional right (I_i, I_j), and the epistemic reliability of our knowledge about the two other factors (R_i, R_j).[39]

Now, I think it is easy to show that none of these factors is unique to optimisation requirements. We need only imagine a norm that relies solely on the abstract

[35] Poscher, 'Insights' (n 8) 433–36; Poscher, 'The Principles Theory' (n 8) 229–33; Poscher (n 3) 141–43.

[36] B Pieroth and B Schlink, *Grundrechte. Staatsrecht II*, 28th edn (Heidelberg, CF Müller, 2012) rn 304; Poscher (n 1) 224. See also Kumm (n 32) 147.

[37] Alexy (n 19) 26.

[38] Alexy (n 9) 446. $W_{i,j}$ stands for the concrete weight of principle '$_i$' in relation to principle '$_j$' under the circumstances of the concrete case. I_i and I_j stand for the intensity of the interference with the respective principle. W_i and W_j stand for the abstract weight of the respective principle. R_i and R_j stand for the reliability of the empirical assumptions concerning what the measure in question means for the non-realisation of principle i and the realisation of principle j under the circumstances of the concrete case. See ibid 444–46.

[39] Alexy (n 19) 23.

weight, or solely on the intensity of the interference with a constitutional right, or solely on the epistemic reliability of our assessment of either weight or infringement, or on any other combination of these factors. If we further consider that all these factors could – if I may say so – *in principle* be modified by numerical values, it becomes evident that the number of norm types that could be construed with the elements of the optimisation requirement is infinite. For example, a norm could require an interest to be twice, three times, 2.5-times, 2.75-times, 'n'-times as important as an opposing interest in order for it to prevail.

Optimisation requirements are just one of the infinite numbers of norm types that require the balancing of the factors that make up optimisation requirements. Thus, optimisation requirements are a specific type of norm, with a specific type of balancing as their content, but there is nothing structurally unique about them. Nothing justifies building a dichotomist ontology of norms around them, with principles as logical equivalents to optimisation requirements, on the one hand, and all other possible norms as rules, on the other.

B. Optimisation as the Fundamental Form of Balancing?

Although balancing is not unique to optimisation requirements, an argument advanced in favour of interpreting norms as optimisation requirements is that anything else would deliver inferior results.[40] Why should we settle for less than the optimal? Why should we not follow the optimal balance of arguments?

This argument confuses different levels of optimisation: namely, the optimisation of arguments about the content of a norm and the optimisation required by a norm that is interpreted as an optimisation requirement. Already in one of my first critiques, I contended that the optimisation idea behind the principles theory might best be understood as a contribution to the theory of argumentation.[41] At the level of argumentation, one could argue that we always aim for the optimal balance of reasons – if there is one[42] – to reach a conclusion. This would also hold true for our arguments supporting an interpretation of a normative text. We aim for the content supported by the optimal balance of reasons (if attainable). Why would we settle for anything less?

However, aiming for the optimal balance of reasons when we interpret a legal text or apply it to a concrete case does not mean that the result of the optimal balance of reasons must be an interpretation of the text in the sense of an optimisation requirement. The overwhelming majority of interpreters of the guarantee

[40] JR Sieckmann, *Rechtsphilosophie* (Tübingen, Mohr Siebeck, 2018) 136.

[41] Poscher, 'The Principles Theory' (n 8) 238–42.

[42] For an overview on the discussion about comparativism in evaluative reasoning and an argument for parity that does not allow for qualifying an alternative as optimal, see R Chang (ed), *Incommensurability, Incomparability, and Practical Reason* (Cambridge MA, Harvard University Press, 1997); R Chang, 'The Possibility of Parity' (2002) 12 *Ethics* 659; R Chang, *Making Comparisons Count: Studies in Ethics* (Hoboken NJ, Routledge, 2014).

of human dignity in the Basic Law, including the Federal Constitutional Court, see the optimal balance of reasons supporting its interpretation as an absolute guarantee. Many authors – drawing on arguments from normative epistemology, democratic theory, the division of powers, and political morality – make the case that the optimal balance of reasons does not support an interpretation of the constitutional proportionality principle as an optimisation requirement but does so only as a protection against obviously disproportionate state action. Inferring from our efforts to optimise our argumentation that, for example, constitutional rights should be interpreted as optimisation requirements would be tantamount to conflating the metalevel of argumentation with the object level of the normative texts our arguments are about.

V. Conclusion

Like all his previous attempts, Robert Alexy's 'new' index principles theory is unable to explain either what principles in his sense are meant to be or why we need them. Everything he has to say and wants to show with the help of 'ideal oughts' can be said and shown by sticking to optimisation requirements. Therefore, Alexy was right the first time he wrote about principles. When he talks about principles, he simply means optimisation requirements. Yet he himself has had to concede that optimisation requirements are rules in the sense of the purported dichotomy of rules and principles, thus calling into question the dichotomy itself. Alexy's theory is a theory of optimisation requirements,[43] and optimisation requirements can be one type of legal principle in the traditional gradualist sense – when they are sufficiently abstract and important. However, they can also be rules in the traditional gradualist sense – even providing for numerically precise results, depending on the objects of optimisation. Whether a legal text codifies an optimisation requirement is a question of legal interpretation and one that is not decided by a purported ontology of principles and rules. Even if the interpretation leads to a norm that requires the balancing of opposing values or interests, optimisation is just one possible outcome. For the doctrine of constitutional rights, the principal consequence is that the theoretical spell of the principles theory is broken. Contrary to the principles theory's suggestion, there is nothing in the theory of legal norms that forces anyone to interpret constitutional rights as optimisation requirements.

[43] See Möller (n 2) 463: 'On a closer look at Alexy's overall argument, it turns out that the difficult sections of the book relating to rules and principles are not relevant to Alexy's conception of constitutional rights because, ultimately, he is interested not in rules and principles but in the necessity of balancing'.

Conclusion

The Alexy–Poscher Debate: Working on the Problems and on the Solutions

DAVID DUARTE*

I. The Principles' Conundrum

It is not without reason that for the past 50 years legal theorists have been discussing the difference, including the possible existence of the difference in itself, between two categories of norms: principles and rules. As a matter of fact, it seems clear that normative systems comprise norms with different properties that point to something envisaged with that classification: there are symptoms of a difference that would justify such categorisation of norms.[1] For instance: (i) some norms have a far wider scope than others; (ii) some norms are much more prone to enter into normative conflicts than others; (iii) some norms seem to materially ground others while these seem to be the mere concretisation of the former without grounding any other; (iv) only some norms seem to be applicable (and applied) by degrees; (v) only some norms seem to be able to reach intermediate deontic solutions when in conflict (combining both norms); and (vi) as also argued, some norms are defeasible ('prima facie' regulation) and others are not (definitive regulation).[2]

It can be said, while observing how normative systems work, that some of these differences exist and, consequently, that they can be exemplified. That is the case

* I am grateful to Andrew Halpin, Pablo Navarro and Jorge Silva Sampaio for valuable comments and suggestions made to a previous version of this paper. But I am also particularly grateful to Pedro Moniz Lopes for years and years of discussion and fruitful exchange of ideas on the present subject matter.

[1] J Raz, 'Legal Principles and the Limits of Law' (1972) 81 *Yale Law Journal* 823, 825; RM Dworkin, 'The Model of Rules I' in RM Dworkin (ed), *Taking Rights Seriously* (Cambridge MA, Harvard University Press, 1977) 22; R Alexy, *A Theory of Constitutional Rights* (J Rivers trans, Oxford, Oxford University Press, 2002); A Aarnio, *Essays on the Doctrinal Study of* Law (Cham, Springer, 2011) 122.

[2] This is not an exhaustive list: other possible differences have been pointed out. Yet, those differences, besides being the most common, are the ones that are relevant for the initial points to be made here. On the other hand, differences between principles and rules based on semantic aspects of their sentences are clearly unacceptable. Similarly, PM Lopes, 'The Syntax of Principles: Genericity as a Logical Distinction Between Rules and Principles' (2017) 30 *Ratio Juris* 471, 472.

with the scope of norms (i). A norm such as the one expressed by 'no one can profit from her own wrong' has a wider scope than the one stated in 'it is forbidden to smoke'. Even though this proposition presupposes 'scope' to be understood as concerning the material domain of norms (related, therefore, to the types of action that are regulated), under such presupposition a clear difference appears: while the first norm encompasses various and even indeterminate action-types, the second one solely concerns 'smoking'.[3] This difference between norms is, however, just a matter of degree (quantitative): the scope can be wider or narrower depending on the variety of actions regulated or, even if only one is at stake, on their comparative grade of specificity.[4]

(i) Assuming a norm with a structure such as '$o_x \Rightarrow O_{\{PA\}}\ x_{\{SA\}}$', in which 'x' stands for the action (for instance, to smoke), 'o_x' for the condition of the opportunity to realise the action, '{PA}' and '{SA}' for the sets of primary and secondary addressees respectively, and 'O' for the deontic modality (here, obligation), it follows that the norm in 'it is forbidden to smoke' can be formalised as '$o_x \Rightarrow F_{\{PA\}}\ x_{\{SA\}}$', in which 'x = smoking'.

(ii) With the same assumption, the norm in 'no one can profit from her own wrong' can be formalised as '$o_x^1 \vee o_x^2 \vee \ldots \vee o_x^n \Rightarrow F_{\{PA\}}\ x_{\{SA\}}$', in which 'x = profiting from wrongdoing'; the difference in the antecedent follows from the fact that the type of action is indeterminate and, consequently, has various, alternative and unrelated opportunities for realisation; in fact, 'profiting from wrongdoing' can be killing one's grandfather to receive the inheritance or burning down a restaurant in order to get the insurance (and so many more).

(iii) It is clear that the scope of 'no one can profit from her own wrong' is wider than the scope of 'it is forbidden to smoke'; it is neither a matter of {PA} or {SA} to have more or fewer addressees, nor a matter of how many opportunities for 'x' will occur (increasing or decreasing the norm's application); it is just that the slice of world covered by the 'x' in 'smoking' is narrower than the one in 'profiting from one's own wrongdoing'.

It seems correct as well to say that there are some norms with more and others with less aptitude to enter into normative conflicts (ii).[5] A norm such as the one in 'it is forbidden to smoke' is visibly less prone to collide than the one expressed by 'freedom of the press is guaranteed'. A reason for this can come from the intuitive fact that there are fewer life situations in which a norm with a contradictory

[3] On the wider scope as a symptom of the difference, see R Guastini, *Le Fonti del Diritto e L'Interpretazione* (Milan, Giuffrè, 1993) 451; G Pino, *Teoria Analitica del Diritto. La Norma Giuridica* (Pisa, Edizioni ETS, 2016) 79.

[4] A difference of degree that does not deny the possibility, as will be seen later on, of an underlying qualititative difference.

[5] See eg D Duarte, 'An Experimental Essay on the Antecedent and Its Formulation' (2012) 16 *i-Lex, Rivista di Scienze Giuridiche, Scienze Cognitive ed Intelligenza Artificiale* 37, 59; PM Lopes, 'The Syntax of Principles: Genericity as a Logical Distinction Between Rules and Principles' (2017) 30 *Ratio Juris* 471, 483.

deontic status on 'smoking' is triggered when compared with freedom of the press, apparently with countless cases that create a normative contradiction, as happens with norms conferring rights to honour or to privacy, usually triggered by any less restrained newspaper article.[6] However, the main and effective reason is given by the antecedent of both norms. The larger scope of 'freedom of the press' means a bigger slice of world covered, which automatically implies increasing the probability of conflicts: the larger the antecedent, the more the opportunities to overlap with other norms and to enter into a conflict. Aptitude to collide is also a difference of degree (quantitative): it is a more or less difference coming from the antecedent's extension.[7]

(iv) 'It is forbidden to smoke' is '$o_x \Rightarrow F_{\{PA\}}\, x_{\{SA\}}$', in which 'x = smoking'; 'freedom of the press is guaranteed' is '$o_x^1 \vee o_x^2 \vee \ldots \vee o_x^n \Rightarrow P_{\{PA\}}\, x_{\{SA\}}$', in which 'x = informing and expressing opinions through the media (print media, broadcast media, internet media, for instance)'.

(v) Accepting that 'the larger the antecedent, the more the opportunities to overlap with other norms and to enter into a conflict' is a true proposition, it follows that freedom of the press is much more vulnerable to entering into conflicts than the prohibition against smoking.

(vi) Such conclusion follows from the fact that a norm such as freedom of the press has a much wider antecedent, formed by the disjunctive opportunities to carry out the various indeterminate actions foreseen (writing news, presenting documentaries, interviewing politicians, for instance).

One of the first detected symptoms of the possible difference between principles and rules was precisely the property of materially grounding other norms: while some norms would be the substantive reason for others, many others would not lead to any subsequent concretisation or, at least, would only lead to some trivial normative development (iii).[8] Yet, it is not that certain that such difference is well designed in these terms. Actually, no matter the kind of norm at hand one can always conceive of a materially dependent norm, working as a concretisation of the former. Be it through the addition of new conditions in the antecedent or by the specification of types of action (in norms in which action is indeterminate), the result is always a relation of 'material dependence'. What can be said instead is that norms with a wider scope naturally give more space to concretisation, this being, under this light, a mere difference of degree also coming from the antecedent.[9]

[6] On the frequent variables of these conflicts, see JJ Moreso, 'Confliti tra Princìpi Constituzionali' (2002) 2 *Diritto & Questioni Pubbliche* 19, 30; D Mendonca, *Derechos, Razón y Emoción: Conflicto y Balance de Derechos* (Asunción, Centro de Estudios Constitucionales, 2016) 48.

[7] Yet, the caveat mentioned in n 4 above is also valid here.

[8] Initially pointing out this difference, J Esser, *Einführung in die Grundbegriffe des Rechtes und Staates* (Vienna, Springer, 1949) 14. See also K Engisch, *Einführung in das juristische Denken*, 9th edn (Stuttgart, Kohlhammer, 1997) 252.

[9] So, it turns out to be a mere quantitative difference. See also G Carrió, *Notas sobre Derecho y Lenguage* (Buenos Aires, Abeledo-Perrot, 1994) 204; JR Sieckmann, 'Los Derechos Fundamentales como Principios' in JR Sieckmann (ed), *La Teoría Principialista de los Derechos Fundamentales* (Madrid, Marcial Pons, 2011) 35.

(vii) The norm in 'no one can profit from her own wrong' ('$o_x^1 \vee o_x^2 \vee \ldots \vee o_x^n \Rightarrow F_{\{PA\}}\, x_{\{SA\}}$', in which 'x = profiting from one's own wrongdoing') can be concretised by, for instance, 'whoever kills a family member loses the right to inheritance'; the latter norm is a material concretisation of the former.

(viii) However, the norm in 'it is forbidden to smoke' ('$o_x \Rightarrow F_{\{PA\}}\, x_{\{SA\}}$', in which 'x = smoking') can also be concretised by 'it is forbidden to smoke in closed spaces' ('$o_x \wedge (cs) \Rightarrow F_{\{PA\}}\, x_{\{SA\}}$', in which 'cs' stands for 'closed spaces'); there is also some material dependence between the former and the latter norms.

(ix) It is visible, though, that these are two different ways of 'concretisation'; in (vii), concretisation is made through the isolation of one of the indeterminate actions; in (viii), concretisation is made through the addition of a condition in the antecedent; yet, 'concretisation' in itself appears in both cases.

It has been claimed that a difference between principles and rules could be based on the possibility that the former would have to be applied by degrees (iv).[10] Yet, this is quite controversial. On the one hand, it seems that a norm regulating an action (or even if it regulates a set of indeterminate actions) covers all its tokens without any kind of variation: if it is mandatory to treat everyone equally, then, whenever there is an assessment of similarity, the same deontic consequence has to be strictly applied. So, whenever only such a norm is being taken into account, no application by degrees can be recognised. On the other hand, there are norms that require a desired state of affairs and, since they establish a goal to be accomplished, they are somehow 'realisable' by degrees. For instance, the norm in 'the state shall promote an ecologically balanced human living environment' imposes a duty on the state to do whatever it takes to achieve an environment with those properties and can be satisfied to a greater or lesser degree. However, two main points are relevant here. The first one is that if only these 'ought to be' norms (as opposed to 'ought to do' norms) were principles, then the category would be rather limited and it would not contain the large majority of norms legal theorists tend to regard as principles (for instance, equality and norms conferring fundamental rights).[11] The second is that one cannot confuse application by degrees with the various outcomes of balancing: application by degrees is often mixed with the multiple situations in which the same norm defeats or is defeated by another. Yet, here the 'variation' comes from the conflict's solution and does not mean that the norm at hand can be satisfied in a progressive way. What it means is that such norm goes

[10] See eg R Alexy, 'Constitutional Rights, Proportionality, and Argumentation' in JR Sieckmann (ed), *Proportionality, Balancing, and Rights: Robert Alexy's Theory of Constitutional Rights* (Cham, Springer, 2021) 2; Pino (n 3) 95.

[11] Since to perform an action is also a sort of state of affairs in itself – See GH Von Wright, 'Ought to Be – Ought to Do' in G Meggle (ed), *Actions, Norms and Values: Discussions with Georg Henrik von Wright* (Berlin, De Gruyter, 1999) 8 –, the notion of 'ought to be' norms is here confined to norms that establish a goal and leave open the actions suitable to achieve it. On this distinction as well, see HN Castañeda, 'On the Semantics of the Ought-To-Do' in D Davidson and G Harman (eds), *Semantics of Natural Languages* (Dordrecht, Reidel, 1972) 675.

more and less far since the outcomes of its various conflicts change in accordance with what the opposite norm is and the context of the conflict.[12] On this understanding, the inevitable consequence is that either principles are only 'ought to be' norms, or variation by degrees (that would be a differentiation of qualitative nature) is not an effective difference between principles and rules.

(x) With 'everyone ought to be treated equally' ('$o_x^1 \vee o_x^2 \vee \ldots \vee o_x^n \wedge (a) \Rightarrow O_{\{PA\}}\, x_{\{SA\}}$', in which 'a = assessment of analogy' and 'x = treat equally'), whenever the condition 'a' (and one of the opportunities) is met, it follows that a similar deontic consequence has to be adopted: there is no variation in treating equally (if agents A and B have the same relevant properties {a, b, c}, agent B has a right to the exact same deontic consequence that was applied to agent A; and one cannot recognise any kind of variation here).

(xi) Yet, 'everyone ought to be treated equally' usually conflicts with the 'general right to freedom' ('$o_x^1 \vee o_x^2 \vee \ldots \vee o_x^n \Rightarrow P_{\{PA\}}\, x_{\{SA\}}$', in which 'x = act [no matter which action]'); in such situation of conflict, the obligation to treat equally can vary by degrees: a professor is not obliged to accord the exact same participation time in class to every student, since each one's personal freedom leads to a more 'relaxed' application of equality; but not being strict on equal treatment only follows from the conflict with the right to liberty.

(xii) A norm such as the one in 'it is forbidden to smoke' is also not applied by degrees: a primary addressee of such norm is always violating such norm whenever she smokes; however, a conflict arises if the normative authority simultaneously enacts 'it is permitted to smoke'; as a total-total conflict unable to be resolved by norms of conflicts (*lex specialis*, *lex superior* and *lex posterior* are not applicable), the deontic status of the action 'to smoke' is only ascertainable through a balancing between the conflicting norms.

(xiii) Since there is nothing else besides the deontic contradiction, any justified solution depends on the context relevant to the 'the deontic status of the action'; so, and most probably, the prohibition will prevail in 'closed spaces', yet not in 'private closed spaces', as the permission will prevail in 'music festivals' or 'football games'; multiple contexts will provide different solutions and the overall outcome is not very different from what has been seen with equality: the norm goes more and less far depending on the conflict.

(xiv) Proper application by degrees can only be recognised in 'ought to be' norms; for instance, with 'the state shall promote an ecologically balanced human living environment' the state can ban the use of plastics, require agents to reduce carbon emissions or execute a plan to plant native species (combined or not); so, the more the state does in its 'promotion', the more such norm is satisfied; here, variation does not come from the 'instability' of a norm being successively defeated or a defeater; it comes from the norm itself.

[12] Which simultaneously is, as Raz says, a scenario also applicable to rules. See J Raz, 'The Argument from Justice, or How Not to Reply to Legal Positivism' in G Pavlakos (ed), *Law, Rights, and Discourse: The Legal Philosophy of Robert Alexy* (Oxford, Hart Publishing, 2007) 17, 34.

When two norms enter into a conflict the usual outcome is the prevalence of one over the other, no matter whether following from the consequence of a norm of conflicts or as the result of balancing. With such 'all-norms-considered' outcome, the norm chosen entirely regulates the case at hand: the deontic status that becomes effective is the one contained in the elected norm. But when the conflict is solved by carrying out a balancing, sometimes it seems possible to create a sort of intermediate solution, in which some compatible aspects of both norms are simultaneously satisfied. And this would amount to another possible symptom of a difference between principles and rules: differently from the latter, the former would be norms that accommodate the possibility of transactional solutions (v).[13] Yet, this seems to be mistaken: any norm can be part of a combined solution, and such possibility depends on the facts of the case and not on the properties of the norms at hand. On the other hand, one would face here a qualitative difference as well: principles would be able to accommodate such transactional solutions while rules would not.

(xv) A norm such as the one in 'freedom of the press is guaranteed' can conflict with the 'right to image': in the famous *Lebach* case, that is what happened with the broadcasting of a documentary also exposing images of a formerly imprisoned criminal; this case clearly allows both binary and combined solutions.[14]

(xvi) If freedom of the press prevails completely, the documentary is fully broadcast (or the other way around, if the right to image prevails completely); but a court can allow the documentary to be broadcast with the removal of some frames related to the imprisoned criminal, satisfying both norms.

(xvii) If the case did not involve a documentary, but rather, an indivisible piece of information (showing a picture of the imprisoned criminal on television, for instance), then no combined solution was possible; in such case either the picture is shown or it is not (depending on the prevalent norm).

(xviii) The conflict between 'it is forbidden to smoke' and 'it is permitted to smoke' also allows for binary and combined solutions; nothing prevents the prohibition to prevail completely regarding smoking inside a hospital; but smoking on an uninhabited island could perfectly lead to the opposite prevalence.

(xix) However, in an awkward situation of an agent dependent on nicotine for her own health, nothing prevents a court from saying that such agent can smoke a cigarette a day, even if in a closed space; this is a combined solution coming from the gradeability of smoking more or less.

(xx) In such case, there was not a complete prevalence of 'it is permitted to smoke' since the agent is mostly forbidden to smoke; but since the agent has been allowed to smoke a cigarette a day, 'it is forbidden to smoke' did

[13] On the topic, see DM Zorrilla, *Conflictos Constitucionales, Ponderación y Indeterminación Normativa* (Madrid, Marcial Pons, 2007) 204; Lopes (n 2) 485.

[14] BVerfGe 35, 202 decision of 5 June 1973.

not completely prevail either; combined aspects of both norms were used for the solution.

One of the most mentioned symptoms of a possible difference between principles and rules is the one that classifies the former as defeasible norms, providing only a 'prima facie' regulation, and the latter as indefeasible, containing a definitive regulation (vi).[15] Yet, this seems to be mistaken, as the famous 1981 example of the military facilities given by Alchourrón has demonstrated.[16] The example clearly showed: (i) that two norms that are rules under any possible criteria can conflict; (ii) that the conflict cannot be solved by any norm of conflicts; and (iii) that one of the conflicting norms will necessarily defeat the other. Later, many other examples have been presented, showing a long list of 'black swans' that totally prevent the truth of the proposition 'differently from principles, rules are indefeasible'.[17] And denying such proposition seems to be more or less evident: any two norms in a conflict that cannot be solved by norms of conflicts (because it is a partial-partial or a total-total with equal hierarchy and time) ought to be weighted (a court is usually under a duty of *non liquet*) and, necessarily, one of them will (partially or totally) defeat the other.[18] The result is unavoidable: probably with the exception of competence norms, each and every norm of a normative system is defeasible. Accordingly, this possible qualitative difference cannot be accepted.

(xxi) A norm such as the one in 'it is obligatory to stop one's vehicle at a red light' is, under any possible criteria, a rule; the same is valid for a norm such as 'it is forbidden to stop one's vehicle close to a military facility'; when there is a traffic light near a military facility and the light turns red, these norms conflict; it is a clear partial-partial type of conflict, which means that there are no applicable norms of conflicts (as addressed below).

(xxii) Consequently, the deontic status of the action to drive (regarding motion) can only be obtained through balancing: depending on the contextual reasons, one norm or the other will prevail (for instance, regarding an inactive military facility, most probably the norm with the requirement to stop would prevail); since this can happen with any rule (norm), then all norms just give a 'prima facie' regulation.

[15] See eg M Borowski, *La Estructura de los Derechos Fundamentales* (Bogotá, Universidad Externado de Colombia, 2003) 48; R Alexy, 'Giovanni Battista Ratti's Critique of Principles Theory' (2023) 36 *Ratio Juris* 153.

[16] Carlos Alchourrón, 'G.H. von Wright y los Desarrollos de la Lógica Deontica' (1981) 1 *Anuario de Filosofía Política y Social* 121, 133.

[17] See eg J Rodríguez, 'La Derrotabilidad de las Normas' (1997) 6 *Isonomia* 149, 158; F Schauer, 'Is Defeasibility an Essential Property of Law?' in J Ferrer and GB Ratti (eds), *The Logic of Legal Requirements: Essays on Defeasibility* (Oxford, Oxford University Press, 2012) 81.

[18] D Duarte, 'Drawing Up the Boundaries of Normative Conflicts that Lead to Balances' in JR Sieckmann (ed), *Legal Reasoning: The Methods of Balancing* (Stuttgart, Franz Steiner, 2010) 57; Lopes (n 2) 483. Also, when considering this notion of defeasibility, see P Navarro and J Rodríguez, *Deontic Logic and Legal Systems* (Cambridge, Cambridge University Press, 2014) 193. Also, and inside the debate, see F Leal, 'Prefácio' in RG Dalla-Barba (ed), *Princípios Jurídicos: O Debate Metodológico entre Robert Alexy e Ralf Poscher* (Belo Horizonte, Casa do Direito, 2022) 27.

(xxiii) With two norms such as 'it is forbidden to smoke at lunch time' and 'it is permitted to smoke when it rains', another partial-partial type of conflict happens when 'it rains at lunch time' (a conflict only solvable by balancing, necessarily leading to a defeated norm); again, with two norms that are rules under any possible criteria, their common defeasibility is clear: one will necessarily be defeated.

All these differences between norms have been signalled as possible grounds to classify them in a distinction that detaches principles from rules. Although some of the differences seem to be mistaken (in the sense that their existence is false), the fact is that legal theorists tend to adopt one of those symptoms and use it as a criterion to separate those two categories. It is not surprising, consequently, that a plethora of different distinctions co-exist in the literature and that defenders of a quantitative distinction base their position on a symptom of mere degree while defenders of a qualitative distinction support their view on a difference of substantive character.[19] It can be said, then, that adopting a quantitative or a qualitative distinction has been more the result of choosing a specific symptom as a criterion for the classification than a result of a comprehensive idea about the whole difference between principles and rules. So, and given that some of the analysed differences are real and effective, one has to recognise that nothing prevents two or more different classifications of principles and rules from being simultaneously correct, even though sustained on distinct criteria and even concurrently leading to opposite quantitative and qualitative theories.

Such a scenario poses a very complex problem over this distinction: what do we really want to achieve with a classification such as this one? Or, in other words, if some (diverse) classifications can be made on the basis of different features that distinguish some norms from others, which is the one that deserves to be selected as the 'best criterion' for dividing norms into principles and rules? Evidently, law itself has no answer for this. A classification of norms is a matter of science and, therefore, some theoretical argument (external) is indispensable.[20]

This conundrum seems to have three possible ways out: (i) to select one of the (effective) analysed differences and wait for some conventional consensus among the epistemic community (which is somehow the failure one faces nowadays); (ii) to entirely drop the classification and just give some distinct 'designations' to the categories isolated by each feature (for instance, norms with wider scope would be a term of a separate classification); or (iii) to select the most explanatory difference; that is, the one that explains by itself a greater number of (other) features.[21]

[19] Exposing the various criteria, see DM Zorrilla (n 13) 76; M Keršić and VG Yzaguirre, 'El "Peso" de los Principios: Descifrando la Metáfora' (2022) 28 *Revista Ius et Praxis* 162, 165.

[20] C Alchourrón and E Bulygin, *Normative Systems* (Vienna, Springer, 1971) 3; Å Frändberg, *The Legal Order* (Cham, Springer, 2018) 42.

[21] The second way out corresponds, more or less, to the growing tendency to drop the distinction. See eg L Alexander, 'Legal Objectivity and the Illusion of Legal Principles' in M Klatt (ed), *Institutionalized Reason: The Jurisprudence of Robert Alexy* (Oxford, Oxford University Press, 2012) 129; B Brożek, 'Legal Theories and Principles: A Theory Revisited' (2012) 17 *i-lex. Rivista di Scienze Giuridiche, Scienze Cognitive e Intelligenza Artificiale* 205, 224; GB Ratti, 'An Antinomy in Alexy's Theory of Balancing' (2023) 36 *Ratio Juris* 48, 54.

Bearing in mind the consolidated technical use of the words 'principle' and 'rule', justifying the search for proper references, the third way out seems to be the right theoretical move.

II. Alexy's Solutions and its Problems

Alexy started to divide principles and rules based on two criteria: (i) how each kind of norm regulates its object (and how it is applied); and (ii) what are the consequences when each kind of norm enters into a conflict. Regarding the former, the main idea was that principles are 'mandates of optimisation', which means that they are norms requiring something to be realised to its maximum extent and only limited by the factual and legal possibilities. On this basis, Alexy also stated that principles are norms that are applied by degrees.[22] In contrast, rules are 'definitive mandates'; that is, they require something that can only be obeyed or disobeyed without any kind of variation: an agent has to do exactly what a rule requires.[23] Regarding the latter, the main idea was that, while principles are subject to a balancing when in collision (in which one of them will circumstantially prevail), rules in conflict either accommodate an exception in order to co-exist or one of them has to be considered invalid.[24] And this was also the support for a statement that became very controversial: balancing is the way to apply principles, while rules are applied by subsumption.[25]

The first criterion was the one that received a greater chorus of criticism. Both Aarnio and Sieckmann contended that a 'mandate of optimisation' cannot be a criterion to separate principles from rules: a mandate works like a rule because either it is or it is not followed.[26] Also Poscher criticised the specificity of principles as 'mandates of optimisation'. He stressed the unworkability of such characterisation for the reason that the object to be optimised is empirical and, in such way, everything can be optimised, no matter the kind of norm by which it is regulated.[27]

[22] Alexy (n 1) 47.
[23] ibid 47.
[24] ibid 48.
[25] Alexy (n 15) 153. However, Alexy has already denied that statement at least twice: R Alexy, 'Two or Three?' in M Borowski (ed), *On the Nature of Legal Principles. ARSP-Beiheft 119* (Stuttgart, Franz Steiner, 2010) 9; R Alexy, 'Deber Ideal' in L Clérico et al (eds), *Derechos Fundamentales, Principios y Argumentación: Estudios sobre la Teoría Jurídica de Robert Alexy* (Granada, Comares, 2010) 28 [ed note: see Chapter 3 for the translated version]. Yet, the point is that such statement keeps being repeated and is seriously misleading (Alexy (n 15) 153). As will be addressed later on, balancing is an intellectual operation that is only pertinent when two (or more) norms enter into a conflict and such conflict is unresolvable by the norms of conflicts that the system contains. Yet, since being applicable is a necessary condition for a conflict between norms to be the case, then a subsumption is a contributory condition for the conflict in itself. In other words, balancing norms (in this precise technical sense) without their previous subsumption (as norms covering the case at hand) is impossible.
[26] JR Sieckmann, *Regelmodelle und Prinzipienmodelle des Rechtssystems* (Baden-Baden, Nomos, 1990) 65; A Aarnio, 'Las Reglas en Sério' in A Aarnio et al (eds), *La Normatividad del Derecho* (Barcelona, Gedisa, 1997) 27.
[27] R Poscher, 'Insights, Errors and Self-Misconceptions of the Theory of Principles' (2007) 22 *Ratio Juris* 425, 438 [ed note: see Chapter 2 for the equivalent text].

Alexy accepted the criticism and changed his original view, now presenting the distinction as based on the difference between 'mandates of optimisation' and 'mandates to be optimised': for the former the object of optimisation is the action under regulation (object of the norm), for the latter the object is the mandate itself (deontic mode of the norm).[28] By conceiving principles as 'mandates to be optimised' (even though using, for simplicity sake, the formula 'mandates of optimisation'), Alexy explains that what is to be optimised is, precisely, the deontic operator of the norm at hand.[29]

(xxiv) Alexy explains, regarding an obligation 'Op', that while 'O Opt p' reveals an empiric object of optimisation ('p'), the proposition 'O Opt Op' concerns an object of optimisation that is normative ('Op'); it is, at a meta level, the mandate itself that ought to be optimised ('Op').

Alexy moves, then, to associate such understanding of optimisation with the idea of principles as norms belonging to an ideal ought. Given that 'mandates to be optimised' are the object of balancing, then they can be designated as an ideal ought (or merely as 'ideals'): the ideal ought is exactly what should be optimised and what, through optimisation, should be transformed into a real ought.[30] Alongside such association, Alexy explains the difference between the real and the ideal oughts: while a formulation such as 'it is mandatory to help those in need' contains a real ought if it requires the addressee to help someone in need on each and every occasion, such sentence contains an ideal ought if the requirement accommodates the condition of not considering what might be in conflict.[31] Hence, the ideal ought constitutes an abstract one, not yet linked with the limited possibilities given by the empirical and legal worlds; it is, therefore, a 'prima facie' ought. And a conclusion follows: while a normative contradiction is possible at the ideal level, in the sense that both norms keep their validity, at the real level such contradiction is effectively impossible.[32]

(xxv) Considering '$O_i p$' and '$O_r p$' as respectively representing the ideal and the real oughts, Alexy presents two axioms: the first is '$\Diamond(O_i p \mathbin{\&} O_i{\sim}p)$' – it means that a contradiction at the ideal level is possible; the second is '${\sim}\Diamond(O_r p \mathbin{\&} O_r{\sim}p)$' – it means that a contradiction at the real level is impossible.

Alexy's conception of the distinction between principles and rules, even if exciting, is problematic for many reasons. The first one is that it is not understandable

[28] Alexy, 'Deber Ideal' (n 25) 16, but already in R Alexy, 'On the Structure of Legal Principles' (2000) 13 *Ratio Juris* 294, 300 [ed note: see Chapter 1 for the equivalent text].

[29] Alexy, 'Deber Ideal' (n 25) 19.

[30] R Alexy, 'Deber Ser Ideal y Optimización' in G Villa Rosas (ed), *Ensayos sobre la Teoría de los Principios y el Juicio de Proporcionalidad* (Lima, Palestra, 2020) 326 [ed note: see Chapter 4 for the translated version].

[31] ibid 319.

[32] ibid 319.

what makes a specific norm a 'mandate to be optimised' (dropping already the initial formulation 'mandates of optimisation'). If a norm is a requirement for its regulation to be taken to the maximum extent possible (in view of the empirical and legal limits existent), then something in its structure has to cause such 'behaviour'. Without identifying the feature that causes a norm to belong to the class of 'mandates to be optimised' one cannot know which norms are principles and which ones are rules. And this is somehow proven by the extension Alexy himself gives to the class of principles: why each and every norm conferring a fundamental right is a principle is something that remains unknown.[33] Is it the case that norms such as 'the prohibition on expelling nationals from their own country' and 'freedom of the press is guaranteed', both conferring fundamental rights, are both principles? And is it the case that a norm conferring the 'right to obtain a copy of an application submitted to a public service' is a rule if imposed at a statutory level, but a principle if included in the constitution? Nobody knows. What is known is that the extension of the category 'principles' is obscure: as far as one can see, no criterion has been provided in order to know what makes a norm a 'mandate to be optimised'.

The second reason is intimately related to the previous one. When Alexy adopted the idea, at a later stage, that principles are 'mandates to be optimised', he clearly stated that the object of optimisation is not the object regulated by the norm; it is, rather, the mandate itself. On such a view, for instance, what is supposed to be taken to the maximum extent is not the action 'to express oneself', but the 'permission to express oneself'; that is, the deontic modalisation of that action. Yet, it seems rather doubtful what might be to 'optimise' a deontic modalisation. As far as it is known, the deontic modalisation of an action is a 'normative predication' without any variation in its intensity (to permit more or less?).[34] For instance, a 'prohibition of torture' only requires the addressee not to carry out any possible token of such action. And from the prohibition follows that whatever constitutes torture of a person is something that has been removed from the realm of the legally permissible and, consequently, that someone who tortures another is violating the law (possibly becoming subject to sanctions foreseen in other norms). So, it is not clear what it is to 'optimise' such prohibition since it behaves in the same way however its antecedent is filled: the act at hand is, always and similarly,

[33] On fundamental rights norms as principles, the mainstream conception of the Kiel School, see Alexy (n 1) 80; JR Sieckmann, 'Los Derechos Fundamentales como Principios' in JR Sieckmann (ed), *La Teoría Principialista de los Derechos Fundamentales* (Madrid, Marcial Pons, 2011) 27; Borowski (n 15) 47; M Klatt and M Meister, *The Constitutional Structure of Proportionality* (Oxford, Oxford University Press, 2012) 27.

[34] Even the idea that optimising a mandate is to transform it from an 'ideal' to a 'real ought' – R Alexy, 'On Balancing and Subsumption. A Structural Comparison' (2003) 16 *Ratio Juris* 433, 300 – looks unlikely to be very helpful. On the one hand, passing from the ideal ought to the real one is just to apply one norm 'all norms considered', which is a transformation strictly connected with the contextual reasons that justify its prevalence: it is not the mandate that is optimised; it is the object of such mandate that is somehow taken as prevalent. But, on the other hand, this is not specific to principles: since rules are defeasible as well, such transformation also happens with them.

not permitted (and just that).[35] Accordingly, it seems that Poscher is right here: the object of optimisation, if there is one, is the content regulated by the norm.[36]

And this leads to the third reason, that mixes the first two. 'Ought to be' norms establish a goal to be achieved and, for such reason, they require that something has to be realised to the maximum extent possible. These norms are effective 'mandates of optimisation' (in Alexyan terminology), since they determine not only that the agent has to carry out all actions suitable to reach the goal at hand but also that such agent has to carry out them in order to go as far as possible (and such variation is intrinsic to the norm individually considered). The example already presented of a norm such as the one expressed in 'the state shall promote an ecologically balanced human living environment' shows this clearly. However, it also shows two other aspects relevant for the present discussion. First, and as stated before, the adoption of a criterion such as the 'compliance by degrees' would lead to the category of principles being the same as 'ought to be' norms, which is a result totally distant from Alexy's conception of the former. Second, the object of optimisation is definitely not the deontic operator: to do whatever it takes in order to promote an ecologically balanced human living environment cannot be more or less required; it is just required and the state is under a very common and basic obligation to act. What is capable of variation here is the object of the norm, specifically how much the state is achieving in order to reach the goal. So, it seems that not even in norms that could be properly qualified as 'mandates of optimisation' one can find any room for maintaining that the object of optimisation is the mandate itself.

A fourth reason for considering Alexy's conception of the distinction to be problematic comes from the difficulty of understanding what is the connection between being a 'mandate to be optimised' and an ideal ought or, in other words, what makes a 'mandate to be optimised', it seems by definition, a command belonging to the ideal level of law. Once it is understood that an ideal ought is, in Alexy's conception, an abstract ought for the reason of being deprived (abstracted) of the possible empirical and legal obstacles, it becomes puzzling why a 'mandate to be optimised' implies such an ideal ought (and vice versa).[37] On the one hand, it seems that one thing has no necessary connection with the other: it has never been explained why abstracting competing norms (or empirical limits) would amount to a norm being one that is somehow realised in various degrees. And such connection is difficult to grasp: abstracting from competing norms plays on the field of considering a norm regardless of others and while varying by degrees is a matter intrinsic to the content of the norm in itself. That is, they are aspects

[35] And this should not be confused with the variation by degrees that, excluding 'ought to be' norms, follows from the various conflicts a norm enters into and not from the morphological nature of the norm at hand (isolatedly considered): either such norm defeats or is defeated in the conflict and, thus, it will be applied or not regardless of the 'intensity of the prohibition'.

[36] R Poscher, 'Theory of a Phantom: The Principles Theory's Futile Quest for Its Object' in JA de Oliveira et al (eds), *Alexy's Theory of Law* (Stuttgart, Franz Steiner, 2015) 134 [ed note: see Chapter 4 for the equivalent text]. Apparently, Alexy also conceded on this. See Alexy (n 30) 326.

[37] Alexy (n 30) 325.

belonging to totally different ontological and methodological standpoints. On the other hand, and while observing any normative system in the way it is linguistically formulated by normative authorities, it is not clear (mainly in its content) either what makes a norm an ideal ought or what makes it a 'mandate to be optimised'. Following Alexy's equivalence, the 'cause' would be common.[38] Yet, this is not explained and, moreover, given the 'distance' between one thing and the other, it is also not easy to figure out.

(xxvi) Alexy presents the equivalence 'O_r Opt p ↔ O_i p' in which the real ought to optimise 'p' implies the ideal ought to 'p' and vice versa; however, not only is it unclear what makes a norm an 'O_r Opt p' or an 'O_i p', but also why they are to be considered equivalent: an ideal ought regarding 'p' only means that such norm has not yet faced its legal and empirical limits; so, it is not discernible why a norm in such conditions would be, by definition, a 'mandate of optimisation' (which seems to be totally unrelated).

A fifth reason is the one associated with the idea that an ideal ought is at the same time a principle and a norm with the condition of not taking into account its empirical and legal obstacles. Intrinsically related to what has been said above about the common defeasibility of principles and rules, the problem is that Alexy's proposition depends on the truth of rules being indefeasible, which seems to be very difficult to demonstrate. Inversely, every norm can be seen with such condition and it is not true, as Alexy says, that a conflict of rules in which they both maintain their validity is impossible.[39] As seen before, rules are norms that can enter into conflicts that are unresolvable by norms of conflicts and, therefore, they are also norms that in a balancing scenario can be circumstantially defeated without being removed from the system (exactly like principles).

III. Poscher's Solutions and their Problems

It seems that Poscher has several good points in his criticism of Alexy's distinction between principles and rules. Yet, the significant number of good points is inversely proportional to the solutions he proposes to explain what might differentiate those two kinds of norms. It is a fact that Poscher assumes the existence of that division and accepts that some norms are principles and some are rules.[40] His approach to the topic is, though, essentially negative: Poscher mostly stresses the

[38] Which is no other than the consequence of assuming a logical equivalence: if A implies B and B implies A, whatever causes A necessarily causes B. On the unclearness of the operator 'Opt', see JP Alonso, 'The Logical Structure of Principles in Alexy's Theory' (2016) 28 *Revus* 53, 58.

[39] Alexy (n 30) 319.

[40] Although he does not address the so-called 'exclusion theorem', as is sustained by Alexy (n 34) 295: from each and every single norm of a system one can say that either it is a principle or a rule (there is no third category). On the 'exclusion theorem', see C Bäcker, 'Reglas, Principios y Derrotabilidad' (2014) 37 *DOXA. Cuadernos de Filosofía del Derecho* 31, 32. On Poscher's acceptance of the category of principles, see Poscher (n 36) 147.

flaws he recognises in this foundational part of the 'theory of principles' without elaborating much on possible alternative solutions. It would be false, however, to say that Poscher is totally mute on the constructive side of the debate. Actually, he says that the difference between principles and rules is gradual and not structural. And he subsequently says that such gradeability can be found in the dimension of the norm's need for concretisation and its relevance to the legal system as a whole.[41] Poscher then says that norms can be called principles if they are particularly important, stressing that that is (more) the case when their impact is not restricted to one area of law.[42]

Poscher's solutions for the distinction seem to have low explanatory power. Two reasons support this assessment. The first one is related to gradeability and is somehow common to all weak theses: those maintaining that the difference between principles and rules is just a matter of mere degree.[43] The general point is that, whenever one assigns to something a quantitative difference, it is crucial to identify which is the property (in variation) that gives the progression at hand. Without such identification, the difference of degree has no grounds and cannot be sustained.[44] On the other hand, sustaining differences of degree also implies the demonstration that no qualitative difference occurs at the opposite points of the scale.[45] And if it seems that Poscher never addressed this latter point, what is more relevant is that, regarding the former, Poscher assigns the 'variation' to inconsequential or vague properties: (i) importance; (ii) need for concretisation; and (iii) abstraction.

Regarding the first of these properties, importance of a norm is not an internal property of such norm; it is the moral or social value a community of agents assigns to a specific normative content. And this implies that being a principle or a rule not only becomes totally dependent on what is the object of regulation but also that the norm's qualification as one or the other diverges in accordance with how agents value such object. Accordingly, besides a significant lack of certainty about qualifying a norm as a principle or a rule, it also follows that the gradeability has nothing to do with the norm in itself.[46] On the other hand, the insufficiency of

[41] Poscher (n 36) 148. Also, stressing that the traditional sense of principles (that he defends) is related to abstraction and importance, R Poscher, 'Resuscitation of a Phantom? On Robert Alexy's Latest Attempt to Save His Concept of Principle' (2020) 33 *Ratio Juris* 134, 147 [ed note: see Chapter 6 for the equivalent text].

[42] Poscher (n 36) 147.

[43] See eg Alchourrón and Bulygin (n 20) 81. See also N MacCormick, *Legal Reasoning and Legal Theory* (Oxford, Clarendon Press, 1978) 260; A Jakab, 'Re-Defining Principles as "Important Rules" – A Critique of Robert Alexy' in M Borowski (ed), *On the Nature of Legal Principles* (Stuttgart, Franz Steiner, 2010) 152.

[44] For instance, Alchourrón and Bulygin (n 20) 81 speak about a difference in 'generality'. However, what might be referenced by such term is totally indecipherable.

[45] As Moniz Lopes once said, discussing this exact same topic, *ad absurdum* the 'difference between humans and chimpanzees is also one of degree (degree of brain activity, bipedalism, body hair and so on)'. See Lopes (n 2) 477.

[46] Which also means that this weak difference is not a difference between norms: it is a difference on the beliefs of agents.

the criterion is not solved with the idea that importance is more significant when the norm at hand is not restricted to an area of law. Areas of law are in some cases controversial and, therefore, it would be rather imprecise to know when a norm is or not restricted to one of them. Moreover, since that particular importance comes from not being restricted to an area of law, it follows that the possibility of 'localised principles' is being denied.[47]

Regarding the second property, it is difficult to grasp what might be the 'need for concretisation'. It seems that one is dealing with a different property than the one analysed before: being able to be concretised. But if the idea of a variation by degrees based on the need for concretisation is somehow related to how much a norm depends on others in order to regulate an action (as it seems to be), then the property either has no object or moves the class of principles to norms that create gaps. A norm such as the one expressed in 'everyone has the right to vote' cannot be exercised by the right-holder while the state does not create, through other norms, the whole electoral apparatus. In that way, such a norm is in need of concretisation.[48] Yet, since a category such as this one would be senseless within the present topic, it seems that Poscher is not making reference to this kind of norm. And once this understanding is removed, one faces the fact that no norm is in need of concretisation. Whatever might be the content of a norm, its applicability (not application, for defeasibility reasons) is guaranteed whenever its antecedent is filled. So, either it is not, and the problem has no pertinency here, or it is, and then the norm at hand regulates the case and no concretisation is needed.

(xxvii) 'No one can profit from her own wrong' ('$o_x^1 \vee o_x^2 \vee \ldots \vee o_x^n \Rightarrow F_{\{PA\}}\ x_{\{SA\}}$', in which 'x = profiting from one's own wrongdoing') is concretised by 'whoever kills a family member loses the right to inheritance'.

(xxviii) Yet, a norm such as '$o_x^1 \vee o_x^2 \vee \ldots \vee o_x^n \Rightarrow F_{\{PA\}}\ x_{\{SA\}}$' is not in need of concretisation: whenever some case matches 'o_x^1' or 'o_x^2', the consequence 'F x' applies; and it is enough to solve the case.

Regarding the third property, 'abstraction' is a term often used by the defenders of weak theses in order to say that principles are more 'something' than rules and, consequently, that it is in this property that one finds the progression by degrees typical of those theses. Yet, what is meant by 'abstraction' is not always the same among legal theorists: it sometimes means a more or less vague idea of distance from the object of regulation, just as it also means a norm with a significantly wide scope or even a norm that is applied on multiple occasions.[49] Given the almost

[47] Which would be the case with norms commonly accepted as principles in undisputed areas of law such as criminal law or tax law: for instance, for the first, *nullum crimen sine lege*; and, for the second, the prohibition of retroactive taxes.

[48] Presupposing that such norm is in a constitution, just conferring the fundamental right. On the need for concretisation with the right to vote, see C Wellman, *An Approach to Rights* (Dordrecht, Springer, 1997) 61; R Martin, *System of Rights* (Oxford, Clarendon Press, 2003) 47.

[49] And what is valid for 'abstraction' is also valid for 'indeterminacy' or even 'generality', which seems to be more or less the same 'undefined thing' in some literature. On the topic and the terminological confusion, see Alexy (n 1) 46.

laconic way in which Poscher makes reference to this property, it is not clear what he means when he says that principles are more abstract than rules. A caritative reading requires that it be understood as a reference to the fact that principles are norms with a wider scope than rules and, if that is the case, it is definitely a difference one effectively finds in norms that are often called principles (as seen before).

The second reason for the low explanatory power of Poscher's solutions is that a variation by degrees based on more than one criterion always poses the traditional problems assigned to multidimensional vague words: namely, that each criterion of variation can manifest itself with different intensities and that they can even have contradictory outputs.[50] So, even if it is a strict theoretical argument, nothing prevents a norm from being of little abstraction and enormous importance. In such cases, it becomes totally undefined whether the norm at hand is a principle or a rule.[51] Of course, one can think about each one of the criteria as a sufficient condition, which would imply that the qualification as a principle ascertains when a norm is evidently important or manifestly abstract (or in objective need of concretisation). Yet, such a strategy also has unpleasant consequences: there would be no uniformity within the category and it would be a category whose members could have opposite relevant properties.[52] Everything considered, it seems that Poscher is a sort of a sceptic. It appears to fit with his approach that: (i) there is no significant relevance in a norm being a principle or a rule; and (ii) such qualifications are used in legal science just to highlight some varying yet inconsequential aspects of norms.

IV. The Indeterminacy in the Variable 'Action'

A norm is a unit of a normative system and, using a quite reasonable criterion of individuation, entails the minimal necessary conditions for regulating behaviour.[53] Hence, it can be said that each and every norm comprehends an action-type (or various types, determinate or not), a deontic modalisation of such action and, at least, since the normative authority can add other conditions, the condition of opportunity to carry out a token of the action foreseen.[54] Since a norm regulates

[50] On the structure of multidimensional vagueness, see JJ Moreso, 'Marry Me a Little: How Much Precision is Enough in Law?' (2017) 9 *Droit & Philosophie* 45, 46; A Escher, 'When It is Vague What is Vague: Identifying Vagueness' in D Duarte et al (eds), *Legal Interpretation and Scientific Knowledge* (Cham, Springer, 2019) 173.

[51] A criticism valid for all defenders of multiple criteria. See eg R Guastini, *La Sintaxis del Derecho* (Madrid, Marcial Pons, 2016) 239; G Pino, *Teoria Analitica del Diritto. La Norma Giuridica* (Pisa, Edizioni ETS, 2016) 88.

[52] Which would be the case with a norm that is 'very important' and of 'little abstraction' and another one 'without importance' but 'very abstract'. They would both be members of the category of principles.

[53] Following Raz, requirements of individuation. See J Raz, *The Concept of a Legal System*, 2nd edn (Oxford, Clarendon Press, 1980) 140.

[54] On the condition of the opportunity, GH von Wright, *Norm and Action* (London, Routledge and Kegan Paul, 1963) 74. Specifying the condition of opportunity as a condition regarding the internal capacity of the agent to perform the action foreseen, D Duarte, 'Rights as Formal Combinations of Normative Variables' (2023) 51 *Revus* 1, 6.

the behaviour of someone, then a norm also entails a universe of agents. And, once one adds correlativity between agents, be it considered absolute or relative (present in all norms or just in some of them), then two subjective universes have to be assigned to the structure of norms (one for primary addressees and another for secondary ones).[55] Taking this all into account, a norm is seen here as the conjunction of these five 'morphological' elements: each one is a necessary condition for behaviour to be regulated; dropping one of them makes such regulation impossible.

(xxix) in order to regulate the action 'to smoke', a normative authority has to decide which is the deontic modalisation of such action; when it decides that it is forbidden, then a universe of addressees becomes targeted by such prohibition; however, such prohibition correlates that universe with another, encompassing the agents that the normative authority might choose (or, at least, those that get the corresponding impact); simultaneously, the prohibition is only applicable whenever there is an opportunity to exercise the action 'to smoke'.

(xxx) a structure such as '$o_x \Rightarrow O_{\{PA\}}\, x_{\{SA\}}$', in which 'x' stands for the action (here, to smoke), shows that the five 'morphological' elements are necessary conditions for regulating the behaviour at hand; if the action-type, its deontic modalisation and the universe of primary addressees {PA} are more or less obvious, the condition of opportunity and the universe of secondary addressees {SA} are logically implied: the former since a token is only the case when possible and the latter under the assumption of the 'correlativity axiom'.

Norms can be classified under the most diverse criteria. Usually, such classifications follow from differences one can observe in the way each element is effectively filled by the normative authority. In other words, each one of those elements behaves as a 'norm variable' and their different possibilities of content lead to criteria with which one can classify norms. For instance, dividing norms into permissive, mandatory and prohibitive is simply to classify norms based on the content inserted in the deontic operator: a norm belongs to one of those classes in accordance with the deontic modalisation adopted for the action-type at hand.[56] In another example, a norm is classified as hypothetical or categorical if its antecedent just has the condition of opportunity to realise a token of the action-type or has additional conditions created by the normative authority. If this classification shows that there are no 'pure' categorical norms, it also shows that the classification depends on the way the variable 'antecedent' has been formulated.[57]

[55] On correlativity of agents (in fundamental rights), see R Alexy (n 1) 111. Defending absolute correlativity (specifically, the 'correlativity axiom'), as it is also presupposed here, M Kramer, 'Rights Without Trimmings' in M Kramer et al (eds), *A Debate Over Rights* (Oxford, Oxford University Press, 1998) 24.

[56] Von Wright (n 54) 71; JJ Moreso and J Vilajosana, *Introducción a la Teoría del Derecho* (Madrid, Marcial Pons, 2004) 76.

[57] Von Wright (n 54) 74; Alchourrón and Bulygin (n 20) 42. Speaking about categorical norms as prescriptions for any possible circumstance as an empty set of facts (which would imply the awkward

(xxxi) A structure such as '$o_x \Rightarrow O_{\{PA\}} \, x_{\{SA\}}$' represents a mandatory norm; it is by changing the deontic modalisation to a prohibition ('$o_x \Rightarrow F_{\{PA\}} \, x_{\{SA\}}$') or to a permission ('$o_x \Rightarrow P_{\{PA\}} \, x_{\{SA\}}$') that the system will have a prohibitive or a permissive norm; the classification follows from the deontic operator's content.

(xxxii) A structure such as '$o_x \Rightarrow F_{\{PA\}} \, x_{\{SA\}}$' represents a categorical norm: its antecedent only has the condition of the opportunity to exercise the action; a structure such as '$o_x \wedge (cs) \Rightarrow F_{\{PA\}} \, x_{\{SA\}}$' represents a hypothetical norm: its antecedent has, besides that condition, another one explicitly formulated.

An important classification of norms is the one that divides general and individual norms; a classification totally related to the way the norm's universe of agents is composed. Usually, such classification is conceived as concerning only one universe of agents.[58] However, once correlativity is assumed as an element of norms, as it is here, then such classification has to be conceived as encompassing the two subjective universes mentioned before. Accordingly, it can be said that a norm is individual whenever both universes are designed as closed classes, which means that there is determinacy regarding who are the members of both classes, primary and secondary addressees. And by 'determinacy' it is meant here, despite epistemic difficulties, that one can know who will be the members of each one of the universes at the moment of enactment.[59] Inversely, a norm is general whenever one or both universes have indeterminate members, no matter if such indeterminacy exists regarding a specific class of some agents (obviously open) or the whole universality of agents. Therefore, indeterminacy of one universe of agents leads to what might be called 'general norms'.

(xxxiii) A structure such as '$o_x \Rightarrow O_{\{PA\}} \, x_{\{SA\}}$' contains two sets of addressees (agents). A set, for instance {PA}, is determinate whenever it is possible to know, at the moment of enactment, who will be its members; for instance {Tristan} or {citizens registered now in Lisbon}. A set is indeterminate whenever that knowledge is impossible; for instance {citizens}, {everyone} or {workers}.

(xxxiv) A norm such as '$o_x \Rightarrow O_{\{citizens\}} \, x_{\{everyone\}}$' has two indeterminate sets; it is general. A norm such as '$o_x \Rightarrow O_{\{State\}} \, x_{\{everyone\}}$' has one indeterminate set; it is general. A norm such as '$o_x \Rightarrow O_{\{everyone\}} \, x_{\{Tristan\}}$' has one

outcome of a norm in permanent application), Navarro and Rodríguez (n 18) 179. On the relevancy of 'non-conditions' as a negation of 'pure' categorical norms, Duarte (n 5) 47.

[58] See eg GH von Wright (n 54) 77; A Ross, *Directives and Norms* (London, Routledge and Kegan Paul, 1968) 110.

[59] Exactly what J Bentham, *On Laws in General* (first published 1782, London, The Athlone Press, 1970) 313 has called 'assignable'. Also, on indeterminacy of addressees, see CS Nino, *Introducción al Análisis del Derecho*, 2nd edn (Barcelona, Ariel, 2003) 77. The main point of inversion that follows from two universes of addressees is that one has to conceive whether indeterminacy in one of them is a sufficient condition for generality. And that seems to be the best solution: the opposite one would lead to absurd results, such as qualifying as an individual norm the one in 'the state shall promote an ecologically balanced human living environment' (which evidently correlates the state with an indeterminate set of agents).

indeterminate set; it is general. Yet, a norm such as '$o_x \Rightarrow O_{\{State\}}\ x_{\{Tristan\}}$' has two determinate sets; it is individual, and it is irrelevant for the qualification that (in)determinacy happens in {PA} or in {SA}.

A different classification can be also based on the difference between determinacy and indeterminacy; now, regarding the occasions to which a norm is applicable. Under this criterion, a norm can be abstract or concrete. It is abstract whenever it is applicable to indeterminate occasions, which means that one does not know, at the moment of enactment, when will the norm be applicable. Inversely, a norm is concrete whenever its applicability is established for a specific occasion (or for a set of determinate occasions).[60] For a norm to be concrete, consequently, the normative authority has to close the norm's antecedent in some way. Usually, such operation is done by adding a condition related to the occasion (or a set of defined occasions) to which the norm is applicable: the opportunity to realise a token of the action-type is only relevant on the occasion foreseen. Therefore, indeterminacy of applicability occasions leads to what might be called 'abstract norms'.

(xxxv) In '$o_x \Rightarrow O_{\{PA\}}\ x_{\{SA\}}$', the exercise of 'x' only depends on an opportunity for 'x'; thus, it is an abstract norm: on each and every (indeterminate) occasion of opportunity, the norm applies.

(xxxvi) In '$o_x \wedge$ (today at lunch) $\Rightarrow O_{\{PA\}}\ x_{\{SA\}}$', the obligation is only applicable to 'today at lunch' (only opportunities at such time are relevant); because it determinates occasion, it is a concrete norm.

Yet, a third classification based on the opposition between determinacy and indeterminacy can be assigned to norms. And it concerns exactly the action-type set out in the consequent. A norm can foresee a determinate action-type (or a set of determinate ones), but it can also include indeterminate actions in its consequent. The relevance of a consequent with such indeterminate actions is that it creates an antecedent in which the condition of the opportunity to realise a token also becomes undefined: it is not only that one has different actions for which there must be an opportunity to act; moreover, one does not know which are those opportunities, for the reason that it is also unknown which types of actions are covered by the consequent. And since each type of action has its own opportunity condition, this leads to an antecedent with disjunctive (but inclusive) conditions of opportunity and always with the disjunctive condition of indeterminacy: 'o_x^n'. A norm that has an antecedent with such condition is a norm one can call a principle.[61] Therefore, under the present approach, indeterminacy of action-types leads to 'principles'.

[60] This classification (abstract or concrete) corresponds to the dichotomy 'general or particular' in von Wright (n 54) 80. On the other hand, it seems that abstraction and concreteness have nothing to do with discretion, as Ross seems to maintain. See Ross (n 58) 113. The point is related to whether examples of the action at hand are restricted to one occasion (or a set of indetermined ones) or simply performable whenever the agent has the mentioned opportunity. And for such alternativity it seems irrelevant whether the agent has discretion or not in the perfomance of the said action.

[61] The present criterion for distinguishing principles from rules is similar (or, at least, leads to similar outcomes) to the one Moniz Lopes (n 2) 479 presented, based on the genericity of antecedents,

(xxxvii) A structure such as '$o_x^1 \vee o_x^2 \vee \ldots \vee o_x^n \Rightarrow F_{\{PA\}}\, x_{\{SA\}}$' matches the sentence 'no one can profit from her own wrong' in which 'x = profiting from one's own wrongdoing'; since 'profiting from one's own wrongdoing' constitutes a set of indeterminate actions-type (as seen before), each one of them has its own condition of opportunity; moreover, given that indeterminacy, it is even unknown which those action-types might be.

(xxxviii) Accordingly, each condition is a sufficient condition to trigger the norm: an opportunity of obtaining advantage occurs either after one has burned down her own restaurant (to get insurance) or killed her grandfather (to get inheritance); such indeterminacy about action-types can be represented in that structure by the disjunctive condition 'o_x^{n}', which shows unknown opportunities that also trigger the norm.

(xxxix) Bearing all this in mind, it follows that a condition 'o_x^{n}' at the antecedent is, under the present criterion, the mark of a norm that is a principle. It necessarily follows from the indeterminacy of action-types in the consequent. Accordingly, a norm that is a rule does not contain such condition; that is what happens with '$o_x \Rightarrow F_{\{PA\}}\, x_{\{SA\}}$' such as, for instance, the structure of 'it is forbidden to smoke' (x = 'to smoke').

A proposal such as classifying as principles norms with indeterminacy on the actions deontically modalised fits the methodological requirement previously assumed: to be the criterion that is the most explicative regarding the effective differences allocated to the possible distinction between principles and rules. Actually, a norm with disjunctive opportunity conditions, and including one like 'o_x^{n}', is a norm with a significantly wide scope. And, for that reason, it is also a norm that is particularly prone to enter into conflicts with other norms: the extension of its antecedent increases overlapping possibilities and, therefore, increases the probability of deontic contradictions. Even though having a wide scope and being more or less apt to enter into conflicts are, by themselves, mere differences of degree, indeterminacy of action-types is a qualitative difference.[62] So, a norm either is applicable to determinate or to indeterminate action-types. And, as happens with 'generality' and 'abstraction', here neither gradeability nor any sort of progression in (in)determinacy can be found.

an approach also followed by JS Sampaio, 'Proportionality in Its Narrow Sense and Measuring the Intensity of Restrictions on Fundamental Rights' in D Duarte and JS Sampaio (eds), *Proportionality in Law* (Cham, Springer, 2018) 77. Yet, besides not being totally certain that genericity leads to disjunctive alternative conditions, two reasons justify the preference for the present approach: (i) while genericity seems to merely take the issue to alternative disjunctive conditions, the main point here rests exactly on the difference made by the disjunctive condition 'o_x^{n}'; (ii) the present solution seems to be simplier and more elegant.

[62] Which denies the Razian claim (based on the criterion of the specificity of the types of behaviour) that the difference is merely one of degree. See Raz (n 1) 838. Actually, if something can be more or less specific, the same cannot be said about something being more or less determinate: one either can or cannot identify, at the moment of utterence, the types of actions described in a sentence.

(xl) A structure such as '$o_x \Rightarrow O_{\{PA\}}\ x_{\{SA\}}$' shows a rule, since 'x' is a determinate action-type (or a set of determinate ones); a structure such as '$o_x^1 \vee o_x^2 \vee \ldots \vee o_x^n \Rightarrow F_{\{PA\}}\ x_{\{SA\}}$' shows a principle, since 'x' is an indeterminate set of action-types.

(xli) The fact that 'x' is determinate or indeterminate is not a matter of degree: one either is capable or not of identifying the action-types contained in the consequence; accordingly, there is no variation by degree from a determinate action-type to indeterminate action-types.

A classification of norms based on the determinacy or indeterminacy of the action-types set out in its consequent, essentially due to the effects that such duality has on the antecedent, creates a division grounded on a structural difference between norms; one is normally able to say whether a norm belongs to the class of principles or to the class of rules. Even though this also leads us to accept a sort of 'exclusion theorem', from such proposition it does not follow that there are no penumbra cases or that it is always easy to make the inherent qualification. As a matter of fact, there are serious problems coming from the difficulties about what an 'action-type' is in itself. Besides the already known complexities surrounding the individuation of action, sometimes it is not clear whether a more or less 'vague' action-type is not effectively a set of indeterminate actions.[63] Yet, this is not a reason to drop the criterion. As happens in many normative situations, it is not the occurrence of penumbra cases that threatens a distinction built on a reasonably clear criterion.

(xlii) While 'profiting from one's own wrongdoing' or 'expressing oneself' are sentences that clearly make reference to indeterminate action-types, 'to smoke' or 'to sleep' point to very clear determinate actions.

(xliii) However, such clarity does not prevent penumbra cases; for instance, 'to teach': although teaching is just transmitting knowledge, 'showing a flag' or 'reading aloud a book' can both be teaching.

On the other hand, the criterion used has a clear expression in the structure of norms and allows us to grasp what is effectively at stake. As seen before, the indeterminacy of types of action projects itself on the antecedent through the disjunctive 'o_x^n' condition, representing the indeterminate (and unknown) conditions of opportunity (for action-types) under which the consequent of the norm is triggered. Such representation seems to give a clear picture of the specific structure of the antecedent of principles and avoids the more or less vague idea of an open antecedent.[64] Actually, it is not clear what is meant by an 'open antecedent', since such an element of norms can be open through diverse ways and some of them

[63] On the problems (and theories about) individuation of action, see eg L Davis, *Theory of Action* (Englewood Cliffs NJ, Prentice-Hall, 1979) 28; L O'Brien, *Philosophy of Action* (New York, Palgrave Macmillan, 2015) 29.

[64] As defended by M Atienza and JR Manero, *Theory of Legal Sentences* (New York, Springer, 1998) 8.

have nothing to do with what might enter the class of principles: for instance, an open antecedent based on a contributory condition.[65] Yet, and as happens with the present approach, an antecedent can be also open when each condition is a sufficient one.

(xliv) In a norm structure such as '$o_x \wedge (m) \Rightarrow F_{\{PA\}}\, x_{\{SA\}}$'), the antecedent is open if the condition 'm', namely for linguistic reasons (vagueness), gives, in borderline cases, the choice '$m \vee \sim m$'.
(xlv) In a norm structure such as '$o_x^1 \wedge o_x^2 \wedge \ldots \wedge o_x^n \Rightarrow F_{\{PA\}}\, x_{\{SA\}}$', the antecedent is open because each one of its conditions is a contributory one.
(xlvi) In a norm structure such as '$o_x^1 \vee o_x^2 \vee \ldots \vee o_x^n \Rightarrow F_{\{PA\}}\, x_{\{SA\}}$', the antecedent is also open but each one of its conditions is a sufficient one.

Sustaining the distinction between principles and rules on the indeterminacy or determinacy of the actions implies that all 'ought to be' norms are, by definition, principles.[66] Since such norms are understood as those that define a state of affairs to be achieved and do not describe in a closed way which actions are mandatory to achieve the goal at hand, it follows that actions appropriate for the goal (exactly those that are under the requirement) are indeterminate.[67] Such nature of those norms is not even denied when, for empirical reasons, only one action-type is appropriate to reach the goal: since different and indeterminate actions are abstractly usable and normatively foreseen, the norm at hand clearly surpasses the 'indeterminate action-types' test. On the other hand, a possible difference in the degree of discretion here plays no role: indeterminacy of action in 'ought to be' norms (also principles) implies the disjunctive condition 'o_x^n' and that is enough.[68]

(xlvii) In the norm sentence 'the state shall promote an ecologically balanced human living environment' one finds an 'ought to be' norm: there is a goal to be reached through indeterminate action-types.
(xlviii) Since 'x' contains different action-types, its structure is '$o_x^1 \vee o_x^2 \vee \ldots \vee o_x^n \Rightarrow O_{\{PA\}}\, x_{\{SA\}}$' and the antecedent contains the disjunctive condition 'o_x^n'.
(xlix) Indeterminacy in 'x' it is not about banning plastics to a greater or lesser extent or requiring agents to reduce carbon emissions in one way or another; it is indeterminacy about which action-types should be used to get 'x'.

[65] As remarked by GB Ratti, *El Gobierno de las Normas* (Madrid, Marcial Pons, 2013) 166. So, the point is also that it seems to be insufficient to speak about finite and closed antecedents (rules) as opposed to an open list of properties (principles), as Atienza and Manero (n 64) 9 do, since one does not understand either what provokes such outcome or how the difference expresses itself in the antecedent of norms.

[66] Circumscribing principles to 'ought to be' norms, see Zurek, T et al, 'Reasoning with Principles' (2022) 210 *Expert Systems with Applications* 1, 4.

[67] As mentioned in n 12.

[68] Ratti (n 65) 167 minimises the idea of norms with alternatives of action, saying that all norms somehow include a sort of discretion. The point is that he seems to mix two different things: (i) one is the various ways by which one can perform an instance of an action-type; (ii) another, completely different, is to have indeterminate types of action (which, in some way, lead to the scheme that implicitly he also acknowledges '$O(p \vee q \vee \varphi)$'). On the other hand, Ratti also maintains that the difference between 'ought to do' and 'ought

V. Principles as a Mere Category of Norms

A difference between principles and norms based on the determinacy or indeterminacy of the action-types leads to accommodating within the distinction some other differences that necessarily follow from such criterion. Simultaneously, it implies refusing other possible (and alleged) differences that have been claimed to be so in the literature. As to the former, indeterminacy of action-types creates an open antecedent through the disjunctive condition '$o_x^{\,n}$' and, therefore, it causes the norm at hand not only to have a significantly wide scope but also to be a norm that is particularly vulnerable to normative conflicts. Such correlated features explain, accordingly, why norms that are principles are often in conflict and, moreover, that they are in conflicts unresolvable by norms of conflicts. Actually, their antecedent's structure is a fertile land for conflicts of the partial-partial type, a specific kind of conflict to which there are no norms of conflicts available.[69]

(1) A structure such as '$o_x^{\,1} \vee o_x^{\,2} \vee \ldots \vee o_x^{\,n} \Rightarrow P_{\{PA\}}\, x_{\{SA\}}$' in which '$x$ = express oneself' stands for the norm in 'everyone has freedom of expression'; a structure such as '$o_y^{\,1} \vee o_y^{\,2} \vee \ldots \vee o_y^{\,n} \Rightarrow F_{\{PA\}}\, y_{\{SA\}}$' in which '$y$ = harming somebody's reputation' stands for the norm in 'it is forbidden to harm personal reputation'.

to be' norms is merely a difference of the syntactical formulation (ibid 166). One can obviously think about a formulation in which 'O (p V q V φ)') is more or less exhaustively written (as a 'ought to do' sentence), creating a text for 'φ' such as, for instance, 'other actions that are also possible'. Yet, this does not deny that the difference makes sense. In a consequent with an desired state of affairs reachable through indeterminate types of action one can always recognise the definition of a goal. And such goal is absent in a 'ought to do' norm: in 'ought to do' norms, action is in the content of the norm and the goal is whatever it might be; in 'ought to be' norms, the goal is in the content of the norm and action is whatever it might be (although those indeterminate actions are what is being indirectly required). If this makes all the difference, it also shows that the key point is the goal and not the interchangeability between states of affairs and actions. Actually, Ratti's examples are unfortunate (ibid 166): 'it is mandatory to work on workdays' is not the same as 'to stay at work on workdays', not only because both sentences contain 'ought to do' norms ('workdays ⇒ O work' and 'workdays ⇒ O to stay at work'), but also because they require different actions (to work and to stay at the workplace, not necessarily working). In none of these norms does one find the specific property of 'ought to be' norms: the definition of a goal to be somehow achieved. The pair 'men and women are equal' and 'it is forbidden to discriminate between men and women' is also unfortunate, but for other reasons. The former sentence is a description. But, if it is to be understood as a prescription, as it should, than it is a clear case of an 'ought to be' norm, imposing a state of affairs to be achieved, no matter how. And if this prescriptive reading is the right understanding of such sentence, then it has nothing to do with 'it is forbidden to discriminate between men and women' since this latter sentence contains an 'ought to do' norm that forbids carrying out any (indeterminate) action that could treat men and women in an inequal manner. As is visible, they are not examples of interchangeability between states of affairs and actions: each norm requires a different thing; the first one, to promote equality; the second, to forebear from creating (more) inequality (which can also be a way to promote equality, yet does not exhaust what it is to promote equality).

[69] This last statement has to be understood *cum grano salis*. Evidently, norms of conflicts are contingent and a specific system contains these or those norms of conflicts depending on what the normative authority has enacted. However, partial-partial conflicts lead to a material choice between norms (just because of the partial-partial) since no formal difference justifies a prevalence; in a partial-partial there is nothing formal similar to being superior, posterior or more specific. So, it is for the reason that the partial-partial requires a material choice that nobody knows, in any system (as far as it is known), a norm of conflicts applicable to such kind of collision. And no normative authority would create a 'transversal' norm possibly applicable to such kind of conflicts, for the reason that it would be too risky (or impossible) to previously make such material choice.

(li) Since there are instances of '$o_x^{1} \vee o_x^{2} \vee \ldots \vee o_x^{n} \Rightarrow P_{\{PA\}}\ x_{\{SA\}}$' that do not trigger (or are not instances of) '$o_y^{1} \vee o_y^{2} \vee \ldots \vee o_y^{n} \Rightarrow F_{\{PA\}}\ y_{\{SA\}}$' and vice versa, but there are also cases that instantiate both norms, they intersect and are in a partial-partial type of conflict.

(lii) The partial-partial in itself has nothing capable of supporting a formal prevalence of one of the conflicting norms; they have the same structure and each norm is also applicable regardless of the other. This shows that a solution is inherently material; only the contextual reasons of the conflict support a prevalence.

Yet, as to the latter, relevant consequences follow. Once it is assumed as true that variation by degrees is only recognisable in 'ought to be' norms (and that these do not exhaust principles), that any norm in a conflict can support a transactional solution, and that any norm can enter into a conflict and be defeated in such conflict (defeasibility), the outcome is that there are no particularly relevant consequences arising from the distinction between principles and rules. Rigorously, these three possible differences would be the ones that could give some palpable differentiation between the two kinds of norms; they would be the differences that would justify distinguishing normative 'behaviours' from principles and rules in such a way that a norm being one or the other would have effective implications for the solution of legal cases. Nevertheless, and as is claimed here, things do not work that way: having an antecedent with the disjunctive condition 'o_x^{n}', with all the associated properties, does not lead to any consequential differences in the application of law.

Such (apparently poor) conclusion about the division between principles and rules does not prevent the categorisation from being relevant. It is an explanation about significant features of norms and it gives some understanding about important aspects of how norms operate. As an explanation it is valuable for the answers given, which are significantly informative and justificatory. Be that as it may, the main point is that legal science is still divided about what causes a norm to be a principle and it seems to be about time to adopt a simple and comprehensive criterion.

BIBLIOGRAPHY

Journal Articles

Alchourrón, CE, 'G.H. von Wright y los Desarrollos de la Lógica deóntica' (1981) 1 *Anuario de Filosofía Política y Social* 121.

Aleinikoff, TA, 'Constitutional Law in the Age of Balancing' (1987) 96 *Yale Law Journal* 943.

Alexy, R, 'Between Positivism and Non-Positivism? A Third Reply to Eugenio Bulygin' in J Ferrer Beltrán et al (eds), *Neutrality and Theory of Law* (Dordrecht, Springer 2012) 225–238.

Alexy, R, 'Constitutional Rights, Balancing, and Rationality' (2003) 16 *Ratio Juris* 131.

——, 'Giovanni Battista Ratti's Critique of Principles Theory' (2023) 36 *Ratio Juris* 153.

——, 'Grundrechte, Abwägung und Rationalität' (2002) 7 *Ars Interpretandi. Yearbook of Legal Hermeneutics* 113.

——, 'Grundrechte als subjektive Rechte und als objektive Normen' (1990) 29 *Der Staat* 49.

——, 'Jörn Ipsens Konstruktion der Grundrechte' (2013) 52 *Der Staat* 87.

——, 'Kollision und Abwägung als Grundprobleme der Grundrechtsdogmatik' (2001) 6 *World Constitutional Law Review* 181.

——, 'On Balancing and Subsumption: A Structural Comparison' (2003) 16 *Ratio Juris* 433.

——, 'On the Concept and the Nature of Law' (2008) 21 *Ratio Juris* 281.

——, 'On the Structure of Legal Principles' (2000) 13 *Ratio Juris* 294.

——, 'Rechtsregeln und Rechtsprinzipien' (1985) 25 *Archiv für Rechts- und Sozialphilosophie* 13.

——, 'Rights, Legal Reasoning and Rational Discourse' (1992) 5 *Ratio Juris* 143.

——, 'Zum Begriff des Rechtsprinzips' (1979) 1 *Rechtstheorie* 59.

Alonso, JP, 'The Logical Structure of Principles in Alexy's Theory' (2016) 28 *Revus* 53.

Bäcker, C, 'Reglas, Principios y Derrotabilidad' (2014) 37 *DOXA. Cuadernos de Filosofía del Derecho* 31.

Bix, BH, 'A Critique of Alexy's Claim to Correctness' (2020) 33 *Ratio Juris* 124.

Böckenförde, EW, 'Grundrechte als Grundsatznormen' (1990) 29 *Der Staat* 1.

Borowski, M, 'Prinzipien als Grundrechtsnormen' (1998) 53 *Zeitschrift für öffentliches Recht* 307.

Brożek, B, 'Legal Theories and Principles: A Theory Revisited' (2012) 17 *i-lex. Rivista di Scienze Giuridiche, Scienze Cognitive e Intelligenza Artificiale* 205.

Bulygin, E, 'Alexy Between Positivism and Non-Positivism' (2011) 1 *Law of Ukraine: Legal Journal* 51.

Chang, R, 'The Possibility of Parity' (2002) 12 *Ethics* 659.

Da Silva, VA, 'Comparing the Incommensurable: Constitutional Principles, Balancing and Rational Decision' (2011) 31 *Oxford Journal of Legal Studies* 273.

Duarte, D, 'An Experimental Essay on the Antecedent and Its Formulation' (2012) 16 *i-Lex, Rivista di Scienze Giuridiche, Scienze Cognitive ed Intelligenza Artificiale* 37.

——, 'Rights as Formal Combinations of Normative Variables' (2023) 51 *Revus* 1.

Duxbury, N, 'Jhering's Philosophy of Authority' (2007) 27 *Oxford Journal of Legal Studies* 23.

Dworkin, RM, 'The Model of Rules' (1967) 35 *University of Chicago Law Review* 14.

Endicott, T, 'Are There any Rules?' (2001) 5 *The Journal of Ethics* 199.

Esser, J, 'Review: Wilburg, W, *Entwicklung eines beweglichen Systems im bürgerlichen Recht*' (1950–51) 151 *Archiv für civilistische Praxis* 555.

——, 'Review: Wilburg, W. *Entwicklung eines beweglichen Systems im bürgerlichen Recht*' (1953) 18 *Rabels Zeitschrift für ausländisches und internationales Privatrecht* 165.

Gardner, J, 'Legal Positivism: 5½ Myths' (2001) 46 *American Journal of Jurisprudence* 211.

Herget, JE and S Wallace, 'The German Free Law Movement as the Source of American Legal Realism' (1987) 73 *Virginia Law Review* 399.

Jansen, N, 'Die Abwägung von Grundrechten' (1997) 36 *Der Staat* 27.
——, 'Dogmatik, Erkenntnis und Theorie im europäischen Privatrecht' (2005) 13 *Zeitschrift für Europäisches Privatrecht* 750.
——, 'Zum Gedanken einer juristischen Strukturtheorie' (2006) 91 *Archiv für Rechts- und Sozialphilosophie* 277.
Keršić, M and Yzaguirre, VG, 'El "Peso" de los Principios: Descifrando la Metáfora' (2022) 28 *Revista Ius et Praxis* 162.
Klatt, M, 'Taking Rights Less Seriously: A Structural Analysis of Judicial Discretion' (2007) 20 *Ratio Juris* 517.
Klement, JH, 'Vom Nutzen einer Theorie, die alles erklärt. Robert Alexys Prinzipientheorie aus der Sicht der Grundrechtsdogmatik' (2008) 63 *JuristenZeitung* 756.
Kumm, M, 'Constitutional Rights as Principles: On the Structure and Domain of Constitutional Justice. A Review Essay on *A theory of constitutional rights* by Robert Alexy' (2004) 2 *International Journal of Constitutional Law* 574.
——, 'Global Constitutionalism, Human Rights and Proportionality: Institutionalizing Socratic Contestation' (2022) 9 *Journal of Constitutional Justice* 193.
Ladeur, KH, 'A Critique of Balancing and the Principle of Proportionality in Constitutional Law – A Case for "Impersonal Rights"?' (2016) 7 *Transnational Legal Theory* 228.
Leal, F, 'Irracional ou Hiper-racional? A Ponderação de Princípios Entre o Ceticismo e o Otimismo Ingênuo' (2014) 14(58) *Revista de Direito Administrativo & Constitucional* 177–209.
Llewellyn, KN, 'A Realistic Jurisprudence: The Next Step' (1930) 30 *Columbia Law Review* 431.
Lopes, PM, 'The Syntax of Principles: Genericity as a Logical Distinction Between Rules and Principles' (2017) 30 *Ratio Juris* 471.
Marmor, A, 'The Separation Thesis and the Limits of Interpretation' (1999) 12 *Canadian Journal of Law & Jurisprudence* 135.
Michael, L, 'Methodenfragen der Abwägungslehre' (2000) 48 *Jahrbuch des öffentlichen Rechts* 169.
Möller, K, 'Balancing and the Structure of Constitutional Rights' (2007) 5 *International Journal of Constitutional Law* 453.
Moreso, JJ and Vilajosana, J, 'Confliti tra Princìpi Constituzionali' (2002) 2 *Diritto & Questioni Pubbliche* 19.
——, 'Marry Me a Little: How Much Precision is Enough in Law?' (2017) 9 *Droit & Philosophie* 45.
Poscher, R, 'Die Würde des Menschen ist unantastbar' (2004) 59 *JuristenZeitung* 756.
——, 'Insights, Errors and Self-Misconceptions of the Theory of Principles' (2009) 22 *Ratio Juris* 425.
——, 'Resuscitation of a Phantom? On Robert Alexy's Latest Attempt to Save His Concept of Principle' (2020) 33 *Ratio Juris* 134.
——, 'The Potential and Limits of Proportionality in Law' (2025) *Jurisprudence, forthcoming.*
——, 'Theorie eines Phantoms. Die erfolglose Suche der Prinzipientheorie nach ihrem Gegenstand' (2010) 1 *Rechtswissenschaft* 349.
——, 'What Would It Take? The Potential and Limits of Proportionality in Law' (2025) *Jurisprudence* 1–34.
Pound, R, 'Enforcement of Law' (1908) 20 *Green Bag* 401.
——, 'Law in Books and Law in Action' (1910) 44 *American Law Review* 12.
Priel, D, 'Farewell to the Exclusive-Inclusive Debate' (2005) 25 *Oxford Journal of Legal Studies* 675.
Ratti, GB, 'An Antinomy in Alexy's Theory of Balancing' (2023) 36 *Ratio Juris* 48.
Raz, J, 'Legal Principles and the Limits of the Law' (1972) 81 *The Yale Law Journal* 823.
Reßing, M, 'Prinzipien als Normen mit zwei Geltungsebenen. Zur Unterscheidung von Regeln und Prinzipien' (2009) 95 *Archiv für Rechts- und Sozialphilosophie* 28.
Rodríguez, J, 'La Derrotabilidad de las Normas' (1997) 6 *Isonomia* 149.
Schauer, F, 'Prescriptions in Three Dimensions' (1997) 82 *Iowa Law Review* 911.
Schlag, P, 'Rules and Standards' (1985) 33 *UCLA Law Review* 379.
Schlink, B, 'Grundrechte als Prinzipien?' (1992) 39 *Osaka University Law Review* 41.
Sieckmann, JR, 'Prinzipien, Ideales Sollen und normative Argumente' (2011) 97 *Archiv für Rechts- und Sozialphilosophie* 178.

——, 'Rechtssystem und praktische Vernunft' (1992) 78 *Archiv für Rechts- und Sozialphilosophie* 145.
——, 'Zur Abwägungsfähigkeit von Prinzipien' (1994) 53 *Archiv für Rechts- und Sozialphilosophie* 227.
Stavropoulos, N, 'The Debate That Never Was' (2017) 130 *Harvard Law Review* 2082.
Verheij, B et al, 'An Integrated View on Rules and Principles' (1998) 6 *Artificial Intelligence and Law* 3.
Von Wright, GH, 'Deontic Logic' (1951) 60 *Mind* 1.
Walsh, JE, 'Inadequacy of Cost per "Kill" as Measure of Effectiveness' (1957) 5(6) *Operations Research* 750.
Wilburg, W, 'Zusammenspiel der Kräfte im Aufbau des Schuldrechts' (1963) 163 *Archiv für civilistische Praxis* 346.

Book Chapters

Aarnio, A, 'Las Reglas en Sério' in A Aarnio et al (eds), *La Normatividad del Derecho* (Barcelona, Gedisa, 1997) 17–36.
Aarnio, A, 'Taking Rules Seriously' in W Maihofer and G Sprenger (eds), *Law and the States in Modern Times. ARSP-Beiheft 42* (Stuttgart, Franz Steiner, 1990) 180–192.
Alexander, L, 'Legal Objectivity and the Illusion of Legal Principles' in M Klatt (ed), *Institutionalized Reason: The Jurisprudence of Robert Alexy* (Oxford, Oxford University Press, 2012) 115–130.
Alexy, R, 'Abwägung, Verfassungsgerichtsbarkeit und Repräsentation' in M Becker and R Zimmerling (eds), *Politik und Recht. PVS-Sonderheft 36* (Wiesbaden, VS Verlag, 2006) 250–58.
——, 'Alf Ross' Begriff der Kompetenz' in A Hoyer et al (eds), *Gedächtnisschrift für Jörn Eckert* (Baden-Baden, Nomos, 2008) 55–62.
——, 'Comments and Responses' in M Klatt (ed), *Institutionalized Reason: The Jurisprudence of Robert Alexy* (Oxford, Oxford University Press, 2012) 319–56.
——, 'Constitutional Rights, Proportionality, and Argumentation' in JR Sieckmann (ed), *Proportionality, Balancing, and Rights: Robert Alexy's Theory of Constitutional Rights* (Cham, Springer, 2021) 1–10.
——, 'Deber Ideal' in L Clérico et al (eds), *Derechos Fundamentales, Principios y Argumentación: Estudios sobre la Teoría Jurídica de Robert Alexy* (Granada, Comares, 2010) 15–35.
——, 'Deber Ser Ideal y Optimización' in G Villa Rosas (ed), *Ensayos sobre la Teoría de los Principios y el Juicio de Proporcionalidad* (Lima, Palestra, 2020) 317–31.
——, 'Die Gewichtsformel' in J Jickeli et al (eds), *Gedächtnisschrift für Jürgen Sonnenschein* (Berlin, De Gruyter, 2003) 771–98.
——, 'Grundrechte im demokratischen Verfassungsstaat' in A Arnio et al (eds), *Justice, Morality and Society. Festschrift für Aleksander Peczenik* (Lund, Juristförlaget, 1997) 27–42.
——, 'Ideales Sollen' in L Clérico and JR Sieckmann (eds), *Grundrechte, Prinzipien und Argumentation. Studien zur Rechtstheorie Robert Alexys* (Baden-Baden, Nomos, 2009) 21–38.
——, 'Ideales Sollen und Optimierung' in F Saliger et al (eds), *Rechtsstaatliches Strafrecht. Festschrift für Ulfrid Neumann zum 70. Geburtstag* (Heidelberg, CF Müller, 2017) 17–30.
——, 'John Rawls' Theorie der Grundfreiheiten' in J Rawls and W Hinsch (eds), *Zur Idee des politischen Liberalismus. John Rawls in der Diskussion* (Frankfurt, Suhrkamp, 1997) 263–303.
——, 'Probleme der Diskurstheorie' in R Alexy (ed), *Recht, Vernunft, Diskurs* (Frankfurt, Suhrkamp, 1995) 109–27.
——, 'The Weight Formula' (B Brożek and SL Paulson trans) in J Stelmach et al (eds), *Studies in the Philosophy of Law. Frontiers of the Economic Analysis of Law* (Krakow, Jagiellonian University Press, 2007) 9–27.
——, 'Two or Three' in M Borowski (ed), *On the Nature of Legal Principles. ARSP-Beiheft 119* (Stuttgart, Franz Steiner, 2010) 8–18.
——, 'Zum Begriff des Rechtsprinzips' in W Krawietz et al (eds), *Rechtstheorie: Argumentation und Hermeneutik in der Jurisprudenz* (Berlin, Duncker & Humblot, 1979) 59–87.

——, 'Zum Begriff des Rechtsprinzips' in R Alexy (ed), *Recht, Vernunft, Diskurs* (Frankfurt, Suhrkamp, 1995) 177–212.

——, 'Zur Struktur der Rechtsprinzipien' in B Schilcher et al (eds), *Regeln, Prinzipien und Elemente im System des Rechts* (Vienna, Verlag Österreich, 2000) 31–52.

Anderson, AR, 'The Formal Analysis of Normative Systems' in N Rescher (ed), *The Logic of Decision and Action* (Pittsburgh, University of Pittsburgh Press, 1966).

Bäcker, C, 'Rules, Principles, and Defeasibility' in M Borowski (ed), *On the Nature of Legal Principles* (Stuttgart/Baden-Baden, Franz Steiner/Nomos, 2010) 79–91.

Bódig, M, 'Rules, Principles, and the Problem of the Limits of Legal Reasoning' in M Borowski (ed), *On the Nature of Legal Principles* (Stuttgart/Baden-Baden, Franz Steiner/Nomos, 2010) 127–44.

Borowski, M, 'Reconstruction of Formal Principles' in JA de Oliveira et al (eds), *Alexy's Theory of Law* (Stuttgart, Franz Steiner, 2015) 95–109.

Castañeda, HN, 'On the Semantics of the Ought-To-Do' in D Davidson and G Harman (eds), *Semantics of Natural Languages* (Dordrecht, Reidel, 1972) 675–94.

Dreier, H, 'Vorbemerkungen vor Artikel 1 GG' in H Dreier (ed), *Grundgesetz-Kommentar*, vol 1 (Tübingen, Mohr Siebeck, 2013) 42–153.

Duarte, D, 'Drawing Up the Boundaries of Normative Conflicts that Lead to Balances' in JR Sieckmann (ed), *Legal Reasoning: The Methods of Balancing* (Stuttgart, Franz Steiner, 2010) 52–62.

——, 'The Alexy-Poscher Debate: Working on the Problems and on the Solutions' in RG Dalla-Barba (ed), *The Alexy-Poscher Debate on Legal Principles* (Oxford, Hart Publishing, 2025) 137–160.

Dworkin, RM, 'Hard Cases' in RM Dworkin (ed), *Taking Rights Seriously* (Cambridge MA, Harvard University Press, 1977) 81–130.

——, 'The Model of Rules I' in RM Dworkin (ed), *Taking Rights Seriously* (Cambridge MA, Harvard University Press, 1977) 14–45.

——, 'The Model of Rules I' in RM Dworkin (ed), *Taking Rights Seriously* (London, Duckworth, 1977) 14–45.

——, 'The Model of Rules II' in RM Dworkin (ed), *Taking Rights Seriously* (Cambridge MA, Harvard University Press, 1977) 46–80.

Ehrlich, E, 'Über Lücken im Rechte' (first published 1888) in E Ehrlich (ed), *Recht und Leben* (Berlin, Duncker & Humblot, 1967) 30–169.

Escher, A, 'When It is Vague What is Vague: Identifying Vagueness' in D Duarte et al (eds), *Legal Interpretation and Scientific Knowledge* (Cham, Springer, 2019) 161–86.

Fuchs, E, 'Was will die Freirechtsschule?' (1929) in AS Foulkes and A Kaufmann (eds), *Gerechtigkeitswissenschaft. Ausgewählte Schriften zur Freirechtslehre* (Karlsruhe, CF Müller, 1965) 21–63.

Guastini, R, *La Sintaxis del Derecho* (Madrid, Marcial Pons, 2016).

——, *Le Fonti del Diritto e L'Interpretazione* (Milan, Giuffrè, 1993).

Habermas, J, 'Reply to Symposium Participants, Benjamin N. Cardozo School of Law' in M Rosenfeld and A Arato (eds), *Habermas on Law and Democracy* (Berkeley CA, University of California Press, 1998) 381–452.

Hilpinen, R and McNamara, P, 'Deontic Logic: A Historical Survey and Introduction' in D Gabbay et al (eds), *Handbook of Deontic Logic and Normative Systems* (London, College Publications, 2013) 3–136.

Jakab, A, 'Re-Defining Principles as "Important Rules" – A Critique of Robert Alexy' in M Borowski (ed), *On the Nature of Legal Principles* (Stuttgart, Franz Steiner, 2010) 145–60.

Jansen, N, 'Die normativen Grundlagen rationalen Abwägens' in JR Sieckmann (ed), *Die Prinzipientheorie der Grundrechte. Studien zur Grundrechtstheorie Robert Alexys* (Baden-Baden, Nomos, 2007) 39–57.

——, 'Theoriebildung in der europäischen Privatrechtsdogmatik' in R Alexy (ed), *Juristische Grundlagenforschung* (Stuttgart, Franz Steiner, 2005) 29–54.

Jestaedt, M, 'Die Abwägungslehre. ihre Stärken und ihre Schwächen' in O Depenheuer et al (eds), *Staat im Wort. Festschrift für Josef Isensee* (Tübingen, Mohr Siebeck, 2007) 253–75.

——, 'Rechtsprechung und Rechtsetzung. Eine deutsche Perspektive' in W Erbguth and J Masing (eds), *Die Bedeutung der Rechtsprechung im System der Rechtsquellen. Europarecht und nationales Recht* (Stuttgart, Richard Boorberg, 2005) 25–79.

——, 'The Doctrine of Balancing: Its Strengths and Weaknesses' in M Klatt (ed), *Institutionalized Reason: The Jurisprudence of Robert Alexy* (Oxford, Oxford University Press, 2012) 152–72.

Karst, KL, 'Legislative Facts in Constitutional Litigation' in PB Kurland (ed), *The Supreme Court* (Chicago IL, The University of Chicago Press, 1960) 75–112.

Kelsen, H, 'Legal Formalism and the Pure Theory of Law' (first published 1929) in AJ Jacobson and B Schlink (eds), *Weimar: A Jurisprudence of Crisis* (Berkeley CA, University of California Press, 2000) 76–83.

Koch, HJ, 'Die normtheoretische Basis der Abwägung' in W Erbguth et al (eds), *Abwägung im Recht. Symposium und Verabschiedung von Werner Hoppe am 30. Juni 1995 in Münster aus Anlass seiner Emeritierung* (Cologne, Carl Heymanns Verlag, 1996) 9–18.

——, 'Rechtsprinzipien im Bauplanungsrecht. Zur normtheoretischen Basis der planerischen Abwägung' in B Schilcher et al (eds), *Regeln, Prinzipien und Elemente im System des Rechts* (Vienna, Verlag Österreich, 2000) 245–57.

——, 'Zur Methodenlehre des Rechtspositivismus. Das Prinzipienargument' in R Dreier (ed), *Rechtspositivismus und Wertbezug des Rechts* (Stuttgart, Franz Steiner, 1988) 152–61.

Kramer, M, 'Rights Without Trimmings' in M Kramer et al (eds), *A Debate Over Rights* (Oxford, Oxford University Press, 1998) 7–112.

Kumm, M, 'Political Liberalism and the Structure of Rights: On the Place and Limits of the Proportionality Requirement' in G Pavlakos (ed), *Law, Rights and Discourse*: Themes from the Legal Philosophy of Robert Alexy (Oxford, Hart Publishing, 2007) 131–66.

Leal, F, '"Less is More": Against Argumentative Saturation in Legal Decision-Making' in MN de Brito et al (eds), *The Role of Legal Argumentation and Human Dignity in Constitutional Courts* (Stuttgart, Franz Steiner, 2019) 47–55.

——, 'Prefácio' in RG Dalla-Barba (ed), *Princípios Jurídicos: O Debate Metodológico entre Robert Alexy e Ralf Poscher* (Belo Horizonte, Casa do Direito, 2022) 17–39.

Leiter, B, 'American Legal Realism' in WA Edmundson MP Golding (eds), *The Blackwell Guide to Philosophy of Law and Legal Theory* (Malden, Wiley-Blackwell, 2003) 50–66.

——, 'Beyond the Hart/Dworkin Debate: The Methodology Problem in Jurisprudence' in B Leiter (ed), *Naturalizing Jurisprudence: Essays on American Legal Realism and Naturalism in Legal Philosophy* (Oxford, University Press, 2007) 153–82.

Marmor, A, 'Exclusive Legal Positivism' in JL Coleman (ed), *The Oxford Handbook of Jurisprudence and Philosophy of Law* (Oxford, Oxford University Press, 2004) 104–24.

Moore, MS, 'Legal Principle Revisited' in MS Moore (ed), *Educating Oneself in Public: Critical Essays in Jurisprudence* (Oxford, Oxford University Press, 2000) 221–46.

Nelken, D, 'Pound and Ehrlich on the Living Law' in E Kamenka et al (eds), *Rechtstheorie. Soziologische Jurisprudenz und realistische Theorien des Rechts* (Berlin, Duncker & Humblot, 1986) 175–87.

Neumann, U, 'Die Geltung von Regeln, Prinzipien und Elementen' in B Schilcher et al (eds), *Regeln, Prinzipien und Elemente im System des Rechts* (Vienna, Verlag Österreich, 2000) 115–28.

Poscher, R, 'Die Funktionenordnung des Grundgesetzes' in W Hoffmann-Riem et al (eds), *Grundlagen des Verwaltungsrechts. Methoden, Maßstäbe, Aufgaben* (Munich, CH Beck, 2006) 493–532.

——, 'Einsichten, Irrtümer und Selbstmissverständnis der Prinzipientheorie' in JR Sieckmann (ed), *Die Prinzipientheorie der Grundrechte. Studien zur Grundrechtstheorie Robert Alexys* (Baden-Baden, Nomos, 2007) 59–80.

——, 'Interpretation and Rule-Following in Law: The Complexity of Easy Cases' in M Araszkiewicz et al (eds), *Problems of Normativity, Rules and Rule-Following* (Cham, Springer, 2015) 281–93.

——, 'Proportionality and the Bindingness of Fundamental Rights' in E Billis et al (eds), *Proportionality in Crime Control and Criminal Justice* (Oxford, Hart Publishing, 2021) 49–68.

——, 'The Hand of Midas: When Concepts Turn Legal, or Deflating the Hart-Dworkin Debate' in D von der Pfordten and JC Hage (eds), *Concepts in Law* (Dordrecht, Springer, 2009) 99–116.

——, 'The Principles Theory: How Many Theories and What is Their Merit?' in M Klatt (ed), *Institutionalized Reason: The Jurisprudence of Robert Alexy* (Oxford, Oxford University Press, 2012) 218–47.

——, 'Theory of a Phantom: The Principles Theory's Futile Quest for Its Object' in JA de Oliveira et al (eds), *Alexy's Theory of Law* (Stuttgart, Franz Steiner, 2015) 129–48.

Ramos Pascua, JA, 'Die Grundlage rechtlicher Geltung von Prinzipien. Eine Gegenüberstellung von Dworkin und Esser' in G Orsi et al (eds), *Prinzipien des Rechts. Beiträge zur Rechtswissenschaft, vol VI* (Frankfurt, Peter Lang, 1996) 7–33.

Raz J, 'The Argument from Justice, or How Not to Reply to Legal Positivism' in G Pavlakos (ed), *Law, Rights and Discourse: The Legal Philosophy of Robert Alexy* (Oxford, Hart Publishing, 2007) 17–35.

Rossen, H, 'Grundrechte als Regeln und Prinzipien' in C Grabenwarter et al (eds), *Allgemeinheit der Grundrechte und Vielfalt der Gesellschaft* (Stuttgart, Boorberg, 1994) 41–59.

Sampaio, JS, 'Proportionality in Its Narrow Sense and Measuring the Intensity of Restrictions on Fundamental Rights' in D Duarte and JS Sampaio (eds), *Proportionality in Law* (Cham, Springer, 2018) 71–110.

——, 'Proportionality: Measuring Impacts on Fundamental Rights' in M Sellers and S Kirste (eds), *Encyclopedia of the Philosophy of Law and Social Philosophy* (Dordrecht, Springer, 2023) 2863–69.

Schauer, F, 'Is Defeasibility an Essential Property of Law?' in J Ferrer and GB Ratti (eds), *The Logic of Legal Requirements: Essays on Defeasibility* (Oxford, Oxford University Press, 2012) 77–88.

Schilcher, B, 'Prinzipien und Regeln als Elemente einer Theorie des gebundenen Ermessens' in B Schilcher et al (eds), *Regeln, Prinzipien und Elemente im System des Rechts* (Vienna, Verlag Österreich, 2000) 153–92.

Schlink, B, 'Proportionality (1)' in M Rosenfeld and A Sajó (eds), *The Oxford Handbook of Comparative Constitutional Law* (Oxford, Oxford University Press, 2012) 718–37.

Searle, J, 'Prima Facie Obligations' in J Raz (ed), *Practical Reasoning* (Oxford, Oxford University Press, 1978) 81–90.

Shapiro, SJ, 'The Hart-Dworkin Debate: A Short Guide for the Perplexed' in A Ripstein (ed), *Ronald Dworkin* (Cambridge, Cambridge University Press, 2007) 22–55.

Sieckmann, JR, 'Is Balancing a Method of Rational Justification *sui generis*? On the Structure of Justification by Balancing' in C Dahlman and E Feteris (eds), *Legal Argumentation Theory: Cross-Disciplinary Perspectives* (Dordrecht, Springer, 2013) 189–206.

——, 'Los Derechos Fundamentales como Principios' in JR Sieckmann (ed), *La Teoría Principialista de los Derechos Fundamentales* (Madrid, Marcial Pons, 2011) 27–50.

——, 'Zur Abwägungsfähigkeit von Prinzipien' in HJ Koch and U Neumann (eds), *Praktische Vernunft und Rechtsanwendung. ARSP-Beiheft 53* (Stuttgart, Franz Steiner, 1994) 205–13.

——, 'Zur Analyse von Normkonflikten und Normabwägungen' in G Meggle (ed), *Analyomen 2: Perspektiven der Analytischen Philosophie* (Berlin, Walter de Gruyter, 1997) 349–56.

——, 'Zur Prinzipientheorie Robert Alexys. Gemeinsamkeiten und Differenzen' in M Klatt (ed), *Prinzipientheorie und Theorie der Abwägung* (Tübingen, Mohr Siebeck, 2013) 271–95.

Solan, L, 'Vagueness and Ambiguity in Legal Interpretation' in VK Bhatia et al (eds), *Vagueness in Normative Texts* (Bern, Peter Lang, 2005) 73–96.

Somek, A, 'Abwägungsregeln. Ein didaktischer Beitrag zur Grundrechtsdogmatik' in C Hiebaum and P Koller (eds), *Politische Ziele und juristische Argumentation. ARSP-Beiheft 92* (Stuttgart, Franz Steiner, 2003) 113–41.

——, 'Eine egalitäre Alternative zur Güterabwägung' in B Schilcher et al (eds), *Regeln, Prinzipien und Elemente im System des Rechts* (Vienna, Verlag Österreich, 2000) 193–220.

Summers, RS, 'Rudolf von Jhering's Influence on American Legal Theory' in O Behrends (ed), *Jherings Rechtsdenken* (Göttingen, Vandenhoeck & Ruprecht, 1996) 61–76.

Teifke, N, 'Flexibilität der Menschenwürde? Zur Struktur des Art. 1 Abs. 1 GG' in C Bäcker and S Baufeld (eds), *Objektivität und Flexibilität im Recht* (Stuttgart, Franz Steiner, 2005) 142–56.

Von Wright, GH, 'Ought to Be – Ought to Do' in G Meggle (ed), *Actions, Norms and Values: Discussions with Georg Henrik von Wright* (Berlin, De Gruyter, 1999) 3–9.

Waluchow, WJ, 'The Origins of Inclusive Legal Positivism' in T Spaak and P Mindus (eds), *The Cambridge Companion of Legal Positivism* (Cambridge, Cambridge University Press, 2021) 487–511.

Weinberger, O, 'Revision des traditionellen Rechtssatzkonzepts' in B Schilcher et al (eds), *Prinzipien und Elemente im System des Rechts* (Vienna, Verlag Österreich, 2000) 53–68.

Books

Aarnio, A, *Essays on the Doctrinal Study of Law* (Cham, Springer, 2011).
Adickes, F, *Zur Lehre von den Rechtsquelle. Insbesondere über die Vernunft und die Natur der Sache als Rechtsquellen und über das Gewohnheitsrecht* (Kassel, Georg H Wigand, 1872).
Alchourrón, C and Bulygin E, *Normative Systems* (Vienna, Springer, 1971).
Alexy, R, *A Theory of Constitutional Rights* (J Rivers trans, Oxford, Oxford University Press, 2002).
——, *A Theory of Legal Argumentation: The Theory of Rational Discourse as Theory of Legal Justification* (R Adler and N MacCormick trans, Oxford, Clarendon Press, 1989).
——, *Begriff und Geltung des Rechts*, 4th edn (Freiburg, Karl Alber, 2005).
——, *Law's Ideal Dimension* (Oxford, Oxford University Press, 2021).
——, *The Argument from Injustice: A Reply to Legal Positivism* (SL Paulson and BL Paulson trans, Oxford, Oxford University Press, 2002).
——, *Theorie der Grundrechte* (Frankfurt, Suhrkamp, 1986).
——, *Theorie der Grundrechte*, 3rd edn (Frankfurt, Suhrkamp, 1996).
——, *Theorie der juristischen Argumentation. Die Theorie des rationalen Diskurses als Theorie der juristischen Begründung*, 3rd edn (Frankfurt, Suhrkamp, 1996).
Atienza, M and Manero, JR, *Theory of Legal Sentences* (New York, Springer, 1998).
Ávila, HB, *Theory of Legal Principles* (Dordrecht, Springer, 2007).
Barak, A, *Proportionality: Constitutional Rights and their Limitations* (Cambridge, Cambridge University Press, 2012).
Bayles, MD, *Principles of Law: A Normative Analysis* (Dordrecht, Reidel, 1987).
Beatty, DM, *The Ultimate Rule of Law* (Oxford, Oxford University Press, 2004).
Bentham, J, *On Laws in General* (first published 1782, London, The Athlone Press, 1970).
Borowski, M, *Die Glaubens- und Gewissensfreiheit des Grundgesetzes* (Tübingen, Mohr Siebeck, 2006).
——, *Grundrechte als Prinzipien. Die Unterscheidung von Prima-facie Position und definitiver Position als fundamentaler Konstruktionsgrundsatz der Grundrechte* (Baden-Baden, Nomos, 1998).
——, *Grundrechte als Prinzipien. Die Unterscheidung von Prima-facie Position und definitiver Position als fundamentaler Konstruktionsgrundsatz der Grundrechte*, 2nd edn (Baden-Baden, Nomos, 2007).
——, *La Estructura de los Derechos Fundamentales* (Bogotá, Universidad Externado de Colombia, 2003).
Bumke, C, *Der Grundrechtsvorbehalt. Untersuchungen über die Begrenzung und Ausgestaltung der Grundrechte* (Baden-Baden, Nomos, 1998).
Carrió, G, *Notas sobre Derecho y Lenguage* (Buenos Aires, Abeledo-Perrot, 1994).
Chang, R, (ed), *Incommensurability, Incomparability, and Practical Reason* (Cambridge MA, Harvard University Press, 1997).
——, *Making Comparisons Count: Studies in Ethics* (Hoboken, Routledge, 2014).
Coleman, JL, *The Practice of Principle* (Oxford, Oxford University Press, 2001).
Cremer, W, *Freiheitsgrundrechte. Funktionen und Strukturen* (Tübingen, Mohr Siebeck, 2003).
Dalla-Barba, RG (ed), *Princípios Jurídicos: O Debate Metodológico entre Robert Alexy e Ralf Poscher* (Belo Horizonte, Casa do Direito, 2022).
Dalla-Barba, RG and García Amado, JA (eds), *Principios Juridicos: El Debate Metodológico entre Robert Alexy y Ralf Poscher* (Lima, Palestra, 2022).
Davis, L, *Theory of Action* (Englewood, Prentice-Hall, 1979).
Dubislav, W, *Die Definition*, 4th edn (Hamburg, Felix Meiner Verlag, 1981).
Duxbury, N, *Patterns of American Jurisprudence* (Oxford, Oxford University Press, 1995).
Dworkin, RM, *Is Democracy Possible Here?* (Princeton NJ, Princeton University Press, 2006).
——, *Law's Empire* (Cambridge MA, Harvard University Press, 1986).
—— (ed), *Taking Rights Seriously* (Cambridge MA, Harvard University Press, 1977).
Ehrlich, E, *Freie Rechtsfindung und freie Rechtswissenschaft* (Leipzig, Hirschfeld, 1903).
——, *Grundlegung der Soziologie des Rechts* (Munich, Duncker & Humblot, 1913).

Elster, J et al, *Rationale Argumentation. Ein Grundkurs in Argumentations- und Wissenschaftstheorie* (M Kaiser and G Meggle trans, Berlin, De Gruyter, 1988).
Engisch, K, *Einführung in das juristische Denken*, 9th edn (Stuttgart, Kohlhammer, 1997).
Esser, J, *Einführung in die Grundbegriffe des Rechtes und Staates* (Vienna, Springer, 1949).
——, *Grundsatz und Norm in der richterlichen Fortbildung des Privatrechts*, 3rd edn (Tübingen, Mohr Siebeck, 1974).
——, *Grundsatz und Norm in der richterlichen Fortbildung des Privatrechts*, 4th edn (Tübingen, Mohr Siebeck, 1990).
Fischer, K, *Die Zulässigkeit aufgedrängten staatlichen Schutzes vor Selbstschädigung* (Frankfurt, Peter Lang, 1997).
Flavius, G (pseudonym of H Kantorowicz), *Der Kampf um die Rechtswissenschaft* (first published 1906, Berlin, Berliner Wissenschaftsverlag, 2002).
Frändberg, Å, *The Legal Order* (Cham, Springer, 2018).
Frank, J, *Law and the Modern Mind* (New York, Brentano's Publishers, 1930).
Gaido, P, (ed), *La Pretensión de Corrección del Derecho: La Polémica Completa entre Alexy y Bulygin sobre la Relación entre Derecho y Moral*, 2nd edn (Bogotá, Universidad del Externado, 2022).
Geny, F, *Méthode d'interpretation et sources du droit privé positif* (Lausanne, F Pichon et Durand-Auzias, 1899).
Günther, K, *Der Sinn für Angemessenheit. Anwendungsdiskurse in Moral und Recht* (Frankfurt, Suhrkamp, 1988).
——, *The Sense of Appropriateness: Application Discourses in Morality and Law* (J Farrell trans, Albany, State University of New York Press, 1993).
Hain, KE, *Die Grundsätze des Grundgesetzes. Eine Untersuchung zu Art. 79 Abs. 3 GG* (Baden-Baden, Nomos, 1999).
Hare, RM, *Freedom and Reason* (Oxford, Oxford University Press, 1963).
Hart, HLA, *The Concept of Law*, 2nd edn (Oxford, Clarendon Press, 1994).
——, *The Concept of Law*, 3rd edn (Oxford, Oxford University Press, 2012).
Heck, P, *Begriffsbildung und Interessenjurisprudenz* (Tübingen, Mohr Siebeck, 1932).
——, *Das Problem der Rechtsgewinnung* (Bad Homburg, Gehlen, 1912).
Hilgendorf, E, *Argumentation in der Jurisprudenz. Zur Rezeption von analytischer Philosophie und kritischer Theorie in der Grundlagenforschung der Jurisprudenz* (Berlin, Duncker & Humblot, 1991).
Hong, M, *Abwägungsfeste Rechte. Von Alexys Prinzipien zum Modell der Grundsatznormen* (Tübingen, Mohr Siebeck, 2019).
Hurley, SL, *Natural Reasons: Personality and Polity* (Oxford, Oxford University Press, 1989).
Isay, H, *Rechtsnorm und Entscheidung* (Berlin, Aalen, 1929).
Jansen, N, *Die Struktur der Gerechtigkeit* (Baden-Baden, Nomos, 1998).
——, *Die Struktur des Haftungsrechts* (Tübingen, Mohr Siebeck, 2003).
Jestaedt, M, *Das mag in der Theorie richtig sein …: Vom Nutzen der Rechtstheorie für die Rechtspraxis* (Tübingen, Mohr Siebeck, 2006).
——, *Grundrechtsentfaltung im Gesetz. Studien zur Interdependenz von Grundrechtsdogmatik und Rechtsgewinnungstheorie* (Tübingen, Mohr Siebeck, 1999).
Kallmeyer, C, *Ideales Sollen. Eine Analyse der Prinzipienkonstruktion* (Baden-Baden, Nomos, 2016).
Kantorowicz, H, *Der Begriff des Rechts* (Göttingen, Vandenhoeck & Ruprecht, 1939).
——, *Rechtswissenschaft und Soziologie. Ausgewählte Schriften zur Wissenschaftslehre* (Karlsruhe, CF Müller, 1962).
Kelsen, H, *The Pure Theory of Law* (M Knight trans, Clark NJ, The Lawbook Exchange, 2005).
Kingreen, T and Poscher R, *Grundrechte. Staatsrecht II*, 38th edn (Munich, CF Müller, 2022).
Klatt, M and Moritz, M, *The Constitutional Structure of Proportionality* (Oxford, Oxford University Press, 2012).
Larenz, K, *Methodenlehre der Rechtswissenschaft*, 6th edn (Berlin, Springer, 1991).
Lerche, P, *Übermaß und Verfassungsrecht. Zur Bindung des Gesetzgebers an die Grundsätze der Verhältnismäßigkeit und der Erforderlichkeit*, 2nd edn (Goldbach, Keip, 1999).

Lerche, P, *Übermaß und Verfassungsrecht. Zur Bindung des Gesetzgebers an die Grundsätze der Verhältnismäßigkeit und der Erforderlichkeit* (Cologne, Heymann, 1961).

MacCormick, N, *Legal Reasoning and Legal Theory* (Oxford, Clarendon Press, 1978).

Martin, R, *System of Rights* (Oxford, Clarendon Press, 2003).

Mendonca, D, *Derechos, Razón y Emoción: Conflicto y Balance de Derechos* (Asunción, Centro de Estudios Constitucionales, 2016).

Michael, L, *Der allgemeine Gleichheitssatz als Methodennorm komparativer Systeme. Methodenrechtliche Analyse und Fortentwicklung der Theorie der „beweglichen Systeme"* (Berlin, Duncker & Humblot, 1997).

Möller, K, *The Global Model of Constitutional Rights* (Oxford, Oxford University Press, 2012).

Moreso, JJ and Vilajosana, J, *Introducción a la Teoría del Derecho* (Madrid, Marcial Pons, 2004).

Navarro, P and Rodríguez, J, *Deontic Logic and Legal Systems* (Cambridge, Cambridge University Press, 2014).

Neves, M, *Constitutionalism and the Paradox of Principles and Rules* (Oxford, Oxford University Press, 2021).

Nino, CS, *Introducción al Análisis del Derecho*, 2nd edn (Barcelona, Ariel, 2003).

O'Brien, L, *Philosophy of Action* (New York, Palgrave Macmillan, 2015).

Ogorek, R, *Richterkönig oder Subsumtionsautomat? Zur Justiztheorie im 19. Jahrhundert* (Frankfurt, Vittorio Klostermann, 1986).

Park, JH, *Rechtsfindung im Verwaltungsrecht: Grundlegung einer Prinzipientheorie des Verwaltungsrechts als Methode der Verwaltungsrechtsdogmatik* (Berlin, Duncker & Humblot, 1999).

Peczenik, A, *On Law and Reason* (Dordrecht, Springer, 1989).

Petersen, N, *Proportionality and the Review of Legislative Rationality: Fundamental Rights Adjudication in Canada, Germany and South Africa* (Cambridge, Cambridge University Press, 2017).

Pieroth, B and Schlink, B, *Grundrechte. Staatsrecht II*, 21st edn (Heidelberg, CF Müller, 2005).

——, *Grundrechte. Staatsrecht II*, 26th edn (Heidelberg, CF Müller, 2010).

——, *Grundrechte. Staatsrecht II*, 28th edn (Heidelberg, CF Müller, 2012).

Pietsch, J, *Das Schrankenregime der EU-Grundrechtecharta. Dogmatik und Bewertung auf der Grundlage einer Prinzipientheorie der Rechte* (Baden-Baden, Nomos, 2006).

Pino, G, *Teoria Analitica del Diritto. La Norma Giuridica* (Pisa, Edizioni ETS, 2016).

Poscher, R, *Grundrechte als Abwehrrechte. Reflexive Regelung rechtlich geordneter Freiheit* (Tübingen, Mohr Siebeck, 2003).

Pound, R, *Introduction to the Philosophy of Law*, 24th edn (New Haven CT, Yale University Press, 1982).

Prior, AN, *Formal Logic* (Oxford, Oxford University Press, 1962).

Raabe, M, *Grundrechte und Erkenntnis. Der Einschätzungsspielraum des Gesetzgebers* (Baden-Baden, Nomos, 1998).

Ratti, GB, *El Gobierno de las Normas* (Madrid, Marcial Pons, 2013).

Raz, J, *Ethics in the Public Domain. Essays in the Morality of law and Politics* (Oxford, Oxford University Press, 1995).

——, *The Concept of a Legal System*, 2nd edn (Oxford, Clarendon Press, 1980).

Reimer, F, *Verfassungsprinzipien. Ein Normtyp im Grundgesetz* (Berlin, Duncker & Humblot, 2001).

Riehm, T, *Abwägungsentscheidungen in der praktischen Rechtsanwendung. Argumentation – Beweis – Wertung* (Munich, CH Beck, 2006).

Ross, A, *Directives and Norms* (London, Routledge and Kegan Paul, 1968).

Rusteberg, B, *Der grundrechtliche Gewährleistungsgehalt. Eine veränderte Perspektive auf die Grundrechtsdogmatik durch eine präzise Schutzbereichsbestimmung* (Tübingen, Mohr Siebeck, 2009).

Ryter-Sauvant, M, *Allgemeine Rechtsgrundsätze – Analogien zum Privatrecht. Ein Beitrag zur richterlichen Rechtsfortbildung im Verwaltungsrecht* (Bern, Stämpfli, 2005).

Santos de Morais, F, *Ponderação e Arbitrariedade: A Inadequada Recepção de Alexy pelo STF* (Salvador, Juspodivm, 2018).

Schauer, F, *Playing by the Rules: A Philosophical Examination of Rule-Based Decision-Making in Law and in Life* (Oxford, Oxford University Press, 1993).

Schlink, B, *Abwägung im Verfassungsrecht* (Berlin, Duncker & Humblot, 1976).
Sebok, AJ, *Legal Positivism in American Jurisprudence* (Cambridge, Cambridge University Press, 1998).
Sieckmann, JR, *Modelle des Eigentumsschutzes. Eine Untersuchung zur Eigentumsgarantie des Art. 14 GG* (Baden-Baden, Nomos, 1998).
——, *Recht als normatives System. Die Prinzipientheorie des Rechts* (Baden-Baden, Nomos, 2009).
——, *Rechtsphilosophie* (Tübingen, Mohr Siebeck, 2018).
——, *Regelmodelle und Prinzipienmodelle des Rechtssystems* (Baden-Baden, Nomos, 1990).
Somek, A, *Rechtliches Wissen* (Frankfurt, Suhrkamp, 2006).
Stelzer, M, *Das Wesensgehaltsargument und der Grundsatz der Verhältnismäßigkeit* (Vienna, Österreich Verlag, 1991).
Tamanaha, B, *Formalism and Realism on Judging: Beyond the Divide* (Princeton NJ, Princeton University Press, 2009.
——, *Law as Means to an End* (New York, Cambridge University Press, 2006).
Toulmin, SE, *The Place of Reason in Ethics* (Cambridge, Cambridge University Press, 1950).
Von Bülow, O, *Gesetz und Richteramt* (Berlin, Duncker & Humblot, 1885).
Von Jhering, R, *The Struggle for Law*, 2nd edn (John J Lalor trans, Chicago IL, Callaghan and Company, 1915).
——, *Scherz und Ernst in der Jurisprudenz. Eine Weihnachtsgabe für das juristische Publikum* (Leipzig, Breitkopf & Härtel, 1884).
Von Wright, GH, *A New System of Deontic Logic: Logical Studies* (London, Routledge and Kegan Paul Ltd, 1957).
——, *An Essay in Deontic Logic and the General Theory of Action* (Amsterdam, North Holland Publishing, 1968).
——, *Norm and Action* (London, Routledge and Kegan Paul, 1963).
Wellman, C, *An Approach to Rights* (Dordrecht, Springer, 1997).
Wilburg, W, *Die Elemente des Schadenrechts* (Marburg, Elwert, 1941).
——, *Entwicklung eines beweglichen Systems im bürgerlichen Recht* (Graz, Kienreich, 1951).
Wittgenstein, L, *Philosophical Investigations*, 4th edn (GEM Anscombe, PMS Hacker, and J Schulte trans, Malden, Wiley-Blackwell, 2009).
Zorrilla, DM, *Conflictos Constitucionales, Ponderación y Indeterminación Normativa* (Madrid, Marcial Pons, 2007).
Zurek, T et al, 'Reasoning with Principles' (2022) 210 *Expert Systems with Applications* 1.

INDEX

www.ingramcontent.com/pod-product-compliance
Ingram Content Group UK Ltd.
Pitfield, Milton Keynes, MK11 3LW, UK
UKHW020741190926
475689UK00003B/203